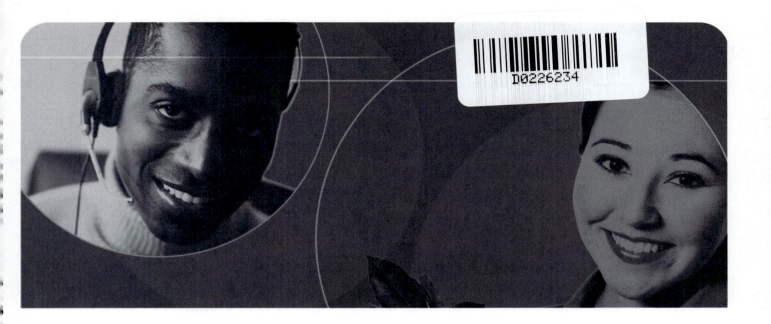

# the world of
# CUSTOMER SERVICE

*Lesley,*
*It was great*
*meeting you at the*
*conference. Thanks*
*for attending our session*
*on customer service.*
*Hattie*
*Nov. - 03*

**THOMSON**
★
**SOUTH-WESTERN**

Australia · Canada · Mexico · Singapore · Spain · United Kingdom · United States

## The World of Customer Service
Pattie Odgers, EdD

**Editor-in-Chief:**
Jack Calhoun

**Vice President/ Executive Publisher:**
Dave Shaut

**Team Leader:**
Karen Schmohe

**Executive or Acquisitions Editor:**
Joseph F. Vocca

**Project Manager:**
Dr. Inell Bolls

**Marketing Coordinator:**
Lori Pegg

**Production Editor:**
Darrell E. Frye

**Production Manager:**
Tricia Matthews Boies

**Manufacturing Coordinator:**
Charlene Taylor

**Compositor:**
Carlisle Publishers Services

**Printer:**
Edwards Brothers
Ann Arbor, MI

**Design Project Manager:**
Stacy Jenkins Shirley

**Internal Designer:**
Whizbang

**Cover Designer:**
Whizbang

**Photo Researcher:**
Darren Wright

For permission to use material from this text or product, contact us by
Tel (800) 730-2214
Fax (800) 730-2215
http://www.thomsonrights.com

ISBN: 0-538-72668-7

# the world of
# CUSTOMER SERVICE

is a practical, common sense text that provides coverage on the basics of customer service, the use of technology, and how to professionally handle difficult customers. For additional customer service resources, check out these other South-Western titles:

## Call Centers: Technology & Techniques

*Greene*    0538726865

Develop the essential communication, interpersonal and problem-solving skills needed for success as a call center, customer service or help desk representative or manager.

## Professional Development Series: Customer Relations & Rapport

*Forde*    0538725273

This short guide will teach you how to build, maintain, and nurture customer relationships, and how to handle dissatisfied customers.

## Professional Development Series: Interpersonal Skills

*Carolselli*    0538726075

This short guide covers key topics such as improving people skills, handling conflict, and thinking on your feet. Advance personal career goals and contribute to the competitive advantage of your company.

## 10 Hour Series: Telecommunication Skills

*Moore*    0538726520

Learn the skills for using telecommunications equipment, practicing etiquette and using technology to solve business communication problems.

## Business 2000: Customer Service

*Career Solutions Training Group*    0538431261

Gain knowledge on the importance of customer service, understanding and satisfying the customer's needs, and ways to interact with all customers. You will also learn how to provide superior customer service, ways to handle difficult situations, and more!

## Business 2000: Selling

*Greene*    0538431458

Learn how to determine your customers needs and wants, prepare to sell, develop the sale, and close the sale. Skill development for successful selling and incorporating technology into the sales process are also included.

## Business 2000: Retail

*Townsley*    0538431563

Retail introduces retail merchandising concepts by providing you with information on the retail industry, planning a business strategy, and merchandising. Also included are ways to evaluate the store's location, manage other business functions, and legal and ethical retailing.

**THOMSON**

**SOUTH-WESTERN**

Join us on the Internet at www.swep.com

*The World of Customer Service* is written in a practical, commonsense manner and reflects current customer service accepted wisdom, concepts, and hints. This multidisciplinary textbook is designed to teach exemplary, yet "down-to-earth," applied customer service thinking in business organizations—public or private, domestic or international.

Increasingly, the customer service function is a critical element in the success and future of all businesses competing in today's economy. With global markets more crowded than ever, it is a major challenge for organizations to attract and retain customers because more companies are competing for the *same* customer. The result appears to be that the secret in getting and keeping loyal customers today comes in creating new business and a commonsense approach for serving customers. As we enter the new millennium, successful organizations are emerging with a common focus—*customers*. Further, these thriving organizations live the mantra that *every* member in an organization is *involved in delivering* exemplary customer service. As Sam Walton, founder and former CEO of Wal-Mart, so fittingly put it, "There is only one boss—the customer. And he can terminate everybody in the company, from the chairman on down, simply by spending his money somewhere else."

## Audience for Text-Workbook

*The World of Customer Service* is designed to be used at any level of higher education or for corporate training programs in business and industry. For example, students may be enrolled in a customer service course offered in community/junior colleges or career schools. At the university level, courses in customer service issues and technologies continue to be critical to an organization's overall success.

## Text-Workbook at a Glance

**Part 1:** In the opening section, we introduce the user to the basic concepts in customer service and begin by describing what customer service is and how a customer is defined. Discussions proceed to identifying what exceptional customer service is and how it has changed. Finally, Part 1 discusses the goals of customer-oriented organizations, the importance of hiring the right person to perform the role of delivering outstanding customer service and the collective effect of each in earning and retaining customer loyalty.

**Part 2:** This part focuses on the numerous essential personal skills that a customer service representative (CSR) must demonstrate on the job. The chapters in this section discuss attitude and personal approach with customers when dealing with problems and complaints, as well as how to recover from and win back the customer who is angry. An overview of the skills CSRs need in managing the customer service role, including problem-solving, time-management, and stress-management skills is included.

**Part 3:** Essential communication skills needed for effective customer service are covered in Part 3. These skills include an understanding of the fundamentals of communicating to the importance of nonverbal communication, dress, manners, and listening skills. Communicating on the telephone and writing letters and messages to customers are also discussed.

Part 4: The final part discusses the future of customer service by addressing the profound impact that new technology and improved telecommunications media are having on the delivery of customer service. This part begins by discussing the growth, opportunities, and challenges that businesses experience when serving customers online. Moreover, the impact that the increased use of the customer relationship management (CRM) strategy software is having when business interact with customers is covered. The concluding chapters further identify the critical need to train, empower, and reward CSRs, as well as the role and responsibility of managing and measuring the effectiveness of customer service in organizations.

## Features

*The World of Customer Service* has an abundance of high-interest features to capture and hold the student's attention:

- *Quotations* introduce each chapter with thoughts from famous people or historians that prompt and focus interest.
- *Customer Service Tips* in each chapter provide practical suggestions from customer service providers today.
- *Ethics/Choices* found in each chapter demonstrate ethical dilemmas as students talk about customer service issues in class discussions.
- *Guidelines* provide a unique way of reviewing central issues in each chapter while serving as a reference tool for solving on-the-job problems at a later date. "Need to know" topics that may require procedural steps to follow, tips to remember, and checklists to refer to are examples of Guideline features.
- *Concluding Message for CSRs* is the last item in each chapter and summarizes or highlights in conversational tone each chapter's main ideas with the intention of reinforcing critical information that is to be applied or remembered.
- *Industry Profiles* introduce each of the four parts and profile customer service providers or managers who explain their jobs while sharing personal information about attitude, education, and work experience as applied to essential elements of customer service.

## Text-Workbook Activities

Most projects in the text-workbook are based on a fictitious company, called On-Time Technology Products (OTP), a medium-sized computer products manufacturing company located in a suburb of Chicago, IL. At the end of each chapter, these applied activities incorporate, for the most part, technology-based, Internet-research projects.

- *Questions for Critical Thinking:* Designed to stretch the reader's thinking, these questions interrelate the content with the reader's philosophy, value system, and work experience.
- *Online Research Activities:* These two projects require students to conduct research online to update chapter content and are designed to augment current thinking on chapter topics and customer service in general. Guided instructions and suggested URLs are provided to assist students in gathering pertinent data for completing these projects.
- *Communication Skills at Work:* This project is intended to present opportunities for students to apply their communication skills to solve customer service problems effectively.
- *Decision Making at Work:* This situational activity provides students the opportunity to apply their decision-making skills as they think through and effectively solve customer service concerns.
- *Chapter Case Studies:* Two cases are designed to reinforce chapter content. For the most part, they use real-life scenarios to deal with important issues in the workplace that include human relations and worker attitude problems.

You, the user, will assume the role of Layla Barsa, customer service representative for On-Time Technology Products for the text-workbook projects at the end of each chapter. As the CSR, you work with five other CSRs, and each of you report directly to the supervisor, Mary Graeff. On-Time Technology has a product line of more than 10 major items. It serves approximately 400 customers on a regular basis from around the world. Following is the current organizational chart for OTP.

## NOTE:

An icon [🖳] will appear next to the project title throughout the text-workbook if the project is on the student CD.

**Organizational Chart
On-Time Technology Products**

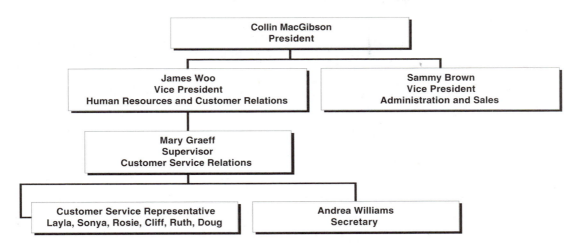

The files are prepared in Windows 2000 using Microsoft Word 2000.

Because many of the projects that follow are based on your assuming the position of CSR at On-Time Technology Products, periodically you will need to refer to the organizational chart above to get a better feel for employee names and their respective positions.

## Supplements Available

- **Facilitator's Guide** available on CD-ROM includes lesson plans, chapter outlines, teaching suggestions, chapter tests, solutions to text-workbook activities, and projects for each chapter. The CD-ROM also includes PowerPoint slides for each chapter summarizing the main topics, issues, and competencies covered in the chapter material.
- **Student CD** contains end-of-chapter activities for use online and in a distance learning environment.

## Acknowledgments

The development of this text-workbook has been a living document, undergoing several practical and constructive revisions and ongoing updates. I would, therefore, like to recognize and thank all those who helped, particularly, colleagues and instructors throughout Arizona and California who practice great customer service and who have shared even better information. Special thanks to Lee Vadnais and the outstanding reviewers for this edition:

Cheryl Carr
Mississippi ACTE
Madison, MS

Helen T. Hebert
EA-Remington College
Maple Heights, OH

Candance Schiffer
Tri State Business Institute
Erie, PA

## About the Author

For over 25 years, Dr. Pattie Odgers has taught a variety of courses in computer applications and systems, business and human resources management, and office skills to high school, community college, and university students in Arizona. She has also taught overseas in West Berlin and Stuttgart, Germany. She received her bachelor's and master's degrees from Arizona State University and a doctorate from Northern Arizona University. She is past president of the Arizona Business Education Association and recently was recognized and honored by the state association as its Outstanding Post-Secondary Business and Computer Educator in Arizona.

Dr. Odgers teaches computers to nearly 150 students each semester at Coconino Community College in Flagstaff,

Arizona. As an adjunct professor at Northern Arizona University, she has taught graduate-level adult and higher-education classes for several years. Dr. Odgers still finds time to own and operate a successful computer consulting and training business that serves Northern Arizona. She has found this experience invaluable as a means to "keep in touch" with what's happening in customer service in the workplace. Earlier in her work career, Dr. Odgers worked in marketing and sales for IBM Corporation on both the East and West Coasts.

A nationally recognized speaker and published author, she writes journal articles on the information workplace, the training of adult learners, and customer service. Dr. Odgers has authored seven textbooks, including *Office Skills* and *Administrative Office Management.*

# Contents

# PART 1

## CALL CENTERS PROFILE

by Rob Pasell,
Sturner and Klein

Customer service is the single most important aspect of any call center organization, regardless of whether its purpose is sales or help desk support or if its focus is inbound, outbound, or a combination of both. Customer service is the cornerstone of my company's philosophy, which states "Quality can never be made up for in quantity."

Call centers are growing in number across America. That is, many companies choose to contract out their customer service and sales work to companies such as ours. We have several large corporations for whom we provide services. Today, reliable call centers are in demand from many corporations because often the only contact their customers will ever have with the company is through a call center such as ours. It is vital, therefore, that each contact results in a positive experience, or those customers may not buy the company's product or use its service again.

To perform the job well, a call center representative must possess many core skills. One of the most important, in my opinion, is to be able to empathize with the person the rep is talking to. When you empathize with customers, you make them feel at ease because, more than likely, they aren't the only ones having this problem. Most people are going to have a question or a problem that will need to be answered during the course of the phone contact. The rep must be able to provide a solution or a way for the customer to get a solution before proceeding with the nature of the call.

# ROB PASELL

Another essential skill for those working in a call center is to be able to listen well. You really have to concentrate on what the customer is trying to tell you and continue to ask questions until you are sure you understand the problem. Once you understand the problem, then you can solve it.

For the most part, call centers prepare a scripted response to most problems and issues that a rep will run across. Usually, the rep can just follow the procedure for that issue; however, occasionally the rep will need to think on his or her feet, and that is another very essential skill. Being able to adapt to situations and to solve problems on the spot, while maintaining a positive attitude, are critical skills to have in call centers.

In summary, the major skill sets our company looks for when hiring a call center employee are listening skills, empathy, problem solving, and a positive attitude. Our focus on delivering a quality service to major corporations is why Sturner and Klein can compete as a relatively small company in the world of call centers. The level of quality and customer service that we and our reps provide keeps our clients coming back and referring us to other companies that have call center needs.

# CHAPTER 1

# Introduction to Customer Service

*There is only one boss—the customer. And he can fire everybody in the company, from the chairman on down, simply by spending his money somewhere else.*

SAM WALTON, FOUNDER OF WAL-MART

## OBJECTIVES

**AFTER COMPLETING THIS CHAPTER, YOU WILL BE ABLE TO:**

1. Define customer service.
2. Describe a customer's concept of good customer service.
3. Provide an example of an organization's mission statement.
4. Distinguish between external customers and internal customers.
5. Contrast traditional customer service with exceptional customer service.
6. List several types of customer contact points.
7. Identify required customer service skills and competencies.
8. Describe the working environment of a call center and of a help desk.

Businesses—large or small, industrial or retail, new or established—cannot survive without customers. Customer service is not about fancy products or intricate corporate culture; it is about dedicated, trustworthy employees and loyal, satisfied customers. Today, with more and more competitors vying for customers' attention, exceptional customer service is no longer optional—it's essential to staying profitable in business. Although nobody would claim that customer service is simple, the basic foundations and concepts should be.

As a result of studying the world of customer service, you will have a clear competitive edge in getting and keeping a job in today's fast-paced business world. Since service occupations are projected to account for the largest percentage of jobs between now and 2010, the approach in this book is to place you, the reader, in the role of a customer service provider. If not in your current job, then sometime in the near future, much of your on-the-job success may be influenced by your ability, knowledge, and willingness to provide exceptional customer service.

In general, Part 1 of this text serves as an overview of the key aspects of customer service, which begins by describing what customer service is and how a customer is defined in Chapter 1. Discussions then move to identifying what *exceptional* customer service is and how it has changed; finally Part 1 discusses the goals of customer-oriented organizations and the importance of hiring the right person to perform the role of delivering exceptional customer service.

## Defining Customer Service

Even though customers are unique, they all expect three things—a quality product, reliable service, and reasonable prices. In other words, customers want to receive what they feel they have paid for. Because you are an employee of an organization, a customer views *you* as the company, regardless what your job description says.

Customer service means different things to different people. In reality, however, the only perspective that matters is the customer's concept and perception of good customer service at the time service is needed and delivered. Some examples of good customer service are

- For a busy traveling executive, a flight that leaves on time
- For a harried office manager, working with a dependable office supply store, which keeps a good inventory of products on hand and delivers regularly and on time
- For a lonely retiree, conversation and kindness from a waitress when frequenting a neighborhood restaurant
- For a college student entering a new school, competent and caring advice from an advisor on the best program of studies with an emphasis in business and computers

Simply stated, **customer service** is the process of satisfying the customer relative to a product or service, in whatever way the customer defines his or her need, and then having that service delivered with efficiency, understanding, and compassion.

### CUSTOMER SERVICE TIP

**1.1** *It has been said that one way to exceed customer expectations is to promise good but deliver great!*

### Mission Statement, Values, and Goals of Customer Service

Organizations, like people, require direction and focus in order to achieve stated goals. How many times have you heard the statement that, if you don't have an idea of where

you're going, you probably don't know where you've been, are confused as to where you are, and most certainly won't know it when you get to where you ought to be? In like fashion, employees who have no idea of where they are going flounder aimlessly, trying to get through the day with no sense of purpose, loyalty, commitment, or urgency. This is not what customers have a right to expect from organizations they buy from.

The quality of customer service that a customer receives is greatly influenced by an organization's mission statement and vision of doing business. As simple as the statement "Good service is good business" can be, it may say all that is necessary to represent a company's mission statement or general values. Another example of a purpose statement is the Ritz-Carlton Hotel's motto, which states, "We are ladies and gentlemen serving ladies and gentlemen." If employees at this hotel follow the motto to the letter, they provide the finest personal service and facilities for their guests, who will always enjoy a warm, relaxed, yet refined hotel experience.

Companies must have planned goals to ensure that daily decisions, actions, and behaviors are totally customer-focused and are designed to adapt as needed to changes in customers' needs, desires, and expectations. Many corporations consider Nordstrom's department store as a premier example of, or benchmark for, superior customer service. When serving customers, top management at this fine department store has empowered employees with two simple phrases that reflect its core values: (1) use good judgment in all situations and (2) there will be no additional rules.

In most cases, when companies ask employees to put themselves in the place of their customers, doing so will usually guide the employees' efforts to provide the same treatment and service that they would expect to receive if they were the customers. If this sounds like the Golden Rule, "Do unto others as you would have them do unto you," it is. For lack of a stated mission and values statement, many companies use the Golden Rule as a guiding principle when serving customers.

Customer service is not new, but there appears to be much confusion as to its importance and degree of practice in today's marketplace. Guideline 1.1 describes some common customer service myths and corresponding facts that speak to an organization's corporate values.

## GUIDELINE 1.1 Common Customer Service Myths

| Myth | Fact |
|---|---|
| 1. We are providing good service, but there is a perception outside the organization that we are not. | • You may, in fact, already be providing good customer service, but it is not good enough; you can improve it. More important if you are providing good service but the customer's perception is that you are not, then you have a problem that needs to be corrected—to the customer, perception is reality. |
| 2. You can't improve service without more people and a larger budget. | • It is far more costly to provide poor service than it is to provide high-quality service. Eliminating contentious, long, repetitive customer interactions and responding to customer complaints more efficiently saves time and money. |
| 3. Why all the concern over customer service? If customers don't like the service we provide, they can try getting it elsewhere. | • This "take it or leave it" attitude is unacceptable. If enough customers receive poor service, they will eventually complain to management or an elected official in a way that can be very uncomfortable for you and/or your organization. |
| 4. You can't provide high-quality customer service when the requirements you must implement force you to tell customers "no." | • Quality customer service is not saying "yes" to everything customers request. People can accept a "no" if it is presented in the right way, but they cannot accept loss of dignity and loss of control. |
| 5. Our customers have conflicting objectives; we will never be able to satisfy them. | • You can do only what legal requirements authorize you to do. However, you cannot let what you cannot do be an excuse for not doing all that you are authorized to do. This includes providing warm, friendly, caring service that is responsive, efficient, and accurate. |
| 6. I don't need to worry about customer service because I don't deal with the public. | • You cannot provide high-quality service to your external customers until you provide high-quality service to your internal customers. |

When organizations commit to a way of treating customers by writing down their mission statement, values, and goals, they create a corporate culture that is better understood and lived by all who work there. According to Peggy Morrow, in her book *Customer Service—the Key to Your Competitive Edge*, there are critical steps organizations can take to create and ensure a customer service culture. Those measures are explained in Guideline 1.2.

## External and Internal Customers

To be successful, one of the first things any organization must do is to identify its customers and to learn as much about them as possible—including their age, gender, income level, lifestyle, and occupation. This demographic information, once collected, creates a **customer profile,** which explains who the customers are and what they want in terms of service. Companies identify their main customers for a very good reason—so that they can develop and market the goods and services their customers want.

Most organizations have two main sets of customers: external and internal customers. **External customers** are the customers whose needs we traditionally think of serving, because these customers are the persons or organizations that purchase and use a company's products and services. **Internal customers,** on the other hand, are identified as other people or departments within a company that rely on colleagues to provide the support they need to serve their own internal and external customers. If you were working at an organization's computer help desk, for example, your internal customer would be anyone who requests your assistance in using the software packages or hardware components on your company's computer network system.

In many firms, unfortunately, internal customers are often ignored or taken for granted—an attitude that compromises the productive flow of work throughout a company. Employees should respect and service internal customers as if they were paying clients. Typically, the ways in which internal customers are treated translate into how a company is perceived by its external customers.

## GUIDELINE 1.2  Keys to Creating a Customer Service Culture within Organizations

1. Management must make the measurement of service quality and feedback from the customer a basic part of everyone's work experience. This information must be available and understood by everyone, no matter what his or her level in the organization. The entire organization must become obsessed with what the customer wants.

2. Be very clear about specifying the behavior that employees are expected to deliver, both with external customers and with their coworkers.

3. Explain why giving excellent customer service is important—not only for the company but also for the world. What does your company do that makes life easier for everyone? What does your product or service add? Be sure to include this in the reasons for achieving customer service excellence.

4. Create ways to communicate excellent examples of customer service both within and outside the company. Institute celebrations, recognition ceremonies, logos, and symbols of the customer service culture and its values. This is where you want the mugs, buttons, and banners. Have a customer service bulletin board to feature service incidents that were special. Seize every opportunity to publicize the times when employees do it right.

5. Indoctrinate and train all employees in the culture as soon as they are hired. Disney is famous for this. Disney puts all newcomers through a "traditions" course, which details the company history with customer relations and how it is the backbone of Disney. Your orientation program is a key part of the ultimate success of your customer service efforts. Make sure that it contains more than an explanation of benefits and a tour of the facilities. It can be an important element in planting the customer service culture of the company, so that it can flourish and grow.

6. Encourage a sense of responsibility for group performance. Help employees see how their performance affects others. Emphasize the importance of "internal customer service." Help everyone see that, if you don't serve each other well, you can never hope to serve your ultimate customer.

7. Establish policies that are customer-friendly and that show concern for your customers. Eliminate all routine and rigid policies and guidelines. Knock yourself out to be a company that is easy to do business with. Never let your customer service representatives say, "Those are the rules I have to follow; there's nothing I can do about it." There is always a way to satisfy the customer. You must give your employees the power to do so.

8. Remove any employees who do not show the behavior necessary to please customers. Too many companies allow frontline service representatives to remain on the job when they are not suited to a customer service position. If employees don't want to serve the customer in the best way possible, document their behaviors and use this information to help them change or to move them to areas away from customer interaction. Everyone, from the top down, must believe that he or she works for the customer.

SOURCE: Peggy Morrow, *Customer Service—the Key to Your Competitive Edge*, Advantage Plus Publishers, September 1995.

The external customer buys a company's product or service.

Never take for granted the importance of serving internal customers well.

## The Service Industry

According to the U.S. Bureau of Labor Statistics, the services division is the largest industry, both in number of establishments and number of employees. Further, this industry is growing, with the prediction that 80 percent of all U.S. jobs will soon be service jobs. From 1990 to 2000, employment in services grew each year and reached 40.5 million workers in 2000. This represents an increase of nearly 45 percent from 1990 to 2000. In contrast, employment for the economy as a whole increased only 22 percent from 1990 to 2000. Moreover, the average hourly earnings of U.S. workers in services were $13.91 in 2000, compared with an average of $13.75 for all workers.

The services division, according to the U.S. Department of Labor, includes establishments engaged primarily in providing a wide variety of services for individuals, business, and government establishments. Service businesses include hotels and other lodging places; establishments that provide personal, business, repair, and amusement services; health, legal, engineering, and other professional services; educational institutions; membership organizations; and other miscellaneous services.

As can easily be seen, the service occupations vary considerably and include the vast majority of jobs. According to the *Occupational Outlook Handbook,* published by the U.S. Department of Labor, Bureau of Labor Statistics, the types of occupations in major service industry categories include

- Cleaning, buildings, and grounds service (janitors, lawn service, cleaning services)
- Food preparation and beverage service (chefs, cooks, food and beverage services)
- Health service (dental, nursing, and medical assistants and aides; occupational and physical therapists)
- Personal service (beauticians, flight attendants, home health and personal care aides, child care workers, veterinarian assistants)
- Protective service (correction officers, guards, police, firefighters, private investigators)

Today, the fastest-growing service industries include fast-food restaurants, government, health care, and amusement and recreation. Computer, legal, and other business services also are expanding rapidly. Guideline 1.3 shows recent employment projections provided by the Bureau of Labor Statistics, reflecting the 10 industries with the fastest wage and salary employment growth from 2000 to 2010.

## Understanding the Evolving Role of Customer Service

The Internet and mobile/wireless technologies, which have progressively become more a part of our lives, have caused an unparalleled shift in the balance of power from companies to their customers. Customers, armed with instant 24-hour access to information, not only are reshaping the products that a company offers and the distribution channels it uses but also are demanding a higher level and quality of service than ever before.

That power shift from companies to their customers underlies the new **customer economy.** What counts in the new customer economy? American businesses are realizing

**GUIDELINE 1.3** Fastest Wage and Salary Employment Growth—2000 to 2010

| Industry | Employment | | Change | |
|---|---|---|---|---|
| | 2000 | 2010 | Number | Percent |
| Computer and data-processing services | 2,095 | 3,900 | 1,805 | 6.4 |
| Residential care | 806 | 1,318 | 512 | 5.0 |
| Health services, not elsewhere classified | 1,210 | 1,900 | 690 | 4.6 |
| Cable and pay television services | 216 | 325 | 109 | 4.2 |
| Personnel supply services | 3,887 | 5,800 | 1,913 | 4.1 |
| Warehousing and storage | 206 | 300 | 94 | 3.8 |
| Water and sanitation | 214 | 310 | 96 | 3.8 |
| Miscellaneous business services | 2,301 | 3,305 | 1,004 | 3.7 |
| Miscellaneous equipment rental and leasing | 279 | 397 | 118 | 3.6 |
| Management and public relations | 1,090 | 1,550 | 460 | 3.6 |

SOURCE: U.S. Department of Labor, Bureau of Labor Statistics.

now more than ever before that the depth of their relationships with customers and the loyalty of those customers to the company are linked directly to profit margins and, ultimately, to their overall sustained existence.

## Traditional vs. Exceptional Customer Service

The very nature of customer service has changed dramatically over the past decade. In the past, organizations provided what could be called *traditional* customer service. Put another way, if customers needed service, they went to the organization's Customer Service Department. The implicit message to the customer was "This department is the *only* place you'll get customer service in this company."

Today's customers, however, expect something more than traditional customer service. They want a company and its employees to exceed their expectations, to demonstrate that the organization cares for them, and to work immediately and decisively on their behalf. In other words, customers today demand *exceptional* customer service. To that end, a successful company recognizes that its competitors may easily be able to copy its products, its prices, and even its promotions, but competitors cannot copy an organization's employees and the distinctive and exceptional service each employee provides.

Each time customers come in contact with an organization, they get an impression of service and the overall products they think they will receive. Everyone in an organization touches customers. The employee's behavior and attitude affect how the customer feels about the company. As the **customer service representative (CSR),** or frontline person who deals with customers on a day-to-day basis, you come to signify all that your company stands for—both good and bad. To the customer, you are the voice and personality of your organization. Customers who experience exceptional customer service will come back for more. They will be less likely to shop around as a result of how they were treated by you.

## Multichannel Customer Contact Points

As a customer service representative, there are several situations in which you will serve customers, and these are typically referred to as **contact points.** Customer contact occurs in person, on the phone, through written communications, or while online. To the customer, it doesn't matter where the interaction takes place. What does matter is that the frontline employee, the CSR, takes ownership of the problem. The CSR must apply the Golden Rule or other course provided by the organization's values statement and must follow it through to the satisfactory outcome expected by the customer. This is not difficult to do, provided that the CSR has all the knowledge, tools, and authority needed to take care of each customer's problem in a positive way.

A caring, friendly atmosphere and quick solutions to problems create *positive* points of contact. Clean, neat surroundings—whether in an office, a store, or a restaurant—say, "We pay attention to details because we value them as important to our success." Accurate invoices, shipment by dates promised, and phone calls returned promptly always convey a positive impression.

On the other hand, examples of *negative* points of contact include letting your phone ring five or six times before answering it, leaving the customer on hold for two or more minutes, and not replying promptly to an e-mail request for information. This translates to the customer as "We don't value your time." Long lines, out-of-stock items, faded signs, and unclean surroundings give customers the impression that the organization doesn't care about them. In the same way, some customers may also wonder whether the company cares about the product or service it sells.

Any successful company strives to make sure that all its points of contact with customers are positive ones. In the final analysis, *all* customers deserve exceptional service at each point of contact, regardless of the means they use to seek customer service.

## The Tiered Service System

In years past, most thriving companies gave all their customers special attention, regardless of the size of their purchase. The thinking then was that, after all, the customer who makes a small purchase today might make a large purchase tomorrow. Today, however, the mindset of treating customers differently is based on certain criteria—their actual or potential value, for example. It is an idea that is beginning to make economic sense to more and more businesses. In other words, many companies today are asking themselves, "Why invest the same amount of customer service effort and expense in a one-time customer as we would in a customer who has a multimillion-dollar history with our business?"

This new approach to serving customers is referred to as a **tiered service system,** and it is becoming increasingly popular. It is an approach to serving customers that is used with customer transaction records, which have been stored and analyzed with the help of computers and customer relationship management (CRM) software. In Chapter 11, the concept and use of CRM software will be more fully discussed. Briefly, however, the underlying principle of CRM is that every interaction with a customer is part of a larger relationship, which the company should be able to maximize and use in helping increase customer loyalty.

What does tiered service look like? Whether we realize it or not, we are already familiar with and are served by this concept each time we choose to fly. Airlines, for example, usually place their customers into three tiers of service: basic, or coach-class; enhanced, or business-class; and premium, or first-class. For the customer, the good news with a tiered service system is that there are a lot more choices on price, convenience, and comfort, and people have the option of upgrading. On the other hand, the not-so-good news for customers is that companies can invisibly identify individuals who don't generate profits for them and may decide to provide them with inferior service. Although tiered service exists, customers should never feel that they are getting a certain level of service because of a certain level of business. All customers should feel that they are receiving the same level of customer service when it comes to assistance with problems or the handling of complaints.

## Describing the Role of Customer Service Representatives

Superior service doesn't just happen; it is a process. Next to a company's product, excellence in customer service is the single most important factor in determining the future success or failure of a company. Regardless of what a company does to make a profit in terms of the product or service it provides, the company is in the business of providing customer service.

If you look at companies that are not doing well or have gone under, one of their common threads is failure to deliver superior customer service. Look at today's successful companies and you will find that they all understand and deliver what their customers want. More important, they are believers in the value of hiring the right person and providing customer service training for not only frontline employees but for management and all other support workers as well.

### CUSTOMER SERVICE TIP

**1.2** *Always strive to improve by focusing on the little things that mean a lot to customers.*

Top organizations select people carefully for the CSR job. Companies train them and foster a supportive working environment, because CSRs *count* in these companies. A customer service representative can work in a variety of settings and have any one of a number of job titles. For instance, a CSR might work in a telephone call center, at a help desk, with customers at a counter face-to-face, on the phone in the role of telemarketing, or on the Internet, providing hospitality and technical information to both internal and external clients. Regardless of the setting or job title, the CSR's role is to answer customers' questions, to solve problems, to take customers' orders, and to resolve complaints.

### ETHICS/CHOICES

**1.2** Assume you are answering a customer's inquiry about a product. After an amicable conversation with you, the customer realizes she cannot afford your product and thanks you. You know that a competitor offers the same product in her price range. What do you do?

### Required Customer Service Skills and Competencies

Although the responsibilities of a CSR are many and varied, depending on the type of organization, most companies write the job description to include the following duties:

- Provides in-house support for salespeople whenever a customer requires information or help

- Assists communication between levels of management and customers
- Represents the customer's interests, rather than those of a department within the company
- Helps develop and maintain customer loyalty
- Handles customer complaints and strives to have the company set them right
- Alerts upper management to trends or any conditions within the company's products or services that lead to customer dissatisfaction and recommends solutions to problems

The fundamental service skills needed by all customer service professionals involve knowing how to

- Build rapport, uncover needs, listen, empathize, clarify, explain, and delight customers
- Handle customer complaints, irate customers, and challenging situations
- Avoid misunderstandings, manage expectations, and take responsibility
- Work in teams and build internal cooperation and communication within the organization
- Show a positive customer service attitude

## Hiring the Right Person

The CSR's task is always to resolve the customer's problem as quickly and completely as possible. This requires three critical skills: (1) exercising judgment, (2) possessing knowledge (business literacy product knowledge, customer history, company information, and competitive data), and (3) using that judgment, knowledge, and common sense.

When hiring customer service professionals, companies should look for a helping attitude. You can teach anyone almost anything, but the feeling of customer service has to come from within the person. First-rate CSRs know what irritates customers. For example, seemingly unimportant issues, such as the way cartons are labeled or late deliveries, *are not unimportant* if they bother customers.

The most important task in hiring CSRs is to select an individual who fits in with the company's customer service culture and has a demonstrated skill and an interest in working with the public. Companies look for a variety of character traits, skills, and experience for customer service

jobs; however, in a perfect world, the profile for the exceptional CSR includes the following characteristics:

- *Initiative.* Takes the initiative to resolve issues before they become problems; ensures that customer needs are met
- *Responsiveness.* Looks for speedy solutions to problems; goes the extra mile to please the customer; responds quickly and effectively
- *Relationship building.* Is friendly and courteous; easy to talk to; tactful and diplomatic; respectful and considerate
- *Sensitivity.* Shows an understanding of and an interest in customers' needs and concerns
- *Objectivity.* Is open-minded; is respectful to others; treats others equally and fairly; tolerates different points of view
- *Resistance to stress.* Works effectively under stressful conditions; remains calm; copes well when under pressure
- *Resilience.* Is open to criticism; feelings are not easily hurt; tolerates frustration well
- *Problem solving.* Provides appropriate solutions to problems; capably handles customer requests; finds positive resolutions to problems
- *Positive attitude.* Is optimistic; maintains a cheerful attitude; looks for positive resolutions to problems

## The Workplace Environment

Not too long ago, most customer service representatives worked at retail stores or corporate headquarters. Today, if you work in customer service, you might be located in a retail store or an office, but CSRs are just as likely to work at a remote call center, at a help desk for a computer software company, or for a web-based company. As the number of web-based companies grows almost daily, a need for more CSRs to professionally and accurately take orders, answer questions, handle complaints, and track customer information using technology is growing steadily. You might be called a customer service representative, a customer care representative, a help desk assistant, a telesales representative, a telemarketer, or any other job title.

A **call center** is a location where groups of people use telephones to provide service and support to customers. Increasingly, this area is also referred to as a **contact center,** because it uses more technologically sophisticated devices when interacting with customers. Contact center representatives don't just answer the phones; they also respond to customers' e-mail messages and, in some cases, participate in live-chat sessions with customers from a web site.

Call centers can be inbound, outbound, or both. That is to say, some call centers handle only inbound calls, such as customer orders and questions or complaints about service issues. Others are outbound centers, where CSRs call customers to promote products or services or to conduct polls about anything from product testing to opinions about recent purchases. Still other call centers perform both inbound and outbound functions.

At a **help desk,** customer service representatives answer customer questions by phone, fax, e-mail, and web-based technologies. Help desk software is available to assist CSRs in quickly finding answers to commonly asked questions about particular products and services.

## The Customer Service Challenge

As previously stated, customer service begins with hiring the right people. It is difficult to teach customer service skills to employees if they don't have a certain type of personality or service attitude. As the workforce has changed, it has become more important to identify, very specifically, the things that employees need to learn about serving customers. Things that we used to take for granted—such as smiling at customers and saying "thank you"—may have to be taught. One of the major challenges of customer service today is the shortage of customer-oriented employees.

An additional challenge most companies face is finding and training staff that can live up to the potential of the technology. Consider the changes technology and the CSR have seen in the past few years: e-mail, text-based Internet chat (the ability to hold a real-time conversation over the Web by typing back and forth), voice-over Internet protocol (the ability to have a real-time verbal conversation over the Internet), and push technology (the ability to send a customer a specific image over the Internet to the customer's computer screen).

With the growth of the Internet and dot-com companies, CSRs must be able to manage digital contacts effectively. Quick, accurate, and appropriate responses by e-mail to customers' concerns can prevent the risk of losing customers to a competitor in seconds with just a few clicks of the mouse. If call center representatives aren't familiar or comfortable with instant messaging, chat rooms, and customer-friendly e-mail responses, they may be left behind in these critical skill areas.

Is it any wonder that customer service training—especially with the new generation of workers—is taking on greater importance? The new breed of CSR will need to be able to handle not only the latest technology but also the most complex customer interactions—those requiring extensive problem-solving and negotiating skills. Making matters even more challenging, these CSRs will have to be able to communicate both verbally and in writing. Increasingly, companies are realizing that the most significant investment they can make is not in purchasing their databases or computer systems but in making the best decisions when hiring their customer service staff. Moreover, once customer service representatives are hired, it is quite a challenge to keep them trained and ready to do their jobs in this technology-driven society.

## Concluding Message for CSRs

Marshall Field said, "Those who come to me with a complaint, teach me. Right or wrong, the customer is always right." He was saying that a complaint gives a service provider the chance to show just how good he or she can really be. Field wasn't saying that the customer is truly *always* right; some customers are very wrong. What Field meant was that, in dealing with complaints, you're dealing with people's perceptions. Although a customer's perception of a problem may be shortsighted or distorted, in the eyes of the customer that perception is right. When most people complain, they truly feel they have a legitimate concern.

The customer service representative is often the customer's first impression of the competence, quality, and tone of the company. The CSR serves as the company's first line of defense against an unhappy customer. Research shows that a well-handled complaint builds more loyalty in customers than any other strategy.

Further, customers are more likely to listen to reason and to a different perspective of their problem if frontline providers have product knowledge, express understanding, and treat each customer as if he or she is the most important customer. To customers, that human touch of treating them as valued people is often more important than price.

## Summary

- Customer service is the process of satisfying a customer relative to a product or service, in whatever way the customer defines his or her need, and then delivering that service with efficiency, understanding, and compassion.

- When organizations commit to a way of treating customers by writing down their mission statement, values, and goals, they create a corporate culture that is better understood and lived.

- Most organizations have two main sets of customers—external and internal customers.

- Service occupations vary considerably and are part of the fastest-growing industry in the United States, in both number of establishments and number of employees.

- The power shift from companies to their customers underlies the new customer economy, in which the depth of relationships with customers and loyalty to those customers are critical to organizations' success.

- Today, interactions with customers take place using multichannel customer contact points, such as in cyberspace, on ground, and through the mail.

- Customer-centered companies believe in the value of hiring the right person and providing customer service training for frontline employees, management and support personnel.

- Regardless of the setting or job title, in general the customer service representative's duties are to answer customer questions, to solve problems, to take customers' orders, and to resolve complaints.

- One of the most important tasks in hiring CSRs is selecting an individual who fits in with the company's customer service culture and has a demonstrated skill and an interest in working with the public.

- The new breed of CSR will need to be able to handle not only the latest technology but also the most complex customer interactions—those requiring extensive problem-solving and negotiating skills.

### QUESTIONS FOR CRITICAL THINKING

1. Cite two examples of a customer's concept of good customer service.

2. Why are organizations' mission statements for customer service different from each other?

3. In your opinion, which type of customer is more important in the long run to an organization—external or internal customers?

4. In what ways is traditional customer service different from exceptional customer service?

5. What are two advantages to organizations of providing customers with multichannel contact points?

6. If you owned your own business, would you provide your customers with a tiered service system? Why or why not?

7. What are five critical skills and competencies a customer service representative must possess?

8. Of the various working environments presented in this chapter, which one would you prefer to work in and why?

## On-line Research Activities

### Project 1.1: Outstanding Customer Service

Assume you are doing a report on *the top (outstanding) customer service organizations in the United States.* Use the Internet to research information and use the search engine *alltheweb.com* to do an *advanced search.* Specifically locate only the publications within the past six months and only from *.com* domains. As a result of your search, outline three items (and their URLs) of current information you might use in your report.

### Project 1.2: Customer Service Training Topics

**Situation**

Your supervisor, Mary Graeff, has asked you to conduct research via the Internet and locate at least three outside sources that On-Time Technology Products can use to provide training on customer service. Consider all types of training materials as possibilities. For example, you'll want to research videos on customer service, as well as bringing in an outside consultant to train in-house, and consider subscribing to magazines that focus on customer service issues.

*Refer to Describing the Role of Customer Service Representatives section, which describes the role, duties, and skills needed by a customer service representative as you evaluate the information in each of the sources. Using file PRJ1–2 on your student CD, key responses in the following table format that will inform Ms. Graeff where you got the information, what training information is provided, the cost (if available), and the advantages to On-Time Technology Products of selecting this source.*

| Source or Web site URL | Description of Training Topics | Costs | Advantages |
|---|---|---|---|
| 1. | | | |
| 2. | | | |
| 3. | | | |

## Communication Skills at Work

### Project 1.3: Customer Service Culture Task Force

**Situation**

Assume you have been asked to participate on a task force to come up with ways to improve the customer service culture at On-Time Technology Products with two coworkers, Doug and Rosie. Using the list of eight items from Guideline 1.2, prioritize the top five methods that you feel represent the approach you would recommend that your company follow.

*Retrieve file PRJ1–3 from the CD and complete the following form by listing five items in column 1; in column 2, state the reasons you support each item.*

| Methods | Reasons for Supporting Each Method (One or Two Sentences) |
|---|---|
| 1. | |
| 2. | |
| 3. | |
| 4. | |
| 5. | |

**Decision Making at Work**

## Project 1.4: Tiered Service—a New Approach

Collin MacGibson, President of On-Time Technology Products, recently returned from a Manufacturing Technology Conference in downtown Chicago; as a result of talking with leaders of other companies, he is now considering establishing a tiered service system, an idea he shared with Mary Graeff. Mr. MacGibson's basic thought is to reward the customers who give On-Time Technology Products $100,000 worth of business an end-of-year check based on 5 percent discount on all yearly purchases. In addition, those customers would receive a commitment to next-day turnaround time on the resolution of all customer service problems. Moreover, the customers who purchase $500,000 or more annually would receive a 10 percent discount and a commitment to a four-hour resolution of customer service problems.

Prior to responding to Mr. MacGibson's idea, Ms. Graeff has asked you and the other five CSRs your opinion, because she has some customer service concerns about this new proposal.

*Respond to the following questions:*

1. As a CSR, what is your initial reaction to this new tiered service recommendation by Mr. MacGibson?

_____

_____

_____

_____

2. In your opinion, what are some advantages of going to a tiered service approach at On-Time Technology Products?

_____

_____

_____

_____

3. In your opinion, what are some disadvantages of going to a tiered service approach at On-Time Technology Products?

_____

_____

_____

_____

## Case Study

### 1.1 "Customer Orders Are Perfect or They Don't Pay"

Thunderbird Technology Products president, Darrell Williams, stormed out of his office and said, "Customers' orders are perfect or they don't pay." At first, those in earshot thought he must be kidding, but the seriousness with which he made that statement and his demeanor said differently.

#### Questions

1. In your opinion, can a company literally afford to live by this statement? Why or why not?

_____

_____

_____

_____

_____

2. Can you think of any situations in which an organization may have difficulty honoring such a customer pledge?

_____

_____

_____

_____

_____

3. What are some hidden and actual benefits to Mr. Williams's company by setting such a standard?

_____

_____

_____

_____

_____

## Case Study

### 1.2 Customer Service Job Description

Because sales have been increasing over the past few months, On-Time Technology Products is planning to advertise for an additional customer service representative. As a result, your supervisor has asked you to review the following draft of a job description, which will be printed in the local newspaper next week. Your opinion has been requested as to its wording and appropriateness in attracting the right fit for a new CSR at On-Time Technology Products.

We are currently seeking to hire a superior customer service representative. The ideal candidate must be familiar with technology and computers. In addition, a postsecondary degree or certificate in information technology is a plus. Those who apply should possess an enthusiastic personality, have excellent problem-solving skills, and work well under pressure. As part of the team, responsibilities involve dealing with customers over the phone, providing pricing, technical, and order-processing information. Strong communication and interpersonal skills are a must. Contact Ms. Graeff at 555-1111 for more information.

Answer the following questions:

1. What is your first reaction to the wording of this job announcement?

_____

_____

_____

_____

2. What recommendations to improve the intent and wording would you suggest?

_____

_____

_____

_____

_____

# CHAPTER II

# Customer Behavior, Customer Loyalty, and Exceptional Service

*It's the little things that make the big things possible. Only close attention to the fine details of any operation makes the operation first class.*

J. WILLARD MARRIOTT

## OBJECTIVES

**AFTER COMPLETING THIS CHAPTER, YOU WILL BE ABLE TO:**

1. Describe customers' buying behavior relative to their basic needs.

2. Cite examples illustrating excellent customer service.

3. Distinguish between customer satisfaction and customer loyalty.

4. List actions companies can take to earn customer loyalty.

5. Cite examples of the three types of customer turnoffs—value turnoffs, systems turnoffs, and people turnoffs.

6. State the relationship between customer expectations and customer perceptions.

7. Cite examples a customer may describe as a great first impression of an organization.

8. Detail reasons that customer service is difficult to manage.

9. Describe methods companies use to measure customer satisfaction.

In a business sense, customers can be considered as assets. Most companies regard assets as items that must be protected and their value maintained and even maximized over time. From the customer's viewpoint, virtually all customer service activities, from billing accuracy to courtesy and accessibility of personnel, are prime components of excellent customer service. The trend in customer behavior and attitude is to expect that excellent customer service will be provided during all customer contacts.

Since recent data show that 40 percent of even satisfied customers will defect to a rival, companies who are intent on retaining their customers must cultivate loyalty by establishing a common ground and showing concern for customers through listening and using humor, among other things.[1] Contrary to popular belief, increased technology isn't the way to create customer loyalty. In fact, it appears that, the more high-tech the business world becomes, the more challenging it is to build customer rapport, and, despite their obvious conveniences, e-mail, voicemail, fax machines, palmtops, and many other technological marvels

_____

[1] Laura Michaud, "Beyond Satisfaction," *CMA Management* (March 2000): 15.

of today take attention *away* from customers and eliminate the human touch needed to build long-term customer relationships.

In general, Chapter 2 describes customer behavior and underlines the importance of exceptional customer service and its effect on customer loyalty. Specifically, however, this chapter explores how companies cultivate and maintain loyalty, how the role of exceptional service keeps customers satisfied, and which elements should be considered when measuring satisfaction with customer service.

## Understanding Customer Behavior

The primary mission of perfect customer service is to experience repeat business and to increase business from present customers. This goal requires specific knowledge about customers' behavior—*why* they buy, *how* they buy, and particularly *what* causes them to return and increase their purchases over time. The following are several types of customers:

- An individual buying
  - For him- or herself
  - For relatives or friends
  - As an agent for others
- An individual who
  - Receives the service or product but does not order it or pay for it
  - Orders or pays for the service or product but does not receive it
  - Is a noncustomer but whose informal advice is sought by family, friends, and acquaintances
- An individual within the organization (an internal customer) who is dependent on others in the organization to complete certain tasks of his or her own

Although the reasons that consumers buy vary considerably, they are manifested from basic needs that each of us has, as shown in Figure 2.1. Regardless of the industry or business, customers have four basic needs when deciding where to spend money on products and services:

1. *The need to be understood.* Emotions, customs, and language barriers can get in the way of properly understanding the needs of customers. Every effort should be made to be able to work with these challenges.

2. *The need to feel welcome.* That first impression a customer gets from service professionals is critical. Anyone doing business with a company and is made to feel like an outsider will probably not return for future goods and services.

3. *The need to feel important.* Little things mean a lot. Acknowledgment, name recognition, and eye contact make a person feel more important and appreciated.

4. *The need for comfort.* People need physical comfort—a place to wait, rest, talk, or do business. They also need psychological comfort—the assurance and confidence they will be taken care of properly and fairly.

Organizations that understand customer behavior and make the transition to customer-driven service are characterized in two ways: (1) the organization is regarded by customers as easy to buy from or deal with and (2) the organization depends on systems and organization (not speeches and slogans) to see that its service fits the customer's needs at a price the customer is willing to pay.

**FIGURE 2.1**
Our basic needs drive our decisions to buy from certain companies, while not buying from others.

## ETHICS/CHOICES

**2.1.** If you were being verbally "beaten up" by a customer about an issue you knew was caused by a colleague who was just fired last week, would you tell the customer who it was that caused the problem? Explain.

In various industries, excellent service is often driven by customer behaviors and needs—for example,

1. *The retail business.* A customer-oriented retail organization provides for consumers a wide variety and selection of merchandise, convenient shopping hours, parking, reasonable policies on returns and exchanges, and ready availability of trained and courteous sales and service personnel.

2. *The consumer direct-marketing or mail-order business.* The nature of this business requires a high degree of customer trust and, in general, centers on immediate access to advertised products, prompt delivery, a liberal exchange and return policy, and hassle-free dealings.

3. *The banking and financial services business.* This area has shown tremendous advances in customer service recently, with its automatic teller machines, effective and interactive phone systems for handling account queries, increased availability and higher skill levels of customer service personnel, faster turnaround on loans, and quick resolution of money problems through immediate access to the financial institution's web site links.

## Earning Customer Loyalty

The consumer services manager at Ben and Jerry's Homemade, Inc., describes how "euphoric service" can move customers from mere satisfaction of purchasing their ice cream into passionate loyalty like this: "Customer satisfaction is only a feeling—an attitude—that does not predict future customer performance because satisfied customers will still purchase from your competitor. Customer loyalty, on the other hand, is a behavior. When you make a personal connection with your customers and let them know that you hear what they're saying and then prove it by being responsive to their needs, you're building loyalty that influences behavior. Loyalty is always going to be based on relationships and that's what you want."[2]

In companies across America, a disconnect between intentions and reality may be driving away customers. Of-

Companies who have earned customer loyalty.

ten, companies do not live up to customer expectations. Incredibly, the disappointments that customers experience are often the result of expectations that the company has set up for itself. For example, customers are routinely surprised because many businesses fail to meet their own promised deadlines, fail to back up their products adequately, provide only limited availability of their advertised products, or provide inconsistent product service and support after the sale. Clearly, customer loyalty is not earned in these ways.

### How Loyalty Is Earned

Profound changes have transformed the business world. Ask most managers what is different in the new economy and they will tell you that markets are more crowded with global competitors and that it is harder than ever to attract and retain customer attention. In other words, an increased capacity to produce products and information has created an overcrowded marketplace, as more and more companies compete for the *same* customers.

Interestingly enough, a momentous shift has occurred—we have, in effect, entered an age of *customer scarcity.* The end result of this shift is that customers have become the most precious of all economic resources to businesses. Earning and keeping their loyalty, therefore, is not undervalued by successful companies.

---

[2]Gary Henderson, "Ben & Jerry's Euphoric Service Makes Customers More Confectionate," *The Supervisor's Guide to Improved Customer Service & Retention* (Sample Issue 2002): 3.

Customers tend to stay with organizations that enable them to experience positive, meaningful, and personally important feelings, even if an organization cannot always provide everything customers want or cannot solve all their problems. Surveys reveal that most people shift from one supplier to another because of dissatisfaction with service, not price or product offerings. It is the service provider's responsibility to manage the emotions in customer service exchanges.

According to Technical Assistance Research Programs, Inc. (TARP), a Washington, DC, consulting firm, 68 percent of the customers who go elsewhere do so because of a perception of indifference.[3] Indifference in this regard means that customers believe that their loyalty is wasted on a company that couldn't care less if they remained customers. Thus, they vote with their feet and walk out the door, seldom or never to be seen again. Establishing lasting customer relationships can be extremely difficult, because one bad experience—or even a mediocre one—can cause a customer to take his or her business to a competitor.

There is an equation for keeping customers. It's not exactly a secret, considering the multitude of books on the topic. It is as follows: Take a good, first reaction with the customer; add in reliability, a quick response time, quality services and products, plus empathy; and you end up with a satisfied customer. Take away any of these factors, and customer loyalty will begin to wane. Guideline 2.1 lists some tips that are useful to earn repeat business from customers.

There is a cost benefit of building customer loyalty. Companies that frequently and periodically survey their customers to find out how happy they are and what suggestions they have to offer to improve products and services are doing the right thing. The names at the top of the list of corporations that have taken these steps and, thus, have earned the right to experience deep customer loyalty are Cisco, GE, Microsoft, Intel, Yahoo!, Home Depot, Wal-Mart, and Oracle. These are some of the companies that actively seek out from the customer better ways to serve them. The entire purpose of improved service is ultimately to honor customers by caring enough to meet their needs. Loyalty is earned when intentions and reality blend and become one.

---

[3]Joan Fox, "How to Keep Customers from Slipping through the Cracks," *The Small Business Journal* (May 2001): 2.

| GUIDELINE 2.1 | Tips to Earn Repeat Business from Customers |
| --- | --- |
| Ask questions. | Never make assumptions about what customers expect in terms of quality and service. |
| Be honest. | For long-term success, honesty is not just the best policy; it's the only policy. |
| Fix the problems. | When a mistake occurs, give your customers two things: an apology and a fix to the problem at no expense to the customer. |
| Learn from the competition. | Pay attention to the service provided by competitors; then try to improve on that level when you are dealing with your customers. |
| Back up your company's promises. | Nothing ruins credibility more than when customer service representatives promise what their company cannot deliver. |
| Offer "one-stop" service. | Customers don't like being passed along from one person to another. Always try to take care of the problem up-front and immediately. |
| Build on emotion-friendly service culture. | To deal effectively with customers' emotions, employees must be aware of the full range of their own emotional states—both positive and negative. |

## Customer Turnoffs

Attracting replacement customers is an expensive process, because research indicates that it costs five times as much to generate a new customer as it does to keep an existing one. Unfortunately, few companies even track customer-retention rates, much less inquire about what issues might be driving their customers away. Could it be fear about discovering the answers that prevents businesses from ever asking the question "What turns you off as a customer?"

If asked, customers would probably cite three categories of turnoffs, as illustrated in Figure 2.2:

1. *Value turnoffs.* This means not getting what the customer pays for. Value turnoffs include inadequate guarantees, a failure to meet quality expectations, and high prices relative to the value perceived of the product or service.

**2.1**  *Don't pass blame. When a customer calls with a problem you personally did not create, don't rush to point out, "I didn't do it," or "It's not my fault." Instead of dodging the issue or blaming someone else, apologize for the customer's inconvenience and immediately begin to take action to solve it.*

2. *System turnoffs.* These irritations arise from the way a company delivers its products or services. When transactions are unnecessarily complicated, inefficient, or troublesome, customers experience system turnoffs. For example, employees who lack the knowledge to answer customer questions and organizations that have just one person capable of fulfilling a key function are symptomatic of system failures. So are voicemail menus that are unnecessarily complicated. Slow service, lack of delivery options, cluttered workplaces, unnecessary or repetitive paperwork requirements, poor product selection, and inadequate reordering processes are additional examples of system turnoffs.

3. *People turnoffs.* These are the things customers most often associate with poor service from customer service representatives. These turnoffs include lack of courtesy or attention, inappropriate or unprofessional behavior, and an indifferent attitude. In short, any behavior that conveys a lack of appreciation, care, or consideration for the customer is a people turnoff.

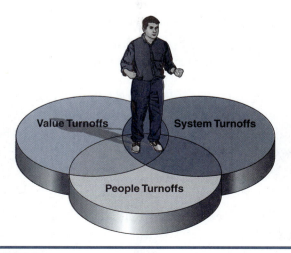

**FIGURE 2.2**
What drives customers away?

According to Jill Griffin and Michael Lowenstein, co-authors of *Customer WinBack,* there are seven primary reasons that customers defect from an established relationship. Guideline 2.2 itemizes these reasons and goes on to suggest approaches companies can take to reduce customer defections.

## Offering Exceptional Customer Service

Exceptional customer service is in the eye of the beholder— the customer. How does the customer determine whether a company has provided exceptional customer service? It usually depends on two factors: the customer's expectations and perceptions.

**Customer expectations** are what a customer wants *before* a transaction. Typically, a customer forms expectations

**GUIDELINE 2.2**  **Why Customers Defect and Approaches to Reduce Defections**

**Why Do Customers Defect from an Established Relationship?**

1. They don't know where or how to complain to the supplier.

2. They are too busy and can't, or won't, take the time to resolve a concern they have.

3. They consider complaining to be an annoyance that they would rather avoid.

4. They don't believe the company will do anything about it, anyway.

5. They don't see any direct value or benefit to them from complaining.

6. They fear some postcomplaint hostility or retaliation on the part of the company.

7. They can get what they want from a competitor, so it is simpler and easier to switch.

**Steps to Reduce Defections**

1. Make it easy for customers to complain.

2. Train CSRs to use good questioning techniques to uncover complaints.

3. Get resolution to customer problems more quickly.

4. Positively acknowledge every complaint as soon as possible.

5. Enforce a closed-loop complaint management system, in which complaints are routinely gathered and analyzed for insights.

**Source:** "Customer Retention Is a Critical Challenge for CSRs," *Customer Service Newsletter* (July 2001): 1.

from several sources: advertising, previous experience, word of mouth, and the competition. **Customer perceptions,** in contrast, are created *during and after* a transaction. A customer's perception is based on how actual service measures up to his or her expectations. If customers get more than they expected, the end result is **exceptional customer service.** However, if customers get anything less than they expected, they perceive a performance gap; in that gap lies customer disappointment. Disappointed customers will leave an organization and take their business elsewhere, and poor customer service is responsible for much of the disappointment experienced by customers.

## CUSTOMER SERVICE TIP

**2.2** *Respect your customers' time. Once you show that you respect your customers' time as much as you value your own, they will give you their time freely.*

In practice, what does exceptional customer service really mean? Perhaps it is when a company seriously tries to determine what is truly unique about the company and what makes its customer experience better than that of its competitors. It is also important to remember cautiously that, when you define what better customer service means for your customers, that definition is based on how they feel right now, and it doesn't necessarily mean that the definition won't change in the future. Defining exceptional customer service is an ongoing, fluid process.

For those reasons, strong organizations keep in touch with their customers on a regular basis and are not afraid to receive negative comments. In fact, they welcome negative comments that help them improve. The overriding thought by these companies is that it is infinitely better to have customers tell their complaints to the companies than for the customers to tell someone else.

## The Value of Exceptional Customer Service

Exceptional customer service matters. Customers who experience world-class customer service return for more products and services and are less likely to shop around. Knowing what is on the customer's mind, therefore, is the smartest thing a business can do. Successful companies focus on what the customer is saying and then tailor their products or services to meet customer needs.

Profits and customer service go hand in hand. The value and economic effects of exceptional customer service are realities businesses are recognizing. According to a myriad of customer service surveys and resulting statistics, on average:

- Most people tell 10 other people about great service they have received (and are willing to pay more just to have it) but will tell up to 20 people about poor service they have gotten.
- Depending on the industry, it costs between 2 and 20 times more to gain a new customer than it does to satisfy and retain a current one.
- Ninety-five percent of the customers whose problems are fixed quickly continue to do business with the company.
- Today, $1 spent on advertising yields less than $5 in incremental revenue, whereas $1 spent on a good customer experience yields more than $60 in incremental revenue.

Paying attention to the little details is the special touch that will make a company stand out from the crowd. Some of the most effective extras are really very basic concepts of conducting good business, although customers are often surprised when these actions take place. Little details that contribute to exceptional customer service include

- Treating customers respectfully and courteously at all times
- Greeting customers by name and promptly answering their questions (if you can't answer promptly, get back to them with an answer as quickly as possible)
- Standing behind your product or service and doing whatever it takes to right a customer service concern in a manner fair to both sides

*Moment of truth* is a term coined by Jan (Yon) Carlzon of Scandinavian Airlines Systems (SAS) in turning around his company as a result of a tremendous loss of profits in 1981. Simply put, a **moment of truth** is an episode in which a customer comes in contact with any aspect of the company, however remote, and thereby has an opportunity to form an impression. This moment of truth happens in a very short time period, from 7 to 40 seconds. That is the amount of time you, as a CSR, have to make a good impression on your customer. It is this impression that will guide the rest of the encounter.

If the moment is favorable, the whole interaction will be pleasant. If not, a positive customer relationship has been tarnished. Carlzon's idea is that, if his company's 10 million passengers had an average contact with 5 SAS employees, the company had 50 million unique, never-to-be re-peated opportunities, or "moments of truth." With these moment-of-truth events, the company in two years re-couped from an $8 million loss to a profit of $71 million.

## Critical First Impressions

According to an old saying, "You never get a second chance to make a first impression." Nowhere is this more applicable than in business situations, whatever the industry, because how you communicate with people the first time is key to your overall and continued success. In general, most consumers prefer to spend their money where they are treated well.

Research suggests that, within the short time span of up to four minutes, when two individuals meet for the first time, they make a decision whether they want to continue the relationship or not. It is evident that this decision is based on assumptions. Perhaps the scariest fact of all is that this initial illusion usually lasts a lifetime. In other words, if that initial interaction with the customer is poor, even if a fairly good relationship ensues, the brain won't let go of that very first impression.

Positive first impressions are critical. Several types of communication can be used to create a positive first impres-sion: the physical place of business (both the environment and the way in which people are greeted), the telephone, voicemail and e-mail, printed materials, and the way in which you present yourself and your company outside of the office. First impressions are also influenced by a customer service representative's personal habits. When a CSR's hair is groomed, hands and fingernails are clean, clothing is ap-propriate and clean, and general grooming reflects profes-sionalism on the job—these practices send a positive impression to those who do business with your company.

Indicative of the age of quick response time that we live in, returning calls promptly, delivering products or services quickly, and using modern technology to decrease response time are also smart business moves, which help create supe-rior first impressions. Customers simply are not willing to wait. Beware of using on-hold time to deliver information about your business. A waiting customer can easily take offense at being forced to endure your advertising or your taste in music. If at all possible, have enough phone lines (and enough people to answer them), so that callers don't get a busy signal or get put on hold for longer than 45 seconds.

In terms of making a favorable first impression, a good rule of thumb is to exceed customer expectations consis-tently. Since many consumers have modest expectations to begin with, this may be easier than it sounds. Keep in mind, however, that a positive first impression isn't going to do much good in the long run if a subsequent negative experi-ence eclipses it. The best way to maximize the value of a positive first impression is to reinforce it with extraordinary approaches to customer service and other favorable experi-ences throughout the course of future interactions.

**CUSTOMER SERVICE TIP**

**2.3** *Undeliverable promises can do more harm than saying "no" to a customer.*

## Extraordinary Approaches to Customer Service

To go beyond client satisfaction, make every effort to exceed your clients' expectations, every time. An age-old rule that is followed by customer-savvy organizations is to "under-promise and overdeliver." For example, if you think it will take two months to complete a project, quote a two-month time frame. If you get the job done a week or two early, you have underpromised and overdelivered. Tactics such as these empower people in the organization by giving them freedom to act in customers' best interests, and they yield enormous dividends for the company.

Stellar customer service is a mindset that defines each company's culture. It is pervasive, out in the open, and everyone's responsibility. Obviously, this unity of purpose begins with hiring and training the right people, but it also requires organizations to keep the basic company functions in superior shape, so that CSRs do not get bogged down by

**ETHICS/CHOICES**

**2.2.** Time after time, as you enter your company's employees' break room, you overhear other CSRs talking about how bad the management is at your company—specifically, your manager. What is your reaction to this situation? Would you enter the dis-cussion to express your personal views, would you ignore the dis-cussion, or would you try to reason with your coworkers and advise them against spreading negative thoughts? Explain.

the grind of cleaning up problems, correcting errors, or being on the defensive with customers. The following are six ways companies can improve performance and apply extraordinary approaches to customer service:

1. *Decide who you are and what you can deliver.* It's important to know what you can and cannot provide. Make sure you are true to your company's mission. Decide who you want to provide exemplary service to. Decide what you want to deliver and deliver it well.

2. *Decide who your customers are and what they want.* What you think customers should value might not really be what they value. Make sure you are in sync with customers.

3. *Deliver more than you promise.* Make sure that you give your customers more than they request, but, when doing so, ensure it is something they will value.

4. *Review your rules.* Look at both formal and informal rules. Some rules might have evolved from previous stressful times in your company. Examine which rules obstruct serving your customers' needs and get rid of them, if at all possible. Make every effort to favor the customers' needs over internal needs.

5. *Celebrate your diversity.* Some employees might be difficult to work with, but they might be the best fit with some customers. Empower them. They might become your best employees.

6. *Treat your employees as you expect them to treat your customers.* Treat your employees with respect. Put yourself in their shoes. Make them feel special. Make time for them. The result is that they will treat customers the same way. In business, this idea is referred to as the **mirror principle,** which says, your employees won't treat customers better than you treat them.

In this discussion, it is probably prudent to examine what service is not. Service is not easily managed, because so many factors make it unpredictable and difficult to control fully. The following characteristics of service contribute to this complexity and are the other side of the coin. Therefore, when focusing our discussion on serving customers in the best way, remember the following realities, which can cause dilemmas for CSRs:

- Customer service happens instantaneously and right in front of the customer.
- Customer service is created and delivered at the same time.

- Service must be individualized for each customer; it cannot be standardized or routinely applied universally.
- The perception of the customer may not be the same perception as that of the service providers.
- Often, customer requests are complex and unique and cannot be speedily resolved.
- Different customers have different needs; further, the needs of the same customers change constantly.
- Complete customer service requires others in your organization to support you; it requires customer service teamwork, with everyone committed to the same goal.

## CUSTOMER SERVICE TIP

**2.4** *Measuring customer satisfaction is important because research indicates that 84 percent of all sales in America originate from the recommendations of a satisfied customer.*

## Measuring Customer Satisfaction

The case for maximizing customer satisfaction is a strong one, because a customer base will remain if it is built on trust, quality service, and product excellence. What is the best way to measure customer service and satisfaction? The answer is simple—ask your customers. Having customers tell you specifically what you are doing right and what you are doing wrong is the only accurate means of determining how well you are meeting their needs.

There are several ways to gather customer feedback: surveys and assessments, focus groups, and interviews. When conducted at six-month and yearly intervals, these are all first-rate methods for generating qualitative and quantitative information for sound decision making and appropriate changes to the way business operates.

The advantage of quantitative, or numeric, data is the ability to establish baseline performance measures to create a scorecard for ongoing improvement. Gathering qualitative, or narrative, information, on the other hand, results in the personalized feedback and depth of knowledge generated through this practice.

There is a faulty belief in the marketplace that the mere collection of data will result in improvement. That's probably because, in years past, just the act of conducting a survey had some positive impact on customer satisfaction and loyalty, but the bar has been raised. With a smarter customer base with greater expectations, companies can no longer ask if customers are satisfied without acting in a personalized way on the responses they receive. The process of asking customers to set the standards for the level of service they expect from a company

- Shows the company how effective it is
- Helps the company set realistic goals and monitor trends
- Provides critical input for analyzing problem areas
- Assists the company in monitoring progress toward improvements
- Keeps the company close to its customers

Customer service representatives pay attention to performance standards that are measured because they then know what to expect. Customer-focused measures are needed because they explain reasons for lost sales, retention problems, time-consuming and costly complaints, and cost-redundancies. Without measurable performance standards, employees are left to guess what good service is. When that happens, customers become disappointed. The following are some examples of measurable customer service standards:

- Answer telephones by the third ring.
- Serve hot food at a temperature of at least 140 degrees.
- Smile and greet all guests within 10 feet of you.
- Respond to each shopper, so that he or she does not stand in line more than two minutes.
- Offer bell or concierge service to every hotel guest.
- Speak professionally to clients and avoid the use of slang.

How do you ask customers if your service goals are in line with their service expectations? The easiest way is to have a customer response system in place. You can use several methods, such as comment card surveys, follow-up telephone surveys, mail surveys, or other types of surveys and interviews:

- *Comment card surveys.* Hand the card to the customer at the end of the transaction. Ask the customer to please take a moment and complete the survey, as it will be useful to your company in determining how well you are meeting his or her needs.
- *Follow-up telephone surveys.* Have a written framework of questions to ask the customer. When calling, introduce yourself and tell the customer you are conducting a short customer service survey, which will take no more than two minutes to complete. Tell the customer

you would appreciate his or her input concerning a recent contact with your company.

- *Mail surveys.* Include a cover letter explaining the reasons for your survey. Address the short survey to the person who interacted with your company. Include a stamped return envelope.
- *Other methods:* Electronic surveys, in-store shopper surveys, and onsite interviews can also be effective. In addition, create a forum for customer service representatives to provide anecdotal feedback on the market's response to product features, functionality, pricing, and advertising. Nobody knows what customers are thinking better than CSRs do. Examples of customer response methods are shown in Figure 2.3.

**Customer Comment Card**
YOUR CONCERN IS OUR CONCERN

Please provide your comments in the space below.

We appreciate your input. Thank you.

**HOW ARE WE DOING?**
To help us improve our commitment to you, please take a moment to respond with your reactions to our service.

Please rate us on a scale of 1–5 using the following system:

| 5 | Outstanding |
| 4 | Exceeds Expectations |
| 3 | Meets Expectations |
| 2 | Dissatisfied |
| 1 | Unacceptable |

Friendliness        5 4 3 2 1
(For example, how courteous was our sales staff?)

Timeliness         5 4 3 2 1
(For example, was our sales staff able to assist you promptly?)

Helpfulness        5 4 3 2 1
(For example, did our sales staff offer suggestions?)

Overall satisfaction   5 4 3 2 1

Comments: _____

Completed by: _____

**FIGURE 2.3**

Two methods that survey customers' expectations and satisfaction with products and services.

## Concluding Message for CSRs

To be sure, it takes more than "the customer is always right" rhetoric to satisfy today's diverse customers. Customers are not always right, but customers are always emotional. They always have feelings—sometimes intense, other times barely perceptible—when they make purchases or engage in business transactions. When unhappy CSRs in an organization are out of touch with their own feelings, they cannot provide emotional competence or use emotional connections to increase customer loyalty.

Some tips to help you separate your organization from your competition and build strong customer loyalty are

- *Listen to your customers.* Not everyone complains. Those who do complain speak for more people than themselves.
- *Be knowledgeable and accessible.* Nothing is more frustrating than to have customers treated like basketballs—they don't appreciate being bounced from one person to another, never reaching someone who can help. When CSRs are empowered to solve customers' concerns, it is a win-win strategy for everyone.
- *Be honest.* When something goes wrong, tell the truth. If you are wrong, admit it. Once you've lost credibility with your customer, you've lost a customer.
- *Smile.* Greet every customer with a smile. Double that suggestion if it is a customer with a complaint. Being greeted by a sincere smile softens the "attack" and allows the conversation to take a more pleasant tone. Remember, the customer may not always be right, but he or she is always the customer. Some employment specialists say that, when hiring CSRs, it's advisable to hire the smile and train the skill.

## Summary

- The primary mission of perfect customer service is to experience repeat business and to increase business from present customers.
- When customers spend their money on products or services, they are motivated by the needs to be understood, to feel welcome, to feel important, and to experience comfort.
- Earning customer loyalty is critical, because today's economy has an increased capacity to produce products and information; therefore, there is a glut in the marketplace as more and more companies compete for the same customers.

- When customers move from one supplier to its competitor, it is often because they experience turnoffs relative to the product's value, an organization's troublesome systems, or lack of respect and attention from service providers in the organization.
- Customer expectations are what a customer wants before a transaction, whereas customer perceptions are created during and after a transaction.
- In terms of making a favorable first impression, a good rule of thumb is to exceed customer expectations consistently, because first impressions are formed within the first four minutes of a customer contact.
- It is important to realize that customer service is not easily managed, because so many factors make it unpredictable and difficult to control.
- With a smarter customer base that has greater expectations, companies can no longer ask if customers are satisfied without acting on the responses they receive.

### QUESTIONS FOR CRITICAL THINKING

1. In what ways do the four basic needs described in this chapter relate to the reasons people buy from certain companies?

2. Describe an experience you have had or have heard about that demonstrates excellent customer service.

3. Are customer satisfaction and customer loyalty the same in meaning? Why or why not?

4. Of the three types of customer turnoffs—value turnoffs, system turnoffs, and people turnoffs—which do you feel is the most often violated by organizations? Why?

5. In your own words, explain the relationship between customer expectations and customer perceptions.

6. Do you agree with the statement "You never get a second chance to make a first impression"? Why or why not?

7. Are the reasons customer service is difficult to manage just excuses for poor customer service or are they reasonable? Explain.

8. If you were the president of a retail organization, what methods would you use to measure customer satisfaction? Why?

## On-line Research Activities

### Project 2.1: Measuring Customer Satisfaction

Assume you are doing a report on *current methods to measure customer satisfaction.* Use the Internet to research information and use the search engine *altavista.com.* Specifically, locate in your research published information from business journals and business-oriented web sites. As a result of your search, keyboard three items (and their URLs) of current information you might use in your report.

### Project 2.2: Customer Service Books on Loyalty and Retention 🖥

#### Situation

The big push at On-Time Technology Products is to increase sales by doing whatever it takes to retain customers and increase customer loyalty. In the technology business, however, Vice President Woo, who is in charge of customer relations, realizes that there are so many good ideas and outstanding competitors in the technology field that it might be prudent to do some research on the Internet. He specifically wants to survey how customer loyalty is achieved and specifically relative to the technology industry.

*Go to the* Amazon.com *web site and locate three books on customer loyalty and customer retention. Using file PRJ2–2 on the student CD, key responses in the following table format that will inform Mr. Woo what recently published books are available and that you would recommend, along with a brief description of each book.*

| Book and Author | Cost | Description of Book's Contents (One or Two Sentences) |
|---|---|---|
| 1. | | |
| 2. | | |
| 3. | | |

## Communication Skills at Work

### Project 2.3: Moment of Truth Examples 🖥

#### Review

A moment of truth is an episode in which a customer comes in contact with any aspect of the organization, however remote, and thereby has an opportunity to form an impression. In other words, a moment of truth

- Consists of any interaction with a customer
- Determines a customer's perception of your service
- Requires judgment, skill, and understanding by the CSR
- Occurs in less than 40 seconds

*Retrieve file PRJ2-3 and complete the following form by listing actions a customer professional can do in column 2 for each of the four industries itemized in column 1.*

| Industry | What Can You Do to Create and Communicate Positive Moments of Truths to Customers (e.g., Smile)? |
|---|---|
| 1. Hotel | • <br> • <br> • |
| 2. Restaurant | • <br> • <br> • |
| 3. Retail store (e.g., Sears) | • <br> • <br> • |
| 4. Airline (e.g., American Airlines) | • <br> • <br> • |

## Decision Making at Work

### Project 2.4: Customer Turnoffs Discussion

You are sitting in the lunchroom at On-Time Technology Products with other CSRs Rosie and Doug. It's Friday and everyone is looking forward to the weekend, but Doug is relating a customer problem he has just experienced and is asking how you and Rosie would have handled it. You discuss it, then the discussion moves to other examples of situations that turn customers off and how each of you would handle the situations. The following are three major customer turnoffs, which are not specific to the technology industry.

*Respond to these customer turnoffs and state how you or your company might address each:*

1. A customer waiting in line or on the phone

 

 

 

 

2. Red tape—such as refunds, credit checks, and adjustments on account

 

 

 

 

3. Failure to stand behind products or services

 

 

 

 

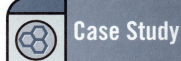

## Case Study

### 2.1 The Mirror Principle

Helen Harrison, marketing director of a major manufacturing plant on the East Coast, was driving back from a noon Chamber of Commerce meeting and was reflecting on a statement made by the luncheon speaker. He described the mirror principle by saying, "Your employees won't treat your customers better than you treat them." Given the increasingly fragile employee morale, decrease in sales, and increase in customer service complaints over the past six months, Helen is wondering if this thing called a mirror principle isn't what is happening at her company.

#### Questions

1. If you were Helen, when you got back to the office in what ways would you translate your feelings into an action plan for improvement?

_____

_____

_____

_____

_____

2. What steps would be included in your action plan to turn this customer service issue around?

_____

_____

_____

_____

_____

_____

## Case Study

### 2.2 Customer Service Satisfaction and the Budget

It's budget time at On-Time Technology Products, and Mr. MacGibson is seeking input from employees in order to develop a realistic budget for next year. One budgeting change he is contemplating is to increase by 8 percent the amount of money allocated to customer service. Mrs. MacGibson (his wife and closest friend) has advised him that just committing more resources to customer service will not necessarily increase customer satisfaction and loyalty. Nonetheless, Mr. MacGibson needs more input and has asked you and the other CSRs to respond to the following three customer service situations to acquire more information as he prepares the budget.

_Answer the following questions:_

1. In what way could a higher budget assist On-Time Technology Products to make credits and adjustments to customer accounts more easily?

_____

_____

_____

2. In what ways could a higher budget assist On-Time Technology Products to provide information and answers to customers in a more timely way?

_____

_____

_____

3. In your opinion, can providing more money really solve customer service problems? Why or why not?

_____

_____

_____

# Let's Discuss...

## Industry: Call Centers

## Call Center Activities

*What are call centers?* Call centers are the areas of every company where customers and prospective customers call, make web site requests, and message through e-mail. Call center areas are where those major customer communications are received and/or answered.

1. *What industries have call centers?* Research your community, city, and state and determine where call centers are. (Usually, call centers don't hang banners on the door, so you might have to do some investigating.) In the following table, column 1 lists some typical industries that have call centers; column 2, categories or names of companies with call center areas. List in column 3 the companies in your area that have call centers established and operating. You may have to call and confirm your suspicions.

| Industry | Examples | Call Centers in Your Area |
|---|---|---|
| Telecommunications | Verizon Wireless, MCI | |
| Financial | Banks and brokerages | |
| Retail | Sears | |
| Travel | Airlines, car rentals | |
| Insurance | Prudential, Farmers | |
| Reservations/tickets | Ticketron, timeshare condos | |
| Internet, or dot-com, companies | ISPs, e-trade, | |
| Others | | |

2. *Size and growth of call centers.* In 1998, there were 69,500 call centers in the United States, and that number is expected to grow to 78,000 by 2003, according to a recent Benchmarking Study. Provide on the following lines three items of information about call centers that you were unaware of. You will find much information by visiting the following four call center web sites: www.callcentermagazine.com, www.callcentermanagement.com, www.callcenternews.com and www.incoming.com.

a. _____

b. _____

c. _____

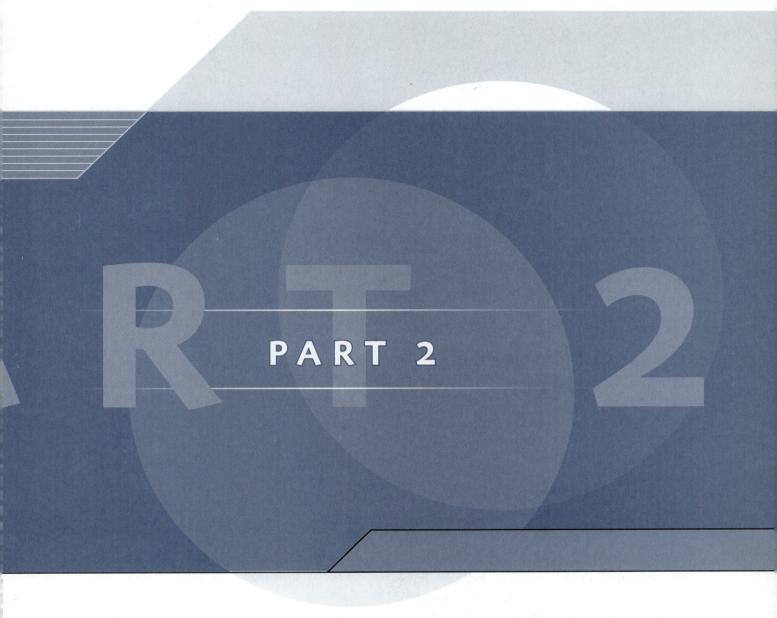

PART 2

## HOSPITALITY AND TOURISM PROFILE

by Leslie Connell,
Flagstaff Convention and Visitors Bureau

I began my career in the hospitality industry cleaning rooms in a small resort ski town in the Canadian Rockies. I hadn't intended to make this my lifelong direction; I just wanted to stay awhile longer in a beautiful location while on a "break" from my educational pursuits. Little did I know that I would begin down the road to a career I would grow to love.

Unfortunately, in those days, customer service was not taken too seriously. Small, busy resort towns can sometimes have an attitude about their attractiveness to visitors. There was the thought that, if customers were unhappy, there would be someone in line behind them, ready to fill that space.

I took a break from the industry for a few years and spent some time walking in the shoes of those visitors I used to serve. By the time I had come back to hotels, it was with a whole new perspective. I joined Marriott in 1984, a company that already knew the importance of customer relationships and great service. I spent 17 years in management positions with Marriott before I got the job of a lifetime—selling the easiest product of all—the wonderful town of Flagstaff, Arizona.

In all my years of hiring the right associates to take care of our customers, I learned some inevitable truths. The hospitality industry is not for everyone. Attitude is everything. Hire great associates who take superb care of your guests, and your job, as the manager, will be easy.

I followed all of the programs and protocol set out by Marriott when making hiring decisions, but I always looked at a couple of things above all else when choosing that right person for the job. Does he or she have the right "people person" qualities in place to be able to interact well with guests and other employees? Does he or she have that "spirit to serve"? Does he or she exhibit the ability to work

# LESLIE CONNELL

well in a team environment? As far as I was concerned, everything else was trainable.

As a manager, I felt that great customer service could not be stressed enough. I might forgive almost any error if it happened while trying to make a guest happy. I empowered my staff to make immediate decisions to fix a situation, instead of having to wait for management authority. Overall, we had very happy guests. From time to time, we encountered someone who was almost impossible to please, but we kept trying. It's important to provide quality training to staff, so that they can perform to a level where mistakes are few, but I think it's more important to provide the type of training that will enable employees to fix something that goes wrong, because Murphy's law guarantees that it will at some point.

Customer expectations are high and ever on the rise. In order to compete in today's marketplace, it is imperative that a company pays attention to how it treats its customers. Customers remember the business that provides consistent service, and return business is almost guaranteed. Gone forever are the days when someone will automatically appear, to take the place of an unhappy customer. Companies are getting wiser to this fact.

Now is a great time for people who are reassessing their goals in life to take a look at the hospitality industry as a possible career change. This is a career that requires flexibility, patience, humility, and a good sense of humor. I know that some of these attributes I possessed when I began down this long road, and some were acquired. Some were acquired the hard way.

Accidental or not, I couldn't have picked a better career path. It's been rewarding and, most of all, fun. I recommend it.

# Attitude and Personal Approach with Customers

*Attitude is the reflection of a person, and our world mirrors our attitude.*

EARL NIGHTINGALE

## OBJECTIVES

**AFTER COMPLETING THIS CHAPTER, YOU WILL BE ABLE TO:**

1. Describe a customer-oriented attitude.

2. Associate self-talk with the concept of positive thinking.

3. Distinguish between outer-level and inner-level customer service.

4. Relate the core elements of the adversity quotient with service attitudes.

5. Describe the customer service benefits of the teamwork approach in organizations.

6. Detail several suggestions to follow when serving customers with disabilities and customers from different cultures.

Customer expectations have a power in and of themselves. Learning to define, meet, and exceed those expectations is key to customer satisfaction. As all the management and quality consultants will tell you, "The customer is king," because it is the customer who remains the final judge of what quality is and what it is not. It is the customer who sets the standard for excellent service.

All customers—internal and external—place different values on different aspects of service attitude and performance. Therefore, it is important to find out exactly which areas are most important to the customer you are currently serving. Customer expectations must be realistic and attainable. Being able to define, meet, and exceed those expectations on a *regular* basis is the key to personal service performance, business growth, and customer satisfaction.

Part 2 focuses on the numerous essential personal skills that customer service representatives must demonstrate on the job. The four chapters in this section discuss customer conflicts and complaints, as well as how to recover from and win back the customer who is angry. An overview of skills you will need in managing the customer service role, including problem-solving, time-management, and stress-management skills are covered.

Chapter 3 begins Part 2 with perhaps the most important characteristic that a customer service representative brings to the job—attitude and personal approach when dealing with customers.

## Servicing with a Customer-Oriented Attitude

Think about the last visit you made to a restaurant and what you remember about it. Is your strongest memory of the food or of the service you received? For most people, it is the service, even though we consciously believe we are going to a restaurant to get a good meal.

Management guru Peter Drucker put it best when he said, "The purpose of business is to create a customer." The logic follows that business is not about making sales, or even making profits. Those come naturally when you create customers—and keep them. Employees who give exceptional customer service have a positive, can-do attitude. They treat customers as important to their success and in an honorable fashion.

### ETHICS/CHOICES

**3.1** Carolyn, a CSR you work with, is having a particularly difficult day. You have overheard her on two occasions sounding short with customers on the phone. Further, you are aware that your company is randomly monitoring customers' calls. Would you call Carolyn aside to talk with her about your concerns?

### The Power of Positive Thinking

It may sound simplistic, but the first step toward creating an appropriate customer-oriented attitude is to begin thinking positive thoughts about yourself and others. The second step is to reflect those thoughts in positive self-talk. **Self-talk** happens inside us, whether we are aware of it or not. We all talk to ourselves, and this self-talk can have a tremendous effect on our attitude. Positive self-talk can help each of us build a positive, winning attitude. On the other hand, negative self-talk can do just the opposite. For example, we become our own worst enemies by telling ourselves things such as "I'll never be any good at this" or "I look terrible today." We feel better if we replace those thoughts with the

following statements: "I'm sure I can do this with just a little practice" and "I look and feel great today."

A positive attitude is not necessarily something you are born with. That's good news, because it means that, even if your attitude is negative from time to time, you can change and create a positive customer attitude that is helpful and dedicated to being outstanding. Today's customers perceive good service as added value. In other words, you need to add that something extra or special to the product or service.

As noted speaker and author Anthony Robbins said, "Our beliefs about what we are and what we can be precisely determine what we will be." In other words, people are not motivated by external sources. Motivation can come only from inside the person. By putting aside preconceived biases and judgments, customer service representatives can better understand what makes their customers tick. Customers can sense positive energy, and the result is that they, too, come away feeling positive.

### The Customer's Attitude and You

In the real world, CSRs serve customers who display a variety of attitudes. For example, there are customers who are

1. *Comfortable.* Customers who believe their needs and expectations will be met
2. *Indecisive.* Customers who cannot make up their minds or may not even know what they want
3. *Insistent.* Customers who make demands and require you to take immediate action
4. *Irate.* Customers who are angry and need to blow off steam before you can begin to work with them

Your attitude toward your customer is not the only thing that can affect the outcome of that customer contact. If some other aspect of your life is bothering you, it can affect the way you interact with your client. Whether your negative thoughts are based in something that happened to you earlier that day or in your negative expectations regarding a particular customer, replace them with positive ones, such as "I'm eager to help" or "Problem solving is something I'm good at." Sometimes, on "off days," we say things we later regret. Guideline 3.1 describes eight statements you should never say to customers.

Following are some survival tips to help you, as a CSR, keep your attitude up all day:

## GUIDELINE 3.1    Eight Statements You Should Never Say to Customers

| Statement | Reason |
|---|---|
| 1. "We don't offer that." | It's fine to say "no"; however, how you say "no" is all-important. For example, when you have to turn away a customer, recommend where the product or service can be found. |
| 2. "All sales are final." | Your business should have a reasonable return policy and warranty plan. This sends a clear message to customers that you believe in what you are selling. |
| 3. "I don't know who does that." | Business is lost, and this type of response frustrates customers. Employees must be familiar with who does what at a business or at least have immediate access to people who do have this knowledge. |
| 4. "Sorry, that's our policy." | Customers faced with this statement will be annoyed at the lack of creativity a company shows in resolving their problem. Be flexible and helpful with customers who deserve a break. |
| 5. "Tell us what you think." | Unless you are prepared to react to all varieties of feedback, be careful with this statement. A method or survey instrument to assess customer satisfaction needs to be designed by companies to handle complaints as well as compliments. |
| 6. "Call us about our special offer." | Make sure everyone who answers the company phones knows about the special if you encourage customers to call. |
| 7. "It will be ready tomorrow." | Unless you are sure it will be ready as promised, don't make this commitment. It is smarter to underpromise and overdeliver. |
| 8. "I don't know." | Don't use that phrase unless it is followed by the phrase "but I will find out for you." Admitting you don't have the answer is fine and can actually improve your credibility, if you make an effort to get the answer for the customer. |

- *Engage in positive self-talk.* Practice healthy thinking. Do not clutter your mind with negatives.
- *Get a calming object.* Use a photo, cartoon, small stuffed animal, or positive notes in your work area that remind you "this, too, shall pass."
- *Focus on successes rather than negatives.* Track the things that go right.

- *Use your break time effectively.* Do something to keep yourself going, something that relaxes you and clears your mind. For example, listen to music, take a short walk, or read. Do not use your free time for complaining to others.
- *Develop a buddy system at work.* Learn from each other and share the load.
- *Take care of yourself.* When the details of work or a particular customer situation are getting you down, step back and look at the big picture. Be kind to yourself. Know that you have choices. Exercise, volunteer, spend time with friends and family, and do other things that add value to your life.
- *Take your sense of humor to work.* Take your work seriously, but don't take yourself seriously. Learn to laugh at yourself.

### CUSTOMER SERVICE TIP

**3.1** *Negative self-talk affects your attitude and interferes with your ability to develop an emotional connection with your customer.*

## Delivering Comprehensive Service

Serving customers well is not a case of *"us versus them."* Put another way, don't look at excellent service as "we lose—they win." When common goals with your customer are established, you are both working toward something you agree is worthy. When you reach those goals, you are both satisfied. Moreover, if you don't reach them, the customer feels that at least you tried and gave an honest effort.

When a customer complains, you need to take corrective action as soon as possible. If the customer complains directly to you, avoid being defensive or judgmental. Do not attempt to explain why the problem occurred. The customer is not particularly interested in reasons for poor service or who is to blame. Customers want to know they are being heard and that their comments are valued. Most of all, they want the problem fixed. Remember that, whenever a customer perceives that he or she is not being served well, that is the customer's reality.

## Delivery of Services

Often, customer service representatives have to deal with customers who perceive services they receive through a filter, or screen. Such a frame of reference depends on several factors:

- How the customer feels that day
- Experiences the customer has had that day
- Experiences the customer has had with the CSR or the company
- Experiences the customer's friends or family members have had with employees in the company
- The setting, environment, and circumstances of the current interaction

All things being equal, there is little difference between an organization and its competition. How service is delivered, therefore, is critical. One small action can make all the difference to a customer on a particular day. In the case of customer service, we can look at delivery of services similar to those in Figure 3.1. The concept of delivery of services can be represented by two circles—one within the other. The inner circle is made up of the basic services and products an organization and its competition provide. Customers *expect* the services and products shown in the inner circle: convenient hours of operation, accurate and timely billing process, adequate computer system, convenient location, and shipping services. In contrast, the outer circle allows a company to showcase its organization, to set itself apart from the competition by providing elements that exceed customers' expectations: customer follow-up, guaranteed appointment times, personal services, child care for shoppers, and assistance to take products to the car.

How important is outer-circle service? It is extremely important. Your inner circle may be perfect because you do everything the customer expects, but what you do might not be enough to guarantee that the customer will come back on a regular basis. To summarize, then, without strong outer-circle service, you may not be offering the customer anything *special enough* to set you apart from the competition.

## CSRs and the Adversity Quotient

Paul Stoltz, author of a book entitled *Adversity Quotient @ Work*, states that companies should hire customer service representatives who have a high adversity quotient (AQ).

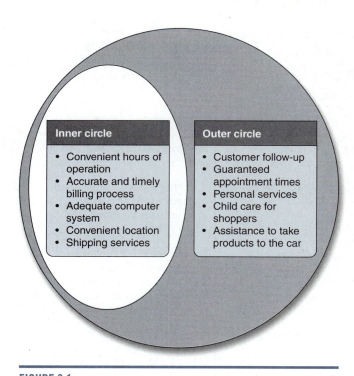

**Inner circle**
- Convenient hours of operation
- Accurate and timely billing process
- Adequate computer system
- Convenient location
- Shipping services

**Outer circle**
- Customer follow-up
- Guaranteed appointment times
- Personal services
- Child care for shoppers
- Assistance to take products to the car

**FIGURE 3.1**
When delivering services to customers, the inner and outer circles of service characterize an organization.

An **adversity quotient** is a precise, measurable, unconscious pattern of how people respond to adversity. According to Stoltz, companies need to hire customer service representatives who not only are nice but also are resilient and have a high AQ. Unless CSRs learn how to maintain control and be energized by tough problems, adversity will take its toll on them and negatively affect the services they provide to customers. The core elements of an AQ, according to Stoltz, are control, ownership, reach, and endurance:

- *Control.* CSRs who have a high AQ perceive that they have influence over adverse customer service situations. For example, if the company has a product recall, CSRs remain calm, project a positive attitude, and reassure customers that the problem will be remedied. On the other hand, low-AQ CSRs become stressed and overwhelmed by adversity.

- *Ownership.* CSRs with a high AQ hold themselves accountable for solving customers' problems. Conversely, low-AQ CSRs are likely to say, "It's not my fault."

- *Reach.* High-AQ CSRs refuse to allow negative situations reach into other areas of their work lives. For instance, if a customer threatens to defect to a competitor, they focus on earning back the customer's loyalty, remaining upbeat, no matter what, whereas low-AQ CSRs view the situation as hopeless and allow their feelings to have an impact on other aspects of their job.

- *Endurance.* High-AQ CSRs can see beyond difficulties and retain their optimism. This gives them the endurance to hang on during adverse encounters with customers. In contrast, low-AQ CSRs reason, "Why try to endure this? It's only going to end in disaster!"[1]

There are a number of skills and personal characteristics that star service representatives have in common. In today's competitive marketplace, you need to do all you can to differentiate yourself in terms of providing excellent customer service. Assume the role of the CSR you want to become and answer each question in Guideline 3.2, to determine how well you might stand out, compared with other service representatives.

## Customer Service Rules and Guidelines

When you work for any organization, there are rules and guidelines that must be followed. To separate our understanding of these rules, we'll refer to them as red and blue rules. Red rules are very prescriptive, because it is essential they be done exactly as specified. One example of a red rule deals with legal issues that say you have a legal obligation to follow particular procedures exactly as outlined. Another red rule might involve safety issues federally mandated by the Occupational Safety and Health Administration (OSHA). For example, requiring that something be done in a certain manner in order to keep the workplace safe is a red rule. In other words, every employee in the organization must follow red rules.

However, there also are blue rules, rules that are optional and can be bent or modified, based on the circumstances. Statements such as "We don't work after 5:00 P.M." and "Late fees cannot be waived" are examples of blue rules. They play into the old saying "There is an exception to every [blue] rule."

It may be the most reasonable and prudent action to bend the rule because it just makes sense and is for the greater good of the situation and the customers involved. The important thing about organizational rules is that you

[1]"Forget the Smile Training—Consider Boot Camp!" *Managing Customer Service* (April 2001): 8.

---

**GUIDELINE 3.2** **QUIZ**

## "Do You Stand Out from the Competition?"

| Yes | No | | Question |
|-----|-----|-----|----------|
| ☐ | ☐ | 1. | Do you spend 60 to 70 percent of your time listening while a customer talks? |
| ☐ | ☐ | 2. | Do you smile more often than most other people? |
| ☐ | ☐ | 3. | Are you better than others at recognizing and responding to customer questions and problems? |
| ☐ | ☐ | 4. | Are you highly effective at identifying and prioritizing customer needs? |
| ☐ | ☐ | 5. | Do you tend to recommend additional products or services that meet a customer's specific needs? |
| ☐ | ☐ | 6. | Do you explain procedures in clear, concise terms? |
| ☐ | ☐ | 7. | Are you highly enthusiastic about attending customer service training seminars and classes? |
| ☐ | ☐ | 8. | Do you listen to motivational tapes and read inspirational books in your leisure time? |
| ☐ | ☐ | 9. | Do you regard yourself as generally upbeat and positive? |
| ☐ | ☐ | 10. | Do you enjoy the work you do? |
| ☐ | ☐ | | Total |

*Note: If you answered 9 or 10 questions "yes," you already have many habits of highly successful CSRs. Eight is an average score. Seven or less indicates that there are still ways you can improve your performance.*

---

have to define clearly both the red and blue rules and give individual employees as much discretion to change blue rules on a case-by-case basis, depending on the situation. In other words, relative to interpreting blue rules, CSRs can be empowered by their organization to use their best judgment.

**CUSTOMER SERVICE TIP**

*3.2 When you are empathetic, you are sensitive to your customer's feelings and thoughts.*

## Building a Teamwork Approach to Customer Service

What do you think of when someone mentions the word *teamwork*? Sports teams most often come to mind, but other situations involve teamwork as well. For example, consider the movie industry. Every time producers decide to make a movie, they have to put together a new team,

Customers feel better taken care of when service providers work as a team.

which includes actors, sound and light crews, makeup artists, clothes designers, and directors, among others. All the members of the team are needed to create a finished product, the movie; however, in order to accomplish that goal with positive results, all the members must work together as a team.

In like fashion, taking a team approach to customer service means working together as a group, with common expectations and goals. What does teamwork show customers? A good team approach shows that the company is organized and that everyone is moving toward a common goal of satisfying the customer.

Because of shared ownership, no team member will let the failure of one member cause the entire team to fail. Team members are accountable to each other; again, customers know that the final objective of the team is their satisfaction.

## Teamwork Communication

Communication is one of the most important considerations for teams to thrive. A team can be effective only if its members communicate well with each other. Everyone needs to know what is going on.

Whenever a team is put together, however, there are always issues, such as different personalities, management styles, and company hierarchies, to deal with. Many times, it is more difficult to exchange honest, open feedback with someone you work with than with your customers. This is sometimes due to the fact that the message you have to share with a fellow worker is not a positive one.

To maintain good working relationships, therefore, it is important that any negative feedback or criticisms you need to offer a coworker be focused on the specific task in question, not on his or her personality. Also, to be constructive, any criticism you offer should be accompanied by a positive suggestion on how to improve the task. By the same token, if a teammate is doing something well, be sure to say so. Again, focus your comments on the task. An effective customer service environment fosters forthright feedback and values honesty.

## ETHICS/CHOICES

**3.2** Your company encourages employees to work in teams. Brent is a fellow CSR with whom you have worked before. On numerous occasions, you have noticed that he really has "an attitude." To you, it appears that he is always angry and seemingly puts others down without thinking that what he is saying may be upsetting and hurtful to others. Most of your coworkers simply ignore Brent and just try to have as little conversation with him as possible. What would be your approach with Brent?

## Benefits of Teamwork

When customer service is built with teamwork as its foundation, many benefits result. One of the most important benefits is that teamwork helps break down walls that can sometimes exist between sections or departments within organizations. Teamwork can also provide new ideas and a new slant on a customer problem. Finally, teamwork can create a more effective method to use in delegating work and any follow-up actions that must be taken.

Because no one is an expert in everything, people need to gather knowledge from others. People who work together tend to learn things faster and retain information longer than do individuals who work alone. Teamwork creates a **synergy,** which means that the combined effect of the efforts of many individuals is greater than the sum of their individual efforts. With synergy, problem solving becomes more effective, and better decisions tend to be made. Guideline 3.3 provides some strategies that team members can adopt to provide exceptional customer service.

1. *Support your teammates with information.* Share what you know freely with your coworkers. Use huddles—brief, informal meetings—instead of formal meetings when time is limited.

2. *Discuss new policies.* Discuss any new policies with your team and jointly create a way to explain changes to your customers in a positive way. Sometimes, using a script can ensure that everyone is consistently following the same plan.

3. *Identify areas for improvement.* Let the ideas flow without judgment in a brainstorming session. Even the craziest ideas sometimes turn out to be the ideas that work the best.

4. *Show pride in yourself and your coworkers.* Celebrate others' successes. Let the customer know you are proud.

# Dealing with Unique Customer Situations

Customer service interactions can be complex under the best of conditions. Add issues of language, race, gender, religion, age, or disability into the mix and, often, otherwise competent employees can be found acting in ways ranging from mildly inappropriate to inexcusably rude.

The customer demographics for most organizations are changing in such a way as to increase the diversity and uniqueness of the populations that are served. This factor makes it imperative that CSRs be aware of how customers perceive their service. Further, how you perceive the needs of your customers may depend on their (and your own) personal and cultural perspectives.

## Customers of Different Cultures

As companies expand across the globe, challenges in customer service grow. In order to avoid cultural collisions with customers—when emotions, habits, or judgments taint service efforts—a CSR needs to be aware of how culture plays a role in the service encounter. A suggestion is for employees to identify their cultural differences and be conscious about not stereotyping any customer. Stereotyping customers leads to misunderstandings and prejudgments that hinder service encounters.

Customers with accents generally know they have an accent, but the responsibility for understanding what is being said still rests with the customer service representative. When serving customers from a different culture, apologize to them when you don't understand them. Be sure to speak to them slowly and clearly. If necessary, ask them to repeat what they have said. This gives you another chance to develop an "ear" for the accent. It is as important for a listener to understand through a heavy accent as it is for the other person to make strides toward improving his or her English skills.

Because some cultures consider feedback or criticism damaging to one's reputation, CSRs might paraphrase to restate what was said to ensure a smooth communication flow. Customer service representatives must be sensitive to the ethnic, religious, and moral values of other cultures. Sensitive companies that provide a good cross-cultural employee training program find it to be very helpful. The content of this training program might include an explanation of the differences between cultures, as well as formal manners and etiquette to follow when serving international customers.

## CUSTOMER SERVICE TIP

*3.3* *If a word or a phrase isn't common knowledge, don't use it with a customer. Always speak distinctly, or you risk failing to connect with the customer.*

## Customers with Disabilities

Discrimination against customers with disabilities is often unintentional. It may stem from a general lack of awareness that many of us have about disabilities. Consequently, it is important for companies to plan ahead to meet the requirements of their customers with disabilities. Wherever necessary and reasonable, service providers should adjust the way they provide their services, so that people who are physically challenged can use them in the best way.

In all cases, it is important to ensure that the dignity of persons with disabilities is respected when services are provided. It is perfectly all right to consult them about how they might be served. It is important that service providers and their organization not assume that the only way to make services more accessible to people with disabilities is to alter the premises physically, such as by installing a permanent ramp or widening doorways. Often, minor measures that are embedded in common sense work wonderfully. One example is to practice patience and to allow more time to deal with customers with disabilities. Listening carefully and responding appropriately helps CSRs meet the requirements and expectations of people with disabilities.

In conclusion, when serving any customer,

- Evaluate how the customer wants to be served.
- Adjust your approach to match the customer's needs.
- Greet all customers and make them feel comfortable.
- Respect personal differences.
- Always thank customers for their business.

## Concluding Message for CSRs

Companies make painful compromises by hiring people with a less than stable work record and a less than acceptable customer service attitude. Employers want service providers who have a history of showing up at work and who are energetic, knowledgeable, kind, and efficient with customers.

Customer service representatives can provide service more consistently if three important guidelines are followed: View all customers positively, establish an emotional connection with customers by giving them your undivided attention, and listen actively to all customer concerns.

## Summary

- The customer is the one who sets the standard for service excellence.
- Employees who give exceptional customer service have a positive, can-do attitude.
- Positive self-talk helps each of us build a positive, winning attitude, whereas negative self-talk does just the opposite.
- There are certain statements that should never be used with customers.
- When a customer complains, corrective action needs to be taken as soon as possible.

- Examples of outer-circle elements of customer service include the extras that many companies do not give, such as customer follow-up and guaranteed appointment times.
- The inner-circle elements are made up of the basic services and products an organization and its competition provide the consumer.
- The adversity quotient is the precise, measurable, unconscious pattern of how people respond to adversity.
- In serving customers, there are legal and safety-oriented company rules that cannot be altered; however, other rules that do not have a legal or safety basis can be bent or modified, based on particular customer circumstances.
- A good team approach shows that the company is organized and that everyone is moving toward the common goal of doing whatever it takes to satisfy the customer.
- CSRs deal with unique service situations, including working with customers who present challenges related to issues of language, race, gender, religion, age, and disability.

## QUESTIONS FOR CRITICAL THINKING

1. How would you describe the best customer-oriented attitude you've encountered relative to services you've received over the past month?

2. In what ways can self-talk affect how people behave and think?

3. Describe a business you've encountered in your city where you feel both its outer-level and its inner-level elements of customer service are par excellence.

4. Do you agree that the way people handle adversity in their lives affects their service and work attitudes? Explain.

5. What are two benefits to a CSR of contributing to team efforts at work?

6. If you were a CSR in the travel industry, what would you keep in mind when booking travel for customers of different cultures and customers with disabilities?

## On-line Research Activities

### Project 3.1: Positive Attitudes at Work

Assume you are doing a report on *the power of a positive work attitude.* Use the Internet to research information and use the search engine of your choice. As a result of your search, keyboard three items (and their URLs) of current information you might use in your report.

### Project 3.2: "Application of the Adversity Quotient In . . ."

#### Situation

In the lunchroom one day at On-Time Technology Products, someone had left the book *Adversity Quotient @ Work* on one of the tables. Several CSRs picked it up and started talking about the usefulness of AQ when applying these concepts in the world of business. You said that you felt AQ could apply to any aspect of our lives to include how we work, play, learn, and are members of families and society, in general. Doug, on the other hand, said he felt AQ applied only to the business world, and Ruth said that, if educators could help students achieve higher AQs, then school environments would be less violent.

*On the Internet, locate the application of dealing with adversity at several web sites. Using file PRJ3-2 on the student CD, key responses in the following table format that will provide information on ways that a high AQ can positively influence each area.*

| Life Situation | Benefit of Applying High AQs |
|---|---|
| 1. In business, in general | |
| 2. In call centers for CSRs | |
| 3. In the home/family | |
| 4. In schools (K–12) | |

## Communication Skills at Work

### Project 3.3: "Action Plan for Improving Your Attitude"

#### Situation

Supervisor Mary Graeff has asked each CSR to develop an action plan to improve on employees' attitudes when working with customers. Give some thought to each of the situations in column 1 and respond in column 2 with an activity that would work for you.

*Retrieve file PRJ3-3 and complete the following form.*

| What Can You Do To . . . | Response |
|---|---|
| 1. Convey interest in your customers? | |
| 2. Keep your attitude positive? | |
| 3. Remain energized and enthusiastic on the job? | |
| 4. Learn more about the organization you work for? | |
| 5. Take initiative when helping a customer? | |

## Decision Making at Work

**Project 3.4:** How to Motivate the Unenthusiastic Teammate

During a weekly team meeting at On-Time Technology Products, you notice that one of your teammates is quieter than usual and acts as if he does not care to be involved in the team's brainstorming session.

*Respond to each of the following statements with an example of what you might say to a team member who suffers from lack of motivation.*

1. Acknowledge your teammate's value.

   _____

   _____

   _____

   _____

   _____

2. Get to the source of the problem.

   _____

   _____

   _____

   _____

   _____

3. Stress the importance of team harmony.

   _____

   _____

   _____

   _____

   _____

## Case Study

### 3.1 "Deal with It!"

On the first day of a 4-day holiday weekend, Samantha was having a problem with her phone and needed to use her neighbor Tim's phone. When she finished talking to the customer service representative at the phone company, she was quite shocked by the service she had received. She told Tim that the CSR told her that she would just "have to *deal with* the inconvenience until Tuesday morning." Samantha ranted and raved to Tim for a good 20 minutes.

#### Discussion Questions

*1. Does Samantha have a legitimate reason to be upset with the phone company?*

_____

_____

_____

_____

_____

_____

*2. If this happened to you, what steps would you suggest to the phone company to improve its customer service?*

_____

_____

_____

_____

_____

_____

_____

## Case Study

### 3.2 "If There's a Rule, I'll Follow It"

Doug, a CSR for On-Time Technology Products, recently experienced a very frustrating civil brush with the law concerning boundary lines between his and his neighbor's property. As a consequence of this negative legal experience, everyone at work recognizes that Doug is a bit straitlaced when it comes to following rules. However, the situation is starting to become disturbing, because his narrow attitude is carrying over to how he is dealing with customers while on the job.

*Answer the following questions:*

*1. Do situations in a person's personal life spill over and affect attitudes on the job? Explain.*

_____

_____

_____

*2. If you were Mary Graeff, Doug's supervisor, how would you explain to him the best way to interpret which rules he is required to follow to the letter and which ones allow him some flexibility?*

_____

_____

_____

*3. If Ms. Graeff were to ask you what steps you would take to help Doug overcome this attitude and get back on track with customers, what would you recommend that she do (i.e., would you just talk to him, reprimand him, send him for training, . . .)?*

_____

_____

_____

_____

# Resolving Customer Problems and Complaints

> *Pursue excellence in what you do and contain mistakes so the customers don't have to experience them.*
>
> TOM REILLY, VALUE ADDED CUSTOMER SERVICE

## OBJECTIVES

**AFTER COMPLETING THIS CHAPTER,**
**YOU WILL BE ABLE TO:**

1. Describe the activities involved in proactive problem solving when dealing with customers.

2. List reasons that customers complain.

3. Distinguish between a disagreement and a conflict and their respective outcomes on customer relations.

4. Itemize the steps necessary to follow when processing customer complaints.

5. Create a typical script to follow when handling a customer service problem.

6. Discuss approaches to use when handling the emotions of customers when they complain and become angry.

7. Identify several examples of behaviors that service representatives can expect from angry customers.

Everyone has tales of very bad service, often so bad the story becomes comical. Customer service seems so simple—treat customers with dignity and respect, and they will reward you with buying loyalty. Companies that are customer-focused do this best when they establish service standards. When resolving customer problems and complaints, they should feel accountable to their customers for these principles.

Handling a complaint becomes a moment of truth in maintaining and developing long-term customer relations. In fact, first-class organizations are finding they can lock in customers for life simply by treating them fairly during a product or service dispute. Customers point to getting a fair resolution as a reason for continuing to do business with a particular product or service provider. As an example, LL Bean built an empire on the simple rule that "no customer should have a product that isn't completely satisfactory."

The goal of Chapter 4 is to provide some approaches for resolving customer problems in a fair manner and within a reasonable time frame in order to regain business. Ultimately, the overall goal is to cultivate a *loyal* customer.

# Solving Customer Problems

Solving problems is one of the primary goals of any customer service professional. When we think of problem solving, however, we generally think of dealing with problems *after* they arise—a sort of crisis-management approach. This is the traditional view of problem solving; however, to exceed customers' expectations and provide exceptional service, successful companies try to anticipate and solve problems *before* they occur. This process is called **proactive problem solving.**

## CUSTOMER SERVICE TIP

**4.1** *Customers would rather have no information than the wrong information.*

## Proactive Problem Solving

When you solve customer problems proactively, you attempt to do the following:

- *Manage customer expectations.* In other words, as you work with your customers, you try to anticipate any problems that could arise with your product or service. Be careful never to overpromise or oversell. For instance, at the time of the sale, educate and inform buyers about extra costs and possible delays.

- *Clarify incorrect assumptions the customer has.* Usually when this situation occurs, the customer has different expectations than you had hoped he or she would have. Perhaps an overeager salesperson at your company promised the customer something the product could not deliver, or the customer assumed you provided a specific service as part of the regular cost but you do not and this was not clarified up-front. When this happens, remember that customers may not always be right, but they are always customers. The following are some steps to take when the customer approaches you with incorrect assumptions about a product or service you represent:

1. Thank the customer for coming to you with the complaint.

2. Deal with the emotions first. Help the customer express dissatisfaction and empathize with him or her.

3. Establish the facts. Get the customer's understanding of the situation. Don't discount what the customer says and, by all means, don't interrupt.

4. Maintain respect. Do not place blame on the customer or on anyone in your organization.

5. Move to problem solving. Look for a way to help the customer. If you are not sure what you can do or if you need additional time to weigh your options, say, "Let me check into this and get back to you." With that said, it is critical that you follow through on any promises you make in a timely manner.

6. Find the best available option. If possible, let the customer be right. If that isn't possible, tell the customer what you *can* do, instead of what you cannot do.

- *Deliver bad news positively.* There will come a time when you must tell a customer that you will not be able to take something back, that the item he or she ordered is out of stock, or that he or she must pay in advance. Following are some suggestions for delivering unavoidable bad news to a customer:

  - Look for an alternative first.
  - Inform the customer as early in the process as possible. Even though it is an unpleasant part of the job, do not put it off.
  - Inform the customer over the phone or in person, not by letter.
  - Get to the point quickly. You can warn the customer that bad news is coming in a kind way by saying something like "You're not going to like hearing this, but . . ." This can sometimes soften the subsequent distress.
  - Treat the customer fairly. Customers remember your courtesy and professionalism long after the actual problem has been forgotten.

- *Sincerely apologize when it is not possible to satisfy the customer.* Sometimes you can't satisfy a customer, no matter how hard you try. When nothing seems to satisfy the customer, take these additional steps:

1. Begin by honestly apologizing that you are unable to help the customer.

2. Ask for a chance in the future to serve the customer again.

3. Do not let this contact affect your disposition and attitude when serving the next customer.

## Timely Problem Solving

The best time to deal with a customer's grievance is while the complaint is happening. In fact, 70 percent of complaining customers will return if the problem is resolved in their favor, according to recent surveys. That number grows to 95 percent if the complaint is resolved on the spot.[1] Within the bounds of reason, you can never do enough for the customer, particularly when the customer appears noticeably upset. How do you recognize an upset customer? Watch the body language of disgruntled customers. Look for any verbal cue or sign of exasperation in the body language.

Organizations save money when they empower employees with the discretionary authority to spend a reasonable amount of money in resolving the customer's concern at the time of the complaint. When the problem is passed along to somebody higher up, it takes more time and involves the risk that the complaint will not be resolved. Employees will never do wrong by doing right for the customer. The disgruntled customer will also become your organization's most effective advertisement as he or she tells friends about the incredible customer service received.

Even the most experienced CSR has experienced a customer who will be satisfied only by talking to a superior. When the customer demands to talk with the manager, the owner, or the president of your organization,

- Ask for information about the problem, so that you can transfer the customer to a superior.
- After the customer gives you the information, offer to handle the situation for the customer yourself, if you are able.
- Transfer the call when necessary—but only after collecting information and explaining the situation to

your manager *prior* to his or her taking the call. In other words, don't ever blindside your boss by giving him or her a problem to solve without prior information.

## Resolving Customer Complaints

Most business owners deal with one to five or more complaints a week. Before you offer to remedy customer complaints, be sure to ask the customer how he or she would prefer the problem be resolved. A customer may be agreeable to the simple solution of your replacing an item or redoing the work at no charge. If a customer will accept only a full or partial refund, it may be in your best interest to honor the request, even when it is not written in your guidelines to do so. Your willingness to help can squash any bad word-of-mouth advertising that could affect future sales.

## Why Customers Complain

Customers complain for a host of different reasons. Most often, however, the overriding reason is because the expectations they have when purchasing a product or service are not met. When voiced, some reasons customers give for product service complaints are

- Poor product quality
- Incompetent or discourteous employees
- Inadequate or poor repair work
- Goods or service delivery delays
- Failure to fulfill product or service warranties
- Billing errors or failure to provide timely refunds and adjustments, as promised
- Deceptive or inaccurate advertising, such as promoting products that are unavailable or are in limited supply

Recently, consumers have become more demanding, expecting fair pricing and high quality. If the customer's current brand doesn't give them what they want, they will go to the competitor.

A word of warning, however: Just because a company isn't hearing complaints, it does not mean the company has satisfied customers. Whereas some customers shout, many customers just leave quietly. Silent attrition is deadly, because companies get no opportunity to remedy problems and retain customers.

---

[1]Kimberly Stansell, "Handle Complaints with Finesse," *Bootstrapper's Success Secrets* (January 31, 2000): 2.

## Disagreement vs. Conflict

When dealing with customer complaints, it is important to distinguish between disagreement and conflict. In general, **disagreements** arise because two people have different interpretations about the product's abilities, or they blame each other for past wrongdoing. Disagreements don't have to be resolved. You can, for example, agree to debate for the fun of it, or even to take the stance that it is okay to agree to disagree.

Any conflict with a customer, on the other hand, is more serious. It can jeopardize productivity, relationships at work, and dealings with customers. The basic meaning of a **conflict** is "If you get what you want, then I can't get what I want." Although most of us dislike being around or participating in conflict situations, it is important to realize that sometimes good can be brought about by conflict. This could happen if conflict

- Produces change for the better
- Results in gains and innovations
- Fosters unity and understanding
- Brings about positive and meaningful changes in behavior

Not all conflict, however, is good. If conflict escalates with customers, you risk becoming enemies and may end up with accusations and threats. Parties get angry and point the finger at each other. In other words, what usually happens during a conflict is

- General issues replace specific issues as the problem goes from being angry over a specific behavior to wanting to sever the relationship completely.
- Concern for self turns into retaliation, and the primary interest becomes hurting each other or getting even.

## The Complaint-Handling Process

The foundation for maintaining customer goodwill in organizations is the existence, promotion, and practice of a sound **customer relations policy.** Any complaint-handling system is structured from this customer relations policy and must operate simply, effectively, and quickly to everyone's mutual benefit. A customer relations policy should encourage customers to communicate their concerns and demonstrate a strong commitment to customer satisfaction. In addition, the policy should spell out how, when, where, and by whom complaints or questions are handled. One person within the company should have the ultimate authority and responsibility for customer relations, although *all* employees should know the guidelines as stated in the policy and how to implement them.

In our global marketplace, where businesses compete both nationally and internationally, effective complaint handling should be a priority for every business. Customer complaints are never easy to hear. If a shift is made from being defensive to opportunistic, however, complaints can be a company's best friend. Thriving companies take the following steps when processing customer complaints:

1. *Screen, log in information, and listen.* Start the procedure by logging in the date a complaint is received and recording all pertinent customer information. A dissatisfied customer wants to know that someone is willing to listen. It is important to be quiet, to pay attention, and to listen carefully to what the customer is saying—without being distracted or sounding impatient. Try not to interrupt, as doing so may cause the customer to argue, withdraw, or simply hang up or walk away. Sometime during this initial contact, remember to thank the customer for bringing the problem to your attention.

2. *Empathize.* After having the opportunity to express dissatisfaction, the customer wants to know that someone understands and cares about the situation. Listen and respond with empathy to acknowledge the customer's feelings (upset, frustrated, disappointed) and the facts of the situation that are causing those feelings. If possible, tell the customer how long it will take to satisfy the complaint, especially if a delay might occur.

3. *Solicit feedback.* Try to get the customer to explain how the problem happened. By asking the customer for feedback on how the problem was created, you convey concern and a willingness to understand the problem in order to arrive at the best solution. For example, asking, "What do you think would be fair in this situation?" appeals to the customer's sense of justice.

4. *Apologize.* The customer wants to hear that you are sorry about the problem or inconvenience, even if you are not necessarily the one to blame. You can apologize without accepting blame by saying, "This situation is unfortunate, and I apologize for it." A genuine apology is often the key to healing wounds. An immediate, sincere apology defuses hostility, no matter how grievous

the injury. Not only is an apology an expected social politeness; it is also a practical step that helps open the door to further communication.

5. *Take ownership and formulate a solution.* If there is one thing that will frustrate a customer, it is being passed from one employee or department to another. The reason customers complain is that they feel something needs to be done. If the problem can be fixed on the spot, do it. If it can't, you should at least call your supervisor or transfer the customer to the appropriate person who can address the problem. In any case, take ownership of the problem and make sure that it is handled appropriately and immediately. Any solution should conform to your established customer relations policy and take into account contractual and/or warranty obligations, customer expectations, your company's expectations, and your ability to deliver on your decision. When you respond, make sure your response is clear and appropriate. Try to avoid technical jargon. A respectful explanation of even an adverse decision can often preserve customer goodwill.

6. *Follow up.* After your response, contact the customer to make sure that the matter has been resolved satisfactorily. Ask for a second chance by saying, "We hope we'll have a chance to serve you again."

In a recent article, Bernice Johnston, author of the book *Real World Customer Service*, tells customer service professionals exactly what to say when customers complain. Guideline 4.1 provides a few real-world problems submitted to Ms. Johnston by service representatives and the responses she recommends they say.

Sometimes, tough calls become more manageable when the customer service representative uses a **script.** Two advantages of using scripts are that they help CSRs deliver consistent responses to common customer problems and assist CSRs in developing their own problem-solving responses. Sometimes, when you use just the right combination of words—coupled with a sensitivity to your customer's position—the result is notable in its impact. When implemented well, appropriate scripts include four key elements:

1. *Empathy.* CSRs should begin their responses by focusing on feelings. This means understanding the situation and feelings from the customer's point of view.

2. *Acknowledgment.* This involves recognizing the validity of the customer's complaint, a key step in the process of reaching a solution to any problem.

3. *Reassurance.* At this point, CSRs need to restore the customer's confidence in the company.

---

**GUIDELINE 4.1    What to Say When Customers Complain**

| Problem | What to Say | Why This Works |
|---|---|---|
| • Your customer is very upset because a company error has resulted in additional charges to her account. | "I can understand how upset you are that these additional charges have shown up because of our error. I'd be upset about it, too. Here's what I can do about it. . . ." | It is important when you have an upset customer that you acknowledge and restate her concern. This shows you have been listening, you understand, and you are personally interested in getting the problem resolved. |
| • The customer seems unsatisfied after you have told him the options to resolving his problem. | "I understand that you are disappointed, and you have every right to be. I'm disappointed, too, that we cannot resolve this. What do you suggest we do next?" | When you have suggested everything you can think of, ask the customer what the ideal solution would be from his point of view. He might say, "All I really want is an apology." That you can do. |
| • Although you have worked very hard to resolve your customer's complaint, she accuses you of sounding hostile by saying, "You are really being testy today, aren't you?" | "I'm sorry that you have this impression of me. What can I do to change your perception?" | Demonstrating a sincere interest in learning what has upset the customer can give you the information you need to turn her attitude around. |

SOURCE: "Tough Customer Complaints Require Quick, Focused Responses," *Dartnell's Customers First* (June 12, 2000): 4.

4. *Action.* It is not enough to empathize, acknowledge, and reassure. The action is what counts.

Guideline 4.2 provides a script from Bernice Johnston's book that demonstrates the four elements in action.

## CUSTOMER SERVICE TIP

**4.2** *When working with customers, focus on determining "how can we," not "why we can't."*

## Dealing with Unruly Customers

Occasionally, every business has to deal with an unruly customer. No matter how carefully you explain your position, there's one customer in a thousand who will misunderstand and take great offense. Although these situations are never pleasant, understanding a customer's emotions and identifying what actions and words trigger extreme anger can help a service provider.

### Why Customers Get Angry

Dale Carnegie said, "The only way to get the best of an argument is to avoid it." Although there are many reasons that a customer may become dissatisfied, they generally have one thing in common: The perceived value of a product or service is less than the customer expected. The following are four shortcomings that can cause a customer to view your product or service negatively:

1. *The customer didn't get what was promised or what was expected.* To overcome this, you must raise the quality of the product or, in some cases, work to make the customer's expectations more realistic.

2. *Someone was rude to the customer.* Whether the employee knew it or not, this was the customer's perception. Remember that a perception is the customer's reality.

3. *Someone was indifferent to the customer.* An employee projected a "can't-do" attitude and left it at that—with the customer feeling frustrated.

4. *No one listened to the customer.* Of all four reasons, this is the most troubling. Failing to listen to a customer is a tragic waste of an opportunity for feedback. This feedback is important in helping improve processes, products, and services.

---

**GUIDELINE 4.2** | **A Sample Customer Service Script**

1. "You sound pretty disappointed with the information I've just told you." *(empathy)*

2. "Before we give up on your request for . . . ." *(acknowledgment)*

3. "I want to make sure there's nothing I'm aware of that's changed." *(reassurance)*

4. "Let me get Ms. Miller in on this conversation and listen to her ideas about alternatives. I'd be interested in hearing them myself. Do you have any objections to this?" *(action)*

**Source:** "Equip Reps to Manage Tough Calls with Effective Use of Scripts," *The Dartnell Corporation,* July 2001, pg. 5.

## Customer Emotions

When customers are dissatisfied, they can become difficult, frustrated, and quick to anger. What CSRs must realize is that an angry customer does not respond to logic. In fact, the more logical you are, the angrier the customer may become. No matter what you say and no matter how you phrase it, you simply will not be able to penetrate the customer's emotional barrier. Before you can work on the customer's problem, you must be able to deal with the customer's emotions.

The first step in calming an angry person is to stay calm yourself. Try to keep your voice calm and relaxed. When you hear your voice sounding rushed or panicked, take a few deep breaths and use positive self-talk to help you gain composure. When you feel your jaw is clenched, relax your face muscles. Once *your* emotions are under control, then turn your attention to calming your customer:

- *Remain calm yourself.* Do not react emotionally, regardless of how upset the customer gets.

- *Allow the customer to vent.* Actively listen and let the customer know you are listening by not interrupting (he or she will just begin again by restating what was just said). Wait until the venting finishes (you might hear a sigh or sense that the customer is winding down).

- *Deal with the emotion first.* You must resolve the customer's emotions before you can begin to solve the problem:
  → *Restate what the customer said.* By paraphrasing, you let the customer know you heard what was said, and it gives the customer the opportunity to clarify your understanding of his or her concerns.

→ *Show empathy.* When you show empathy, you show concern. Concern is not the same as agreement. Statements such as "I can understand why you feel that way" and "I'd be upset if that happened to me" allow you to empathize with the customer but not place blame on anyone in your organization.

→ *Find agreement.* When you find agreement with the customer, you clearly identify the real problem; in other words, you get on the same side as the customer. The enemy is now the problem, not you or your company.

• *Thank the customer for bringing the problem to your attention.* This sends the message that, although it's unfortunate that the customer has a concern, it presents an opportunity to resolve a problem that other customers may experience.

• *Avoid emotional trigger phrases.* Use calming phrases to describe what you can do for the customer to solve the problem. Examples of trigger and calming phrases are listed in Guideline 4.3.

• *Set limits with abusive customers.* In rare circumstances, you will have a customer who is loud or abusive or who simply cannot be calmed down. In this case, gently set limits with the abusive customer by

→ Using the customer's name, if you know it

→ Using a sympathetic tone of voice to request the customer's cooperation and include a help statement (e.g., "Mr. Jones, I really want to help you. I am finding it difficult as long as you continue to use this language. I can help you resolve this. Will you let me help you?")

• *As a last resort, delay action.* It may be time to seek a second opinion or to get a third party involved.

## Approach to Use with Angry Customers

When you deal with an angry customer, try to maintain a clear mental difference between you and your role. Keep in mind that the customer's criticism is not made against you personally but, rather, against the policy or the product or service the customer has received. If you make the issue a personal one, you will become emotionally involved.

If you continue to maintain a reasonable demeanor and a relatively quiet tone, an argumentative person will sometimes tone down to meet you where you are. In other words, people tend to imitate the tone of the person to whom they are talking. Remember, just because the customer is upset, it doesn't mean he or she is wrong. It can sometimes be a challenge to wade through the emotional message and get to the basic issues; however, you must do so, because, until you've found the heart of the problem, you cannot help solve it.

If a customer is verbally abusive, go into an office or another enclosure that offers privacy, where the customer can vent without disturbing others. Once the customer is calm, then decide what can be done about the problem. Keep in mind that, in a confrontational interchange, it doesn't hurt to agree a little. When you ease a complainant by saying, "I understand" or "What can I do to help?" you are not necessarily agreeing with the customer's position, only with his or her right to be angry—if the customer has a valid complaint.

Another approach is to throw the ball in the customer's court. Ask customers what they think can be done to resolve the problem. Your willingness to listen to what they want will make you appear cooperative and helpful, even if you can't meet their expectations. While you are discussing a possible resolution, remember not to make promises that you cannot keep.

**GUIDELINE 4.3  Trigger and Calming Phrases to Use with Customers**

| Trigger Phrases | Calming Phrases |
| --- | --- |
| "It's our policy." | "Here's what we can do . . .; Here's how we can handle this . . . ." (Quote the policy, just don't call it "policy.") |
| "I can't; we don't" | "I can, we do" |
| "What seems to be the problem?" | "How can I help?" |
| "I don't know." | "I can find out." |
| "You should have . . . ." | "Let's do this." (Move to the future, not the past.) |
| "Why didn't you. . . ." | "I can see why." |
| "The only thing we can do. . . ." | "The best option, I think, is. . . ." |
| "I don't handle that; it's not my job." | "Let's find the right person to handle your concern." |

Finally, to avoid confusion, have a clear understanding of what you have agreed upon with the customer. Reviewing the conversation gives both of you a chance to correct any misunderstanding and to value what the other expects. In summary, follow these steps when dealing with angry customers:

1. *Hear them out.* Let customers tell their side of the story. Let them vent while you listen. Listen all the way out. It is all right to ask questions to understand their problem better and to help you find out what it will take to help them, but don't interrupt.

2. *Empathize.* Acknowledge and respond to customers' feelings. Tell them you understand how they feel. In an effort to comfort them, you may want to tell them that a similar thing happened to you.

3. *Ask and answer questions.* Ask customers questions. This allows them to give you information you need to help resolve the situation. Agree with customers if at all possible. Never argue or get angry. Take notes and confirm that everything has been covered. Find some common ground other than the problem.

4. *Take responsibility for assisting customers.* Help customers resolve their situation. Don't blame others or look for a scapegoat. Don't pass the buck; "It's not my job" is never an acceptable response. Respond immediately. The customer wants a solution now. Remember to make a follow-up call after the situation has been resolved.

**CUSTOMER SERVICE TIP**

*4.3 Customer complaints are like medicine. Nobody likes them, but they make us better.*

In customer service, CSRs cannot avoid dealing with angry persons but should always do so with empathy and tact.

Although customers' anger or emotions may not be directed at you personally, you are the one who receives them. To help defuse anger, CSRs must understand *why* customers get emotional, upset, and angry. Although the following five reasons do not constitute a complete list, they are among the most important reasons that angry customers behave the way they do:

1. They had had a prior bad experience.
2. They felt as if they would get the runaround.
3. They resented potential loss of money.
4. They disliked being inconvenienced and having wasted more of their time.
5. They felt a loss of control.

The behaviors of angry customers manifest in various ways. The following are some behaviors you can expect to see when an angry person lashes out. When customers are angry, they

- Blame others
- Are loud and demanding
- Try to make you angry, too
- Have little regard for the rights of others
- Take charge of the conversation by insisting they be heard
- Tend to interrupt the other person who is talking
- Refuse to do what you ask
- Threaten to go to your manager or supervisor

Stressful customer interactions of this nature affect the morale and health of customer service representatives. For employees on the receiving end of an upsetting customer interaction, there is incredible pressure to simply grin and bear it. In the business world, this pressure is referred to as **emotional labor,** the stress that employees face each day when they must manage their emotions on the job.

Research indicates that workers who fake a good mood and who smile away the rudeness of their bosses and customers are more likely to suffer from emotional exhaustion and burnout.[2] Furthermore, laboratory research has determined that physical effects in the form of overworked cardiovascular and nervous systems, as well as weakened immune systems, manifest from this bottling up of emotions.

Dealing with demanding customers gets even tougher for CSRs when managers try to treat all customer complaints *equally*. Some complaints are justified, but some simply are not. If CSRs, for example, are reprimanded for an unjustified complaint by a customer who is truly being unreasonable, they start to resent it because they did nothing wrong.

One solution companies use is to provide CSRs a forum to vent their frustrations. This solution is easy to set up. Each week, a meeting is scheduled, at which service employees can choose to talk openly about their most difficult customer interaction that week. The advantages are many. First, it shows support for and understanding of the stress level of CSRs. Second, it provides a forum for CSRs to learn from each other ways to deal with specific or routine customer problems.

Another strategy that is becoming popular in organizations is to give a short, unscheduled break to the employee who has just handled a particularly tough customer. The employee may need a little time-out pause to regroup her emotions and positive attitude prior to returning to other customers.

[2]Chris Penttila, "Touch Customers," *Entrepreneur* (May 2001): 94.

## Concluding Message for CSRs

The job as a CSR is not designed to be adversarial with the customer. In fact, quite the opposite is true. When you look for common ground, you will find solutions that please the customer as well as make you and your boss happy.

Every business occasionally performs below customer expectations. Organizations can still be perceived as reputable if they have stood behind their guarantees and promises and have handled criticism diplomatically. Handling complaints in an exemplary fashion is an integral part of delivering excellent customer service.

Basically, when customers transact business with companies, they expect two outcomes: (1) a personal interaction with someone who is courteous and has decision-making authority and (2) products and services that have quality, are reliable, and are readily available. By focusing on these two outcomes, resolving customer problems and complaints are minimized.

## Summary

- Handling a complaint is a moment of truth in maintaining and developing long-term customer relations.
- Proactive problem solving means that successful companies try to anticipate and solve problems before they start.
- When delivering bad news to customers, CSRs should try to do so in a positive way.
- The best time to deal with a customer's grievance is while the complaint is happening.
- Before CSRs offer up remedies, they should ask the customer how he or she would prefer the problem to be resolved.
- Most often when customers complain, the overriding reason is because the expectations they have when purchasing a product or service have not been met.
- Conflicts with customers are more serious than disagreements and must be handled carefully, because a conflict can jeopardize future relations.
- A customer relations policy should encourage customers to communicate their concerns.

- When processing customer complaints, CSRs should follow these steps: screen, log in information, and listen; empathize; solicit feedback; apologize; take ownership and formulate a solution; and follow up.
- A script helps CSRs deliver consistent responses to common customer complaints.
- The steps to follow when calming an angry customer include remaining calm yourself; allowing the customer to vent; dealing with the emotion first; thanking the customer for bringing the problem to your attention; avoiding emotional trigger phrases; setting limits with abusive customers; and, if necessary, delaying action or seeking a second opinion.
- Stressful customer interactions affect the morale and health of customer service representatives; this stress is referred to as emotional labor.

## QUESTIONS FOR CRITICAL THINKING

1. In what ways is it more productive for CSRs to use proactive problem solving when dealing with customers?

2. Given the list of reasons that customers complain, prioritize the top three, according to your experiences.

3. Describe one personal example each of a customer situation in which a disagreement occurred and a conflict occurred and their outcomes on customer relations.

4. In your opinion, are the steps necessary to resolve a customer complaint applicable to nearly all incidents? Explain.

5. Assume that your company failed to deliver a product on time to an important customer. Create a simple script that would work well when handling this service problem.

6. What approach would you use to handle a customer who is very angry?

7. Have you recently observed an angry customer at a grocery store, retail outlet, or bank? If so, describe the behaviors of the person you observed.

# On-line Research Activities

## Project 4.1: Working with Angry Customers

Assume you are doing a report on *the effects of angry customers on business profits.* As a result of your search on the Internet, keyboard three items (and their URLs) of current information you might use in your report.

## Project 4.2: Product Return Policy 🖳

### Situation

In tracking customer complaints over the past year, President Collin MacGibson has decided to review the 10-year-old product return policy at On-Time Technology Products. As a result, he needs to know what the return policies are of other technology companies in order to use them as a guideline in developing a new one for On-Time.

*Go to various technology product web sites (e.g., IBM, Dell Computers, Hewlett-Packard) and locate three examples of product return policies. Using file PRJ4-2 on your student CD, key responses in the following table format that will inform Mr. MacGibson where you got your information and what the strengths are of each return policy.*

| Company | Strengths of Product Return Policy (One or Two Sentences) |
|---------|----------------------------------------------------------|
| 1. | |
| 2. | |
| 3. | |

# Communication Skills at Work

## Project 4.3: Handling Customer Emotions and Yours 🖳

Respond to the following three customer situations by describing how you would handle each situation and why you would take that approach.

*Retrieve file PRJ4-3 on the student CD and complete the following form by describing in column 2 the approach you would take to handle each of the following three customer situations. In column three explaining the reason(s) you would take that particular approach.*

| Situation | How You Would Handle It | Why? |
|-----------|-------------------------|------|
| 1. A customer throws a product on the counter and says, "I want my money back now!" | • | • |
| 2. A customer attacks your personal integrity and you can feel your anger ready to erupt. | • | • |
| 3. A customer says, "I'll never do business with you again!" | • | • |

## Decision Making at Work

### Project 4.4: "Take Whatever the Customer Doles Out"

Cliff, a fellow CSR, is noticeably upset at work this morning. Yesterday while on the job, it was incredibly difficult for him, because it seemed he had to deal with *the worst of the worst* customer complaints. Today, Cliff has confided in you that, after talking with his wife last night, he is thinking about quitting On-Time Technology Products because, as he puts it, he just doesn't think "employees should be expected to take whatever the customer doles out." You are aware that Cliff has other things going on in his life—most notably, his aging mother, who has the beginning stages of Alzheimer's disease, has recently moved in with Cliff, his wife, and their two teenage children.

*Respond to the following questions regarding Cliff's situation:*

1. If you were having a private conversation with Cliff, what would you say to support his decision?

_____

_____

_____

_____

_____

2. What would you say to try to get him to stay in your Customer Service Department at On-Time Technology Products?

_____

_____

_____

_____

_____

3. What do you think is really behind Cliff's wanting to quit his job at this point in time?

_____

_____

_____

_____

_____

_____

## Case Study

### 4.1 Relocating the Office

During a recent office relocation, the facilities manager of a local community college consulted with a technical expert on a variety of tools to help communicate among three remote campuses. The tools that the consultant recommended were just what were needed, and several of those items were purchased.

A few weeks later, the college received a bill from the technical company for time spent consulting on the tools that were purchased. To the community college's buyer, this seemed unfair, since the company received a commission on the items already purchased.

#### Discussion Questions

*1. Is there a problem in this scenario? If so, why was it caused?*

_____

_____

_____

_____

_____

*2. Given that the customer's concern has to be resolved, what steps would you recommend the technical company follow to resolve the conflict and preserve the customer relationship?*

_____

_____

_____

_____

_____

_____

_____

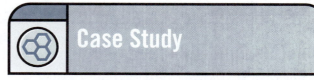

## Case Study

### 4.2 CSR Forums—Reacting to Customer Complaints

On-Time Technology Products has recently instituted a round-table discussion every other Friday at noon, at which CSRs are invited to attend and lunch is served. The purpose of this get-together is to allow each of you to vent and share information about customer issues that might help each other as you react to typical customer complaints. Today, you are discussing six CSR reactions, listed in the following table.

*Using the following table, in column 2 rank the severity of the reactions (1 = Worst; 5 = Best); then in column 3 describe a more positive approach.*

| Action taken | Rank in Severity | A More Positive Approach |
|---|---|---|
| *Apathy:* CSR's attitude of indifference | | |
| *Passing the buck:* Giving the Customer the runaround | | |
| *Being talked down to:* Treating customers as if they don't understand basic information | | |
| *The brush-off:* Trying to get rid of or ignoring a customer because the CSR has other things to do | | |
| *Rudeness:* Treating customers in a disrespectful manner | | |
| *Unresponsiveness:* Not following up on a commitment | | |

# CHAPTER V

# Recovering From and Winning Back the Angry Customer

*If you are patient in one moment of anger, you will escape a hundred days of sorrow.*

CHINESE PROVERB

## OBJECTIVES

**AFTER COMPLETING THIS CHAPTER,
YOU WILL BE ABLE TO:**

1. Describe five types of customers who defect.
2. List the main reasons customers who are unintentionally pushed away no longer buy from a service or product provider.
3. Identify various types of feedback, or survey, instruments.
4. Discuss the advantages of soliciting customer satisfaction comments.
5. Define a mystery shopper.
6. Describe issues to be aware of when interpreting customer feedback.
7. Identify some typical methods a CSR can use to recover from the angry customer.
8. Suggest several reasons that most customers would rather walk away than complain about poor service or products.
9. Identify key points that should be in win-back messages.

Everyone makes mistakes. Processes and procedures fail. That's life. The road to success is always under construction. Customers don't expect companies to be perfect. They do, however, expect companies to care. Companies that care are customer-oriented and know how to respond quickly to customer complaints and make it a priority to keep customers by fixing problems. The following two essential elements help keep customers and turn around disgruntled ones:

- The product-fulfillment system design should have a built-in contingency whereby, in a customer emergency, an order can be moved to the top of the list and filled instantly.
- The customer service representative must be empowered and trusted to make thoughtful, necessary, and appropriate decisions on the spot. Such comments as "Let me talk to my supervisor to see what we can do,

and I will call you back" leave customers feeling angrier, frustrated, and less likely to return.

Chapter 5 provides some reasons that customers leave and some ways to solicit feedback from customers on a regular basis to prevent their leaving in the first place. In addition, the cost of recovering a lost customer and ways to create a win-back customer plan are covered.

## Understanding Why Customers Leave

In a recent book entitled *Customer Winback: How to Recapture Lost Customers—and Keep Them Loyal,* authors Jill Griffin and Michael Lowenstein sort customers who defect into five categories:

1. *Unintentionally pushed-away.* Customers whom you want to keep, but they leave because the company's performance, products, or services do not meet their expectations.

2. *Intentionally pushed-away.* Customers who are, for example, poor credit risks or for whom the service costs are greater than the profits these customers create for the company.

3. *Pulled-away.* Customers who find a competitor who offers a better value or who provides more personable and reliable service; the new provider may be even more expensive and less convenient, but the pulled-away customer's perception is that the overall value is stronger.

4. *Bought-away.* Customers for whom price is all that matters; many competitors make low-ball, introductory pricing offers to get these customers to shop with them. These customers are open to shopping around and typically do not feel a sense of loyalty to any one company. Cutting prices to keep this type of customer is probably pointless, because the company will receive less money, and probably won't keep the customer, anyway. The customer may be bought away again.

5. *Moved-away.* Customers' needs change, perhaps due to age, a life-cycle event, or job relocation. In some cases, if a company has an electronic storefront on the Web, customers can still find the products they are used to buying from the company, even though it is at a distance.[1]

---

[1]Jill Griffin and Michael W. Lowenstein, *Customer Winback: How to Recapture Lost Customers—and Keep them Loyal* (Jossey-Bass, 2001: San Francisco, CA).

The category of unintentionally pushed-away customers is the most critical to understand. The need for earning back a customer's business and recovering a lost customer has more often than not been attributed to this situation. Unintentionally pushed-away customers no longer buy from a service or product provider for four main reasons:

1. *Unhappiness with product delivery, installation, service, or price.* One incident is unlikely to lose a customer, but several incidents of poor service, late delivery, or inaccurate shipment may be the final straw.

2. *Improper handling of a complaint.* Someone who feels a customer complaint hasn't been taken seriously or is displeased with the resolution may search out another competitive product or service.

3. *Disapproval of unanticipated changes.* Whenever companies make a change in the ordering process, price, product, or sales representatives, there is always a risk of offending some customers if they were not alerted in advance.

4. *Feelings of being taken for granted.* New orders and even orders from established customers should not be taken for granted. Every customer should be resold on the quality of the business product or service in every transaction and thanked for their business each time.

## CUSTOMER SERVICE TIP

**5.1** *If possible, do the right thing with customers the first time.*

## Getting Feedback from Customers

Many companies believe that, after years of working closely with customers, they know what their customers want. It is not until some of these companies get into trouble or decide they are facing an obstacle that they think about spending the necessary money to see what customers are thinking and to get their feedback. That is a tragic "too little, too late" approach to customer service. Although customers defect for a number of reasons, Guideline 5.1 describes five of the most obvious signs that indicate customers may be thinking about shopping elsewhere.

## GUIDELINE 5.1    Indications That a Customer is Defecting

| Indication | Approach Recommended |
| --- | --- |
| 1. The squeaky wheel | Companies should track complaints all the way through and make sure that customers emerge from the process happier than when they entered. A customer complaint is a "customer defection alert." |
| 2. The product return | Finding out the reason for returning any product is key. Is the reason because the product is defective, the customer doesn't like the product, or it just wasn't the right size? A string of defective product returns is serious and should be considered a red alert. |
| 3. The quiet customer | When a customer fails to respond to a customer survey or the company hears nothing from its regular customers, there is cause to worry. Make contact with customers. |
| 4. A slow pay | There may be negative issues with your products or services that cause customers to put your company at the bottom of the pay list. Find out what those issues are. |
| 5. Falling revenue and reduced sales volume | When customer spending goes down, it's a very good reason to call customers. It could be that they've either changed their lifestyle or they've found an alternative product or service. |

The most important reason for developing quality standards in many industries is a desire for consistency. Customer feedback—formal and informal—is one of the major driving forces in developing quality standards that prevent organizations from pushing away customers unintentionally. When companies design feedback instruments, the resulting data should serve as a compass to guide the development of products and customization of service offerings to meet identified customer needs.

## Feedback Instruments

Companies solicit customer opinions through a variety of ways—mailed surveys, telephone interviews, feedback forms enclosed with finished jobs, focus encounters, and client relationship meetings. The obvious goal of most customer feedback is to evaluate satisfaction—to discover how happy customers are with service, product quality, delivery,

and overall experience. Some additional benefits derived from this "ask the customer" approach include the opportunities for companies to

1. *Identify unhappy customers before they leave.* The information gathered could signal customer relationships that are in jeopardy. This is important because, unfortunately, most dissatisfied clients walk away and never tell companies why.

2. *Pinpoint the products and services that customers actually want and need.* Surveying customers is a great way to identify new business opportunities and to assess what customers *think* you offer. Customers may not be fully aware of all the products and services you offer.

3. *Solidify customer relationships.* The act of asking customers their opinions shows that they matter and goes a long way in forging strong relationships. Customers may love your product, for example, but be annoyed by such minor incidents as how long they are placed on hold on the phone, how they are treated by the receptionist, or how finished work is packaged. These are issues that companies may be clueless about, but, once brought to the surface, they can be easily and economically corrected.

When developing customer satisfaction feedback instruments, consider measuring the right issues from the numerous customer satisfactions attributes listed in Guideline 5.2. Remember to refrain from using the word *survey.* Few people want to participate in a survey; however, many people are willing to give *feedback.*

## Feedback Sources

There should be few activities as important as finding out what your customers want for products and services and finding out what they think of your current offerings. Fortunately, businesses can use a variety of practical and available sources to get customer feedback:

- *Employees.* An organization's front-line employees are usually the people who interact the most with customers. On a regular basis, ask employees and customer service representatives about products and services that customers are asking for and what issues they complain about the most.

- *Comment cards.* One of the best ways to find out what customers want is to ask them. Provide brief, half-page comment cards on which customers can answer simple

- Ability to meet deadlines and on-time delivery
- Accurate invoice amounts
- Clear and helpful invoices
- Clear and helpful quotes, estimates, and proposals
- Communication of changes in delivery or back-order situations
- Enthusiasm about a customer's business
- Follow-through on commitments
- Overall value and range of products and services
- Presence of competent people and helpful customer service representatives
- Price
- Problem-resolution approach
- Prompt problem solving
- Prompt shipments
- Quality of product or service
- Readily accessible people and information
- Shipments that match orders and specifications
- Understanding of the customer's needs

questions such as "Were you satisfied with our services?" and "Are there any services you would like to see that don't exist?"

- *Competition.* Ask people who shop at your competitors the simple question "What is the competition offering that we could offer to serve your needs better?"
- *Documentation and records.* Using inventory records and sales receipts, companies can take note of what cus-

Customers can help businesses improve their service by providing feedback.

tomers are buying and not buying from them. Better yet, if the data are captured on a computer spreadsheet or database file, chart the data, so that they can be studied to determine buying trends. Also, use the data to prepare comparisons of product inventory.

- *Focus groups.* Focus groups usually consist of 8 to 10 people whom you gather to get their impressions of a product or service.
- *Mail surveys.* You personally might hate answering these surveys, but plenty of people don't—and will fill out and mail back feedback forms, especially if they get something of value in return. Promise survey respondents, for example, a discount if they return the completed form by a certain date.
- *Telephone surveys.* Hire summer students or part-time workers for a few days every six months or so to do telephone surveys.

## ETHICS/CHOICES

**5.1** What would you say to a colleague who wanted to put up a sign in your department for customers to see that says "This office DOES NOT: give legal advice, do research for you, . . . ."?

## The Mystery Shopper

Although many companies spend significant amounts of money on training their employees, few businesses reinforce the training with a monitoring program. One way that today's companies are working to improve the level of customer service is through mystery shopping programs. A **mystery shopper** is a third-party evaluator who visits a business for the purpose of analyzing customer service, product quality, and store presentation. Evaluators follow specific instructions during their visits, complete written reports after leaving the store, and work with management to identify the strengths of and challenges for the business as outlined in the final onsite visit report. Mystery shoppers can perform a variety of activities: unannounced visits, random phone calls to a business, and evaluations of web sites and e-mail responses. This approach provides managers and employees with an unbiased evaluation of their operation's quality, service, cleanliness, and value. The goal of using a mystery shopper is to help in improving productivity, efficiency, and profitability for the company.

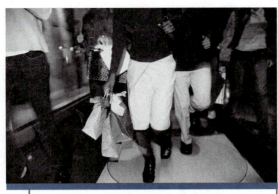

Which person is the mystery shopper?

Companies use mystery shopping services for an assortment of reasons. Some managers use mystery shopping as a way to resolve situations *before* the problem reaches higher-level executives. At other companies, corporate-monitoring programs are established to observe daily and routine operations in order to ensure consistency. Still in other instances, absentee owners monitor critical operations or staff members who play an integral part in the success or failure of the business.

## Interpreting Customer Feedback

When customers stop buying from a business, it is important to ask why. Certain responses to "Why have you stopped buying from us?" are more important than others. Listen very carefully to each reply and be prepared to do something about the customer concern when the reasons customers have stopped buying from you are due to the following:

- The quality of merchandise
- The quality of service
- The attitude of an employee
- A mishandled complaint
- An invoice or billing problem

Such responses are problematic and require companies to take action immediately. Further, when customers expand their response by saying that they informed the company about the problem *before* they stopped purchasing, immediate solutions to these responses are even more important.

Following are four other issues companies must be aware of prior to interpreting and acting on customer feedback:

1. *Use thorough data-gathering and analysis techniques before acting on complaints.* Often, a company will make a change based on feedback from only one or two customers. That type of limited feedback is called anecdotal information; it does not necessarily constitute a trend.

2. *Do not spend lots of time, energy, and money gathering complaint data and then doing nothing with the responses.* That is perhaps the biggest error organizations make when handling complaint data.

3. *Don't take the survey feedback results personally.* The fact is that surveys *invite* customers to criticize, so that a company can improve. Customers that complain the most and the loudest and tell you when there are problems are really your best customers. Addressing those complaints in an honest, forthright manner builds a strong relationship because it demonstrates that you care. You don't want clients who don't complain when they have a problem; the risk is that they will just leave and never discuss it with you. Most likely, however, they will discuss it with several others.

4. *Inform customers about the impact their feedback has had on the way issues will be addressed.* When companies that gather customer data research fail to do this, they lose credibility with clients.

## CUSTOMER SERVICE TIP

**5.2** *As a CSR, remember that, when you are trying to understand the customer's situation, the problem is the enemy, not you.*

## Recovering from the Angry Customer

Most of the time, service mistakes result from situations that are completely out of the control of a customer service representative. Regardless of whether it is a computer glitch or a mistake that a coworker has made, it is important to remember that placing blame will not fix a customer's problem. Instead, focus on how you can help your company recover from the mistake. Without top-notch service recovery, you lose the customers you worked so hard to acquire.

In the long run, business profits are tied to a company's ability to satisfy and retain its customers. With this recognition, the following findings from a summary of recent studies conducted by Technical Assistance Research Programs, Inc. (TARP), a company devoted to helping companies measure and manage the customer experience, should be sobering to any customer service professional:

- About 50 percent of the time, customers who have a problem with a product or service are not likely to tell a company about it.

- Between 50 and 90 percent of these "silent critics" will probably take their future business to a competitor.

- Even when a customer does complain, one out of every two will not be thoroughly satisfied with the company's efforts to solve the problem.

- Dissatisfied customers typically tell eight or more people when they have had an unsatisfactory experience with a company.

- Negative statements have twice the impact as positive information when customers finalize a purchasing decision.

- Word-of-mouth advertising is one of the most important factors influencing a customer's decision to buy from a company.

- It costs between 2 and 20 times as much to win a new customer as it does to retain an existing customer who has a product or service complaint.

Some people would consider it a curiosity that customers, who experience a problem that is politely and quickly resolved, rate companies higher than those who experienced no problems at all. In the TARP studies, customers with happy resolutions to their problems said they were likely to recommend the business more so than did the trouble-free customers. Companies provide terrific customer care by never making any customer jump through hoops to obtain a remedy to a problem or complaint. This is easily accomplished by doing the following:

- Make the response to a customer complaint personal and take ownership of the situation. Stress what you *can* do to help, not what you cannot do.

- Make complaint resolution a one-on-one transaction.

- Contact the customer immediately and resolve the issue quickly. Speed is critical in retaining customers and building loyalty.

The steps for recovering encompass many of the complaint-handling steps already covered in Chapter 4; however, as the list in Guideline 5.3 shows, it goes into greater detail.

## Creating an Effective Win-Back Plan

The key to success in recovering lost customers is having a well-conceived win-back plan. Losing a valued customer is never fun. In most businesses, once customers

| GUIDELINE 5.3 | Steps to Follow in Recovering Lost Customers |
|---|---|
| 1. Listen and empathize. | This is not the time to tell the customer that she is wrong or that, if she had followed your instructions, this would never have happened. Instead, acknowledge that this should not have happened, that there is no excuse for this kind of situation, and that this episode is highly unusual. |
| 2. Apologize. | It is more important to solve the problem than to point out who is to blame. Apologies are very inexpensive, and sometimes that is all the customer wants to hear. |
| 3. Fix the problem fairly and fast. | The faster the problem is solved in a fair manner, the better it is for everyone. |
| 4. Keep your promises. | This is critical. Remember that you have already been unsuccessful once; you cannot afford to fall short again. |
| 5. Make realistic and doable promises. | Don't promise something that is unrealistic to fulfill just because you think it will make the customer happy. Two disappointments will make the customer very unhappy and will result in lost sales and questionable credibility. |
| 6. Thank the customer. | Sincerely tell the customer that you are glad this problem was brought to your attention, so that you can take steps to reassure this will not happen again. |
| 7. Offer some form of compensation. | Find out ahead of time up to what limits of compensation your company will allow you to offer. |
| 8. Follow up. | If you are not the one who will ultimately correct the problem, check back in a few days to see if everything possible was completed to recover the customer's trust and confidence. |

**5.3** *Angry customers need to vent. Telling them to calm down often only makes matters worse.*

make a decision to terminate the relationship, they do not communicate their intent to the company. Four reasons that most customers would rather walk than complain are

1. They often don't know whom to speak to about the problem. Often, customers think, "Is it worth talking to the sales clerk, or will my problem just be moved up the chain?"

2. They feel that complaining won't do any good. Customers perceive that dealing with complaints is a low priority for the company.

3. They think that the complaint will never be acted on so don't want to bother with it.

4. They think that the company really doesn't care about the problem, especially when they hear the line "It's company policy."

The task of determining why companies lose clients may be easier than it seems, because organizations collect an assortment of data about customers and their buying habits. For example, you can review the customer account history by looking for clues in letters, call reports, replacement orders, and the like. By looking at the pattern of past orders, and comparing it with the date of the customer incident, answers might loom before your eyes. Be prepared, however, to hear the unexpected to the question you ask customers, "Why did you stop buying from us?" Subsequent to that response, try to remember to follow up with the most important recovery question: "If we fixed that, would you try us again?"

In summary, when you are reapproaching any lost customer, your win-back message should include the following key points:

- Acknowledge the customer's past patronage.
- Point out improvements and changes made since the customer's decision to stop buying.
- Emphasize the ease with which the customer can reengage and place another order.

- Provide a financial incentive, if possible.

Customer service representatives are a company's frontline of communication, and the quality of their communication greatly affects retention and win-back success with customers. People buy from people, not a company. Upset customers want to be taken seriously. They don't want to hear "You're kidding" or "No way." They want the customer service representative to be a professional who will treat them with respect, as you would any friend. More so, customers want immediate action and to be taken care of now.

**5.2** In your opinion, is it ever acceptable to stand your ground with a customer and not give in to his or her demands?

It's complicated enough dealing with an angry customer; however, when it's your blunder, it makes giving the best and most appropriate response even more complex. Your response must not only soothe this angry customer but also turn this person into a loyal customer. Given these circumstances, it might require you to do something extra to mend fences. Relative to compensation or restitution, customers want someone to pay for the damage done and may ask to be reimbursed for their time and inconvenience in getting the problem resolved.

Customers may just want to be listened to. Sometimes, that is all that is important to them. Remember, apologies are free. If it is your product or service that is the problem, then accept the blame. The customer does not want to hear excuses. If you want to go beyond normal apologies, give a discount coupon, a free product, or free tickets to an event in town. Provide restitution in the form of cash, if that is the only solution to win back the customer.

The secret to successful retention, marketing, and customer fulfillment is to get inside the heads and under the skin of your customers. In other words, think how they think, feel what they feel, and literally become your own customer. In that mindset, everything becomes clear. Always underpromise and overdeliver. Therefore, when the product is received and used, ideally it should be better than what the customer expected. Customer retention is critical to all organizations, because landing new customers costs exponentially more than keeping loyal ones.

## Concluding Message for CSRs

Customer-centered companies make dissatisfied customers feel as if they have been a true agent of change, spurring the company to make improvements, not merely treat symptoms. You can create loyal customers by admitting a mistake, expressing appreciation for help in improving service, and exceeding your customers' expectations by providing something extra.

In review, what are two important recovery steps that customer service representatives need to remember and follow?

1. *Acknowledge the receipt of every complaint immediately.* This says that you are sufficiently concerned about the problem to contact the customer and that the customer service team is on the job to resolve any issue that concerns customers.

2. *Explain exactly how you will remedy the problem.* It is vital to explain in writing to your customer exactly *what* will be done to fix the problem and *when* the customer can expect full resolution. For example, one way to turn a negative customer experience into a positive one is to send a replacement item or refund with a personal note of apology, along with an additional item of value. This unexpected extra, which can be a coupon, product, or discount on a future purchase, helps compensate customers for their time and trouble.

Dealing effectively with difficult customers is the mark of a true customer service professional. Angry customers will remember that you handled a complaint with poise and professionalism long after they have forgotten what the complaint was about.

## Summary

- Five categories of customers who defect are those who are unintentionally pushed away, intentionally pushed away, pulled away, bought away, and who have moved away.
- Companies solicit customer opinions through a variety of ways—mailed surveys, phone interviews, feedback forms enclosed with finished jobs, focus encounters, and client relationship meetings.

- The goal of most customer feedback is to evaluate customer satisfaction with service, product quality, delivery, and overall experience.
- Some very practical and available sources that businesses can use to gather customer feedback are from employees, comment cards, competition, documentation and records, focus groups, mail surveys, and telephone surveys.
- A mystery shopper is a third-party evaluator who visits a business for the purpose of analyzing customer service, product quality, and store presentation.
- Always be concerned when customers say they stopped buying from you due to the quality of merchandise or service, the attitude of an employee, a mishandled complaint, or an invoice or billing problem.
- Placing the blame for a problem will not fix a customer's problem and should be avoided.
- The key to success in recovering lost customers is to have a well-conceived win-back plan.
- The secret to successful retention, marketing, and customer fulfillment is to think how customers think, feel what they feel, and, in essence, become your own customer.

### QUESTIONS FOR CRITICAL THINKING

1. Of the five types of customers who defect, which is the most serious from a win-back point of view? Explain.

2. If you were designing the best feedback survey instrument for the following types of businesses, which one would you create? for a car repair shop? for a four-star hotel?

3. In your opinion, are mystery shoppers fair to use (relative to a company's employees)? Explain.

4. Why is it unwise to always accept any and all customer feedback?

5. Have you ever walked away from a business rather than staying to complain about its service or products? If so, explain why you chose to handle the situation in that way.

6. Write a simple win-back message to a customer who received a product that was of poor quality.

# On-line Research Activities

## Project 5.1: Creating a Customer Survey

Create and keyboard a 10- to 15-question *customer service feedback survey* for an industry or a company of your choice. Research several web sites and locate sample survey customer service questions you might use as guides in completing this assignment.

## Project 5.2: The Feasibility of Using a Mystery Shopper 💻

### Situation

Sammy Brown, vice president of administration and sales at On-Time Technology Products, is interested in researching the impact of using mystery shoppers in technology companies. He feels that using an unannounced third party to visit, phone, or check On-Time Technology Products' web site and e-mail responses could provide meaningful data in evaluating the effectiveness of the company's marketing and customer service areas.

*Log on to your favorite search engine and type the words Mystery Shopper to locate three pieces of recent information from your web site hits that will help Mr. Brown with his research and subsequent analysis. Using file PRJ5–2 on your student CD, key responses in the following table format that will inform Mr. Brown where you got your information and what meaningful mystery shopper data you uncovered.*

| URL of Site | Key Points Discussing Mystery Shoppers (One or Two Sentences) |
| --- | --- |
| 1. | |
| 2. | |
| 3. | |

# Communication Skills at Work

## Project 5.3: Handling Customer Complaints 💻

Respond to the following three statements an angry customer might make to a customer service representative. Then provide an appropriate response to each statement.

*Retrieve file PRJ5–3 on the student CD and complete the following form by describing in column 2 an appropriate response that is customer-friendly and that will help retain the customer.*

| Statement | An Appropriate Response |
| --- | --- |
| 1. "I have waited on the phone for 20 minutes. What takes you people so long?" | • |
| 2. "Your service has been totally unsatisfactory. You promised to deliver my computer three weeks ago, and I haven't heard from anyone since I placed the order. I want my computer delivered—today!" | • |
| 3. "You have done this completely wrong. You are incompetent. I want to see your supervisor immediately, so I can have you fired." | • |

## Decision Making at Work

### Project 5.4: "Bad Product Shipped—Increase in Customer Complaints"

Layla is the most senior CSR at On-Time Technology Products and is the person to whom other CSRs refer most major customer problems. She never fails to service customers in a calm and collected manner and is always kind and courteous to others—coworkers and customers alike. Over the past few weeks, the company has experienced a bad shipment of product; as a result, customer complaints are on the increase. As a result, Layla simply cannot handle the majority of these major customer complaints herself, while the other five CSRs continue to transfer all of these bad-product calls to her.

*Respond to the following questions regarding this situation:*

1. How could On-Time Technology Products have avoided putting its Customer Service Department in the current situation?

_____

_____

_____

_____

_____

2. Given the bad-product situation, what should the other CSRs do now to respond to these increased complaints?

_____

_____

_____

_____

_____

3. What steps should On-Time Technology Products take to avoid customer service situations like this one in the future?

_____

_____

_____

_____

_____

## Case Study

### 5.1  When the News Isn't Good . . .

When Tommy attended a recent customer service seminar at a local hotel, he attended a session at which he was asked what to say and do when CSRs have to turn down a customer's request or to deliver other bad news. Tommy wants to share the following three scenarios with his colleagues and find out how they might respond. If you were Tommy's coworker, how would you respond to each of the following scenarios?

1. *You can't give the customer information on his ex-wife's account balance because it would be illegal.*

   _____

   _____

   _____

   _____

2. *You can't wire flowers to the customer's sister in Phoenix without first receiving payment.*

   _____

   _____

   _____

   _____

   _____

3. *You can't sell weight-loss products to the customer because your dieticians must first evaluate her.*

   _____

   _____

   _____

   _____

   _____

## Case Study

### 5.2  Action Plan: Survey and a Win-Back Plan

On-Time Technology Products has no formal win-back plan, because up to now it has experienced no significant loss in its base of approximately 400 customers. With a recent downturn in the economy, however, some major customers have jumped ship or at least appear not to be ordering as frequently or as much when they do place orders.

On-Time Technology Products wants to contact at least 50 customers over the next six months. Assist in the design of this action plan by suggesting several attributes that measure customer satisfaction and prepare a brief script, using key components of a successful win-back plan that customer service representatives might use.

1. *Using Guideline 5.2 as a reference, select the top five attributes that, in your opinion, On-Time Technology Products should use to measure customer satisfaction.*

   a. _____

   b. _____

   c. _____

   d. _____

   e. _____

2. *Write a brief script that CSRs could use when contacting these upset customers. Use the following steps as a guide to writing the narrative script:*

   a. *Acknowledge the customer's past business.*

   b. *Point out improvements to service and products.*

   c. *Emphasize the ease with which the customer can place another order.*

   d. *Provide a financial incentive.*

   _____

   _____

   _____

   _____

# Skills to Better Manage the Customer Service Role

*People forget how fast you did a job—but they remember how well you did it.*

HOWARD W. NEWTON

## OBJECTIVES

**AFTER COMPLETING THIS CHAPTER, YOU WILL BE ABLE TO:**

1. Describe the steps involved in solving customer problems.

2. Identify techniques to better manage time.

3. List the most troublesome time wasters.

4. Explain the importance of developing organizational skills.

5. Contrast the results of positive stress and negative stress on a person.

6. Cite several consequences of workplace stress on workers.

7. Devise a personal plan that includes several stress-management tips.

How well we solve problems and deal with time- and stress-related issues has to do with our attitudes, beliefs, behaviors, and organizational skills. Even for the most capable of us, it is a stretch to stay on top of the priorities of our jobs and to deliver promises on time and in the best manner possible. Combined with other areas of our lives and given the rush of everyday life, it's commonplace to unconsciously give responsibility and control of our lives to the circumstances around us—be they business, economic, or personal. Chapter 6 addresses problem-solving, time-management, and stress-management skills. CSRs need to learn these practical skills and practice them daily in order to be able to have a quality life at work and at home.

## Practicing Problem-Solving Skills

Effective problem solving in customer service representatives is a highly regarded ability—where situations require you to handle customer problems on a daily basis. CSRs who are considered especially good problem solvers are systematic and analytical and have first-rate interpersonal skills. They not only fix the problem but simultaneously can fix the customer's feelings. Statistics support that fact—70 percent of complaining customers will return if the problem is resolved in their favor. That number grows to 95 percent if the problem is resolved on the spot.[1] How good a problem solver are you? Take the quiz in Guideline 6.1 to find out.

---

[1] "Reduce Cost of Poor Service with Effective Problem-Solving Techniques," *The Dartnell Corporation* (July 2001): 9.

Good service employees deal with complaints on the spot—while the complaint is happening. The benefits of handling complaints immediately are fewer escalations and greater customer satisfaction, which ultimately results in lower customer service costs. Problem solving with customers is a process. It can be easier to do in the following steps:

1. *Determine if the situation is a disagreement or a true conflict of interest.* One way to do this is to ask the customer to state the problem from his or her point of view; then state the problem from your perspective. In that way, you can better understand the areas you agree on already and what needs to be resolved.

2. *Analyze your interests and the customer's interests.* Know ahead of time what concessions management will empower you to make to the customer and which ones you cannot make.

3. *Brainstorm solutions and generate ideas together.* If the issue is complicated, start with the easy issues and then proceed to the tougher ones. Always attempt to establish points of agreement early in the process.

4. *If step 3 doesn't resolve the situation, make some mutual low-priority concessions.* Be patient. You may have to recycle steps 3 and 4 more than once.

Guideline 6.2 offers five additional suggestions for actions that customer service representatives can take to get customers to resolve problems together.

When complaints are passed on to the next level of the organization, the price of service goes up. As you can see, therefore, successful problem solving is critical to a company's financial success. Four factors promote effective problem solving in the most efficient manner:

1. *Accessibility.* When customers call your business, they need to know that they will be getting an answer quickly from an employee who is not only willing to help but also very knowledgeable.

2. *Ownership.* When a customer complains about a problem, CSRs should accept responsibility for the situation (even if it's not their fault) and apologize without assigning blame.

3. *Explanation of policies.* When problems occur because of a company policy, CSRs should provide a clear explanation of *what* happened and *why* the company has this policy.

4. *Follow-through.* When commitments are made to customers, CSRs need to be sure they can deliver as quickly as possible on all promises they make to customers.

In summary, rules for solving customer problems are based on common sense but are not easily put into practice. The following two reminders of actions to take and not to take will help when problem solving with customers:

1. Both parties must state the problem from each one's perspective.
   a. Use "I" statements.
   b. Acknowledge the other person's problem and indicate a willingness to help.
   c. Do not use put-downs or name calling.
   d. Do not answer a complaint with another complaint.
   e. Ask clarifying questions.
   f. Stick to the topic at hand by dealing with one issue at a time.
   g. Look for areas of agreement to move the process along.

2. If the discussion escalates in the wrong direction,
   a. Restate what the misunderstood person has said until the person feels he or she has been understood correctly
   b. State all requests for change in behavioral terms; in other words, don't ask for a change in attitude or for the other person to "feel differently"
   c. Rely more on words when communicating negative feelings instead of nonverbal messages
   d. Withdraw from the current meeting, but not before scheduling the next discussion

## Improving Time-Management Skills

*Webster's Dictionary* defines time as "the period between two events or during which something exists, happens, or acts; measured or measurable interval." We, therefore, have the ability and power to use time in constructive ways. Rather than time controlling us, we can control it. Stated another way, **time management** is not about squeezing more activities into an already overloaded schedule; it is about getting the most important tasks done in a less stressful way.

For most people, it seems that time controls us. This doesn't have to be the case. Time management is self-management. To manage ourselves, we need to gain a better ability to examine our work habits, our environments, and ourselves. The key to improving skills in this area is increasing awareness of our attitudes, thinking, and behaviors regarding how we manage our time and organize our workload. Do we manage it, or does it manage us?

Effective time managers find that the key to controlling how they use time is to write everything down, rather than keep everything in their heads. Write down whatever you have to do in a time-management book. Organize according to current things to do and future action items. Questions to ask yourself during this process include

- What things do I want or need to do and am not currently doing?
- What things do I want or need to complete and have not yet completed?
- What things do I want or need to start and am not starting?
- What things do I want or need to say and am not saying?

After making your list, determine what you are committed to doing and prioritize those items using the A, B, C system that follows. Do the highest-priority items first—A items first, then B items.

- A = Highest-priority and must be completed
- B = Important to be completed, but not absolutely essential for today
- C = Nice to do, if I can get to it

## Time Wasters

Poor time management can interfere with everything you do. To eliminate time wasters, be honest with yourself. How effective a time manager are you? Take the short quiz in Guideline 6.3 and see.

### GUIDELINE 6.3 | QUIZ
### Time Management

| Yes | No | Questions |
|---|---|---|
| ☐ | ☐ | 1. Do you carry little scraps of paper around in your pockets with "to-do" jotted on them? |
| ☐ | ☐ | 2. Do you have trouble focusing on the job or task you are doing because you are thinking of other things that need to be done? |
| ☐ | ☐ | 3. Are you often behind schedule and routinely in a catch-up mode? |
| ☐ | ☐ | 4. Have you started many projects that you cannot seem to complete? |
| ☐ | ☐ | 5. Do interruptions on the job destroy your momentum? |
| ☐ | ☐ | 6. Do you feel overwhelmed when you walk into work and look at your desk and work area? |
| ☐ | ☐ | 7. Do you find you have so many small items on your mind that you get easily distracted from your important work activities? |
| ☐ | ☐ | 8. Are you often remembering other priorities left undone at home while you are at work and vice versa? |
| ☐ | ☐ | 9. Do you arrive home feeling unfulfilled in your job, so tired that you want to escape? |
| ☐ | ☐ | 10. Do you feel that you cannot take time for physical fitness, recreation, or just plain fun? |
| ☐ | ☐ | 11. Do you find that during and after your workday, your stress level is so high that it is hard to calm down and relax? |
| ☐ | ☐ | 12. Do you look for the "quick fix" method of relaxing? |
| ☐ | ☐ | 13. Do you find that you have experienced an increase in the number of near misses, accidents, and injuries? |

*If you answered Yes to more than two or three of these questions, you may be showing symptoms of poor time management. The question is then, "Who runs your life?" Do you control your time, or does time control you?*

From time to time, people get themselves into trouble:

- *They can't say "no."* Be honest about your commitments. Use your schedule to explain why you can't comply with all requests for your attention. Keep in mind that you should probably say "no" to someone if the request is a last-minute, panic request that requires an immediate response, requires skills that you do not have, or demands more time than you can reasonably provide.

- *They are buried in paperwork.* Schedule a specific time for doing paperwork and stick to it. Never look at the same piece of paper twice; deal with it the first time.

- *They procrastinate.* It's said that the hardest part of doing anything is getting started. Once you have started, however, you gain momentum, which makes it easier and easier to keep going. **Procrastination,** defined as the art of putting something off that could just as easily be done today, comes in many forms, as described in Guideline 6.4. If you suffer from this tendency, admit it, analyze it, and make a commitment to get over it today. The enormity of the task could be causing you to stall. Attack the task by taking "baby steps" at first.

### CUSTOMER SERVICE TIP

**6.1** *When you schedule your time, you control your life.*

## Time-Management Tips

Watch your productivity soar when you put the following time-management techniques to work:

1. *Know your purpose.* What do you want to achieve? The first step in time management is to know *why* you are doing something. To change your behavior without a good reason is an uphill, and usually unsuccessful, battle. Write down the goals you want to achieve and look at them frequently to remind yourself why you are spending your time as you are.

2. *Keep your time in perspective.* If you keep a 24/7 time log for a few weeks, here's what you will probably find:
   a. Everything takes longer than you expect it to. In fact, most of us underestimate by 50 percent the amount of time activities take to complete. Learn to build extra time into your plans.
   b. You waste more time than you think you do. Watching TV and surfing the Web aren't necessarily bad activities; however, if they are cutting into time you could use to fulfill your goals, think twice before turning on the TV or computer.
   c. A lot of legitimate activity is pure maintenance. For example, the laundry still has to get done, whether it's a goal or not.

**GUIDELINE 6.4** Forms of and Cures for Procrastination

| Form of Procrastination | Justification | Cure |
|---|---|---|
| Not Wanting to Do Something | Because procrastination usually involves something we don't want to do, we fill our available time with smaller, easier, and more comfortable projects. We avoid tasks, issues, and problems that are uncomfortable to us. | Tackle your biggest project first instead of getting the little ones out of the way. The little ones will be easy to take care of in your spare time. |
| Interrupting Yourself | It's bad enough that we dodge phone calls and interruptions; many of us actually interrupt ourselves. We do that by getting another cup of coffee, stopping to talk with someone, making a quick phone call, or answering e-mail messages. | Set a time frame for the task you are by doing and seat belt yourself to the chair. |
| Making the Project So Big No One Could Be Successful | It is easy to procrastinate when the mountain looks too high to even get started. | Divide your project into bite-size pieces. Then set realistic goals to accomplish each one. |
| Convincing Yourself of Defeat | Why bother trying when you are doomed to fail? The self-talk goes something like this: "I wouldn't make it in school (at that job . . .) anyway." | When you start to think of a negative message, replace it immediately with a positive belief. |
| Rationalizing It Away | We tell ourselves it wasn't that important anyway or that it was too much work. | Look back at your original goal list for the year. There was a reason you put the goal on the list. |
| Feeding Poor Self-esteem | The final outcome for "letting it slide" is a decrease in our own self-esteem. As our esteem takes a beating, we feel less motivated and energized. This in turn feeds future procrastination and leads to a vicious uncomfortable cycle. | Honestly commit to doing it. Evaluate your own process of getting off track when tackling your goals. The only difference between a successful person and a failure is one who did not quit. |

3. *Plan ahead.* Research shows that an hour spent planning is worth three or four hours of just "doing."[2] To avoid interruptions, it's a good idea to do your planning at night, because the current day is fresh in your mind and you know what priorities should be set for the next day. You will then awake refreshed, with a clear mind, and have your day's direction already carved out for you.

4. *Set your priorities.* If everything on your to-do list seems important, ask yourself the following questions to reveal your true priorities:
   a. Will doing this task help me reach a goal I have?
   b. Does the task have a deadline?
   c. Is it an order from a "nonignorable" person (such as your boss or your instructor)?

5. *Break a project into smaller pieces.* To manage projects effectively use the popular "VPIC" process:
   a. *Visualize:* What will the project look like when done?
   b. *Plan:* Break the project into pieces; decide who will do what, when, where, and how.

   c. *Implement:* Monitor your progress to stay on schedule. Adjust activities when necessary.
   d. *Close:* Celebrate and wrap up the project.

6. *Pace yourself.* Know when your peaks of energy are. By honoring your personal time clock, you will have a more balanced life. For example, if you are a morning person, schedule important decisions and activities early in the day, while you are at your prime. If you are a night person, do those important activities in the afternoon or early evening. In other words, do the easy bits and pieces of tasks when you are tired. If you must work past your peak time, give yourself a break by going on a walk, stretching, or phoning someone who cheers you up.

In summary, the principles of time management are simple:

1. Write down all plans and tasks you need to do at work and at home in one place—most appropriately, in your time-management system.

2. Make a written daily to-do list.

3. Prioritize each item on your to-do list according to the A, B, C system.

4. Trust your time-management system, not your memory.

[2]Anne Austin, "How to be Super Productive, *Career World* (Nov/Dec 2001): 22.

5. Handle each paper or item on your desk only once.

6. Check your system before saying "yes" to additional time commitments.

7. Ask yourself frequently, "What is the best use of my time right now?"

## CUSTOMER SERVICE TIP

**6.2** *Enjoy what you're doing while you're doing it. The results will show on your face and in your attitude with customers, coworkers, family, and friends.*

## Organizational Skills

It seems as though today everyone is looking for a more enjoyable, balanced life. What we really need to help put balance in our lives is more time. Unfortunately, we cannot control how many hours are in a day. Instead, we must try to control how we spend the hours we have. Developing effective organizational skills is just one tool that can help add this sense of balance.

Organizational skills can and do help you cope better with the world. These skills provide structure, they create a semblance of order, and they reduce daily stress levels. The organizational skills you apply toward planning each day ensure that you are at least somewhat productive and that you accomplish what you must. More important, they direct the demands on your attention and give you a sense of control.

When you have a large or time-consuming project you must accomplish, organizational skills are essential. Thinking about a large project in its entirety can be overwhelming and discouraging. By applying organizational skills and breaking down any project into smaller, more manageable pieces, it doesn't seem to be as difficult to complete.

People who manage their time well often are also those who tend to be organized and on top of things. What makes some people appear organized and others not? Organized people do most of the following activities as a *routine* matter:

- *Prepare a monthly schedule.* At the end of every month, make a schedule of events and deadlines coming up for the next month. Then use the schedule to highlight or mark off duties as they are met or completed.

Use technology as much as possible to stay organized.

- *Prepare a file folder for each project or event on your schedule.* If you make notes on a particular project and immediately file them in the proper folder, you'll save time by not having to unearth them later.

- *Rely on technology.* Make your computer your electronic assistant by taking computer classes to keep up-to-date on the most useful software. There are several good personal information-management software packages, such as Microsoft Outlook, which allow you to track and schedule your activities and commitments, to take notes, to manage meetings, and so on.

- *Organize your work area.* Arrange your desk and paperwork flow so you are not overwhelmed and confused when you walk into your office each day. Disorganized personal space is a very big time waster.

- *Manage your communications.* If you need to focus on a special project and not be interrupted, let your voicemail or answering machine become your secretary. Return calls every two or three hours—and keep a log of calls and their disposition.

The advantages of taking a few minutes each day to plan your life are considerable:

- Better productivity
- Better organization
- Better memory

- Focused concentration
- Better decisions
- Commitment to goals and aspirations
- Better working relationships with others

## Using Stress-Management Skills

We live in the best of times and the most stressful of times. Human beings have never before experienced the amount of change and number of choices we encounter every day. Everyone has stress, regardless of age, sex, position in life, and income. Each of us, however, is ultimately responsible for our own stress management and personal well-being. No one else can do it for us.

It doesn't matter whether stress comes from the job or from home. Stress is just a part of life. In small doses, stress can help motivate and energize you. However, too much stress can result in medical problems, social difficulties, and the inability to cope at work. Stress is a basic component of most customer service jobs, and it comes in many different forms. In customer service, stress primarily arises from these four main causes: lack of control, leadership issues, interruption or incompletion of tasks, and lack of confidence or self-esteem. Guideline 6.5 explains each one more fully.

---

### GUIDELINE 6.5    Causes of Stress for Customer Service Representatives

- **Lack of control**
  This cause is manifested by not being able to: get things done, get others to cooperate, satisfy customers' needs, and assimilate and organize the workflow.

- **Leadership issues**
  Managers often unknowingly contribute to CSRs' stress level through any of the following omissions: poor communications, unwillingness to delegate, slow to respond to inquiries and requests, changing priorities at the last minute, and perceived discourtesies by managers.

- **Interruption or incompletion**
  When job priorities are changed and others redesign workflow processes, workers find it difficult to complete a task in progress and this builds stress.

- **Lack of confidence or self-esteem**
  Training and various kinds of empowerment including participative management provide tools to deal with lack of confidence and self-esteem.

---

Important aspects of stress management skills are to be able to distinguish between positive and negative stress, the effects of stress, and how to better manage it in our personal and work lives.

## Positive versus Negative Stress

Not all stress is bad. There is such a thing as positive stress. By seeing **positive stress** as a force that motivates and energizes you rather than one that makes you anxious and frustrated, you can channel its energy into productive results. How? You need a little bit of positive stress every so often. If you believe that you do your best work under pressure, you are creating your own stresses. You could be right—you may do your best work under pressure. This is an example of when stress is good.

---

### CUSTOMER SERVICE TIP

**6.3** *Working with positive stress and getting rid of negative stress can be considered a "facelift for the mind."*

---

Let's focus on what kind of stress to get rid of and how to do it:

- *Don't worry.* **Negative stress** comes from worrying about things you have no power to change. By recognizing that sometimes you worry about things that you cannot do anything about, it's easier to channel your worry into something productive. For example, you may not be able to do anything about freezing rain, but you can put salt on the driveway to make sure that no one falls.

- *Set goals.* In other words, stop getting stressed about hating your job and figure out what you want to do about it. You may not know exactly what you want to do about it, but at least your energy will be focused in a positive direction instead of feeling defeated by negative self-talk.

- *Finish unfinished business.* Either make plans to do something about an unfinished task or decide that you will never do anything about it and stop causing yourself stress over it.

- *Resolve conflicts.* Pick up the phone and apologize to a friend, family member, classmate, or coworker that you've had words with. This is the kind of negative stress that can keep you up at night.

## The Effects of Stress

According to the American Institute of Stress, more companies are helping employees deal with stress. The reason is that stress is affecting their bottom line to the tune of $300 billion annually. An estimated 1 million U.S. employees are absent from work each day due to stress-related complaints. Stress-filled workers result in diminished productivity, employee turnover, and increased medical, legal, and insurance fees.

Primary care physicians report that stress is responsible for more than 75 percent of all office visits. Stress leads to high blood pressure and can manifest into infections, which over time can affect the immune system.[3]

On a philosophical level, managing stress means learning how to be flexible and how to adapt to new events. Observations show that it is how people deal with change or any situation that makes them feel out of control and stressed. Among the effects of change and stress are fatigue and lowered response time, loss of focus and attention, tight and tense muscles, and conscious choices to take shortcuts or bypass procedures.

Studies further show that people who see new situations as threats, who feel alienated, or who are out of control have a 50 percent greater chance of getting sick. On the other hand, people who are challenged by change and tend to get involved with life events and other people feel in control and tend to stay in better health.[4]

Early indicators of attitudes and behaviors that cause stress and that can lead to accidents are a decline in job performance, sloppy work habits, poor housekeeping, irritable and quarrelsome behavior, frequent distractions, alcohol and other drug use, an uncooperative attitude, and general negativity toward situations and coworkers. In most organizations, worker burnout and negative office chatter are outgrowths of people who are working under stress.

**Burnout.** Burnout is not only a common occurrence but also one of the biggest reasons that employees quit their service-industry jobs. Surprisingly, however, the more you enjoy your work and the more seriously you take your job of serving customers well, the more vulnerable you may be to the effects of burnout. **Burnout** is defined as a stress-related affliction resulting when people invest most of their time and energy in a particular activity.

To guard against burnout, so that you can keep providing the top-notch service customers have come to expect, try these four tips:

1. *Don't take work too personally.* Keep in mind that, when customers lash out, their frustration is over the difference between what they want and what they are getting; it is not about you personally.

2. *Don't take problems home.* Give complete attention to your job while you are at work, but leave concerns at work when you go home.

3. *Get help from others.* Remember that your coworkers are going through their share of stress-building situations also. It helps to talk over these situations together.

4. *Remember the good news.* When customers approach you with problems, remember that most of them will become satisfied once you've handled their complaint to the best of your ability.

**Negative Office Chatter.** Negative office chatter is a time waster and stress inducer. When you lunch with coworkers, for example, and spend the entire hour complaining about your work, the boss, other coworkers, and customers, it affects your work and attitude. Unfortunately, people absorb the negativity of others through constant repetition. Negative reactions are instantaneous, and you need to stay positive to lessen stress in your life. So that you don't lose your friends or affect your positive attitude through negative office chatter, it is a good idea to establish some ground rules. Friendly ground rules might include any of the following statements: "Let's not talk about work while we are at lunch" or "You can complain no more than five minutes and then you must say what has gone well at work that day."

The work environment needs to be more positive, more appreciative, and healthier. Negative office chatter impedes that process. As the saying goes, if you keep on doing what you've always done, you will keep on getting what you've always gotten. In other words, if you want to change something, you have to change what you are doing before you will get more positive results.

---

[3]Karen Connelly, "Easy Does It," *Inside Business* (April 2001): 47.

[4]Michael Topf, "Managing Change," *Occupational Hazards* (July 2000): 63.

Negative office chatter can be a stress inducer during times that we need to show a positive frame of mind.

## Managing Stress

Part of managing stress is setting attainable goals and not taking on too many commitments at one time. People need to enjoy the process of living, not just be directed on the goal of getting through each day. Most people who are stressed out have very unbalanced lifestyles, because they cannot get in time for some of the things they want to do. Exercise and fitness help rejuvenate us and counteract the loss of concentration that is caused by stress. Customer service representatives who manage stress well make time for relaxation activities and humor each day. In addition, they have developed their own stress-management plans.

**Stress Management Tips.** Devising a stress-management plan that incorporates the following suggestions is a good idea.

- *Learn to pay attention to yourself.* If you can't identify the factors that cause stress in your life, you cannot change or manage them. Write a list of the situations, relationships, and events that are stressful for you. Once you have a stress-awareness checklist, you can begin to make decisions about which ones need your specific and immediate attention.

- *Stop trying to control everything.* You will only wear yourself out. Focus on the situations that you can control

and let go of those you cannot. For example, you can control your reaction to a customer who is angry, but you cannot control that the customer is angry.

- *Alter your lifestyle.* Use an answering machine to screen phone calls. Know when to say "no." Avoid rush-hour traffic. Do not procrastinate. Prioritize tasks. Avoid perfectionism. Use timesaving tools, technology, and know-how.

- *Change your thinking.* Substituting positive thoughts for negative thoughts is one way to change how you perceive a situation. A substitute thought for "I can't do this" is "I don't know how to do this, but I've learned new things before, and I can learn this, too." Drive away anxiety-producing thoughts. Give yourself a pep talk— focus on your good qualities, the kindness you give others, and your many accomplishments.

- *Create a diversion.* Exercise, and do yoga, aromatherapy, or progressive muscle relaxation. Practice imagery or visualization—recalling a vacation at the beach, talking to someone, or keeping a journal. Know how to relax, plan, play, and get silly by taking physical and mental breaks. Nurture and develop your spiritual life by not neglecting matters of the soul. For many people, it brings a sense of inner peace and helps counteract the effects of stress.

- *Be gentle with yourself.* Most people could use a lesson in caring for themselves. What would you say to a friend who had to deal with the stresses that appear on your list? Think about it. Maybe you are actually doing the best you can under the circumstances. Don't be so hard on yourself. If you can't change something, you can at least find ways to make it less stressful. Join a support group, go for counseling, take long walks in the park, meditate, or splurge and get a relaxing massage.

## ETHICS/CHOICES

**6.2** You and others affectionately call a coworker "last-minute Sam." Sam has a good heart and means well, but he always completes projects at the very last minute and stresses out himself and everyone else. Some workers don't let Sam's pattern of procrastination bother them, but increasingly others shake their heads when they call him "last-minute Sam." What would your reaction be if Sam were a colleague of yours? Would you allow his behavior to affect you?

**Relaxation.** Relaxation is a fundamental part of any stress-management program. It is a much-needed activity for overstimulated bodies and minds. When we are under stress, our muscles tense, our breathing becomes shallow, our heart rate increases, and our blood pressure elevates. During relaxation, the opposite happens.

Relaxation means different things to different people. The word *relaxation* refers to a state of being, initiated by you, in which there are physiological and psychological changes. Just feeling relaxed may not mean that you are relaxed, however. Most of us have experienced this from time to time. It can be very frustrating to be unable to relax.

Relaxation is relative to the way each of us defines it. In other words, whatever we would like to do on a day off is relaxing for us. Remember, this is not what we should do; it is what we want to do. We all relax differently, but we all need to relax on a regular basis. Everyone needs 30 minutes every day to do something he or she really enjoys.

**Humor.** Did you know that a child laughs an average of 300 times a day, whereas an adult's count is just 6 to 8 times? A well-balanced life requires laughter and fun every day. One of the best ways to deal with stress in your life is through humor. Humor in the workplace can lead to more productive workers, which enhances profitability. Surrounding yourself with humor that you enjoy and determining the nature of your unique sense of humor is the initial step in using humor to cope with stress.

Laughter helps you reduce muscle tension, release anger, improve your ability to keep panic and anxiety under control, keep a more positive frame of mind, deal with the unexpected, keep your perspective, and increase your sense of control, well-being, and joy. What can you do to promote the spirit of a more amusing workplace? Following are some ideas that companies are promoting to lessen stress through humor:

1. *Sponsor weird apparel days.* Wear silly hats, funny T-shirts, outrageous ties, and so on.
2. *Celebrate holidays.* Dress up for Halloween or sing holiday songs together in December.
3. *Hold match-the-baby picture contests.* Display employees' childhood pictures and see how many matches coworkers can make.

Competing for the fun of it on a local playing field or court promotes unity among coworkers.

4. *Organize lunch-hour board game tournaments.* It doesn't matter if its checkers, Scrabble, or Monopoly, a midday diversion of a fun activity helps us cope better.
5. *Create an office "fun" bulletin board.* Devote the display to amusing cartoons, funny e-mails, and silly photos.
6. *Play games or participate on sports teams, with various departments competing for fun.*

## Concluding Message for CSRs

Staying on top of things, keeping your promises, delivering what you said you would, and doing complete and excellent work are what it takes to be successful at work. In addition, these actions maintain your integrity, and you feel good about yourself. Ultimately, this can lessen stress. It seems difficult, yet it is very simple. This process takes diligence, rigor, and a strong commitment to developing practical skills in problem solving and time and stress management to work smarter and to staying healthy, both on and off the job.

No one is immune to stress. Although we can't avoid it, experts agree that we can learn to manage it. Start with the basics: get plenty of sleep, eat a balanced diet, and exercise regularly. Remember that a key to a healthy, safe, and stress-reduced lifestyle is the successful management of all aspects of life: career, family, financial, recreational, social, physical, mental, emotional, and spiritual.

# Summary

- CSRs who are considered especially good problem solvers are systematic and analytical and have first-rate interpersonal skills.

- When complaints are passed on to the next level to problem solve, the cost of service goes up.

- Rules for problem solving customer situations are based on common sense but are not easily put into practice.

- Time management is not about squeezing more activities into an already overloaded schedule but, rather, about getting important tasks done in a less stressful way.

- Examples of time wasters include procrastinating, not being able to say "no," and being buried in paperwork.

- Applying organizational skills results in providing structure and a semblance of order to activities in our lives and reduces daily stress levels.

- Positive stress can motivate and energize a person, whereas negative stress often makes a person anxious and frustrated.

- Stress-filled workers result in diminished productivity, employee turnover, and increased medical, legal, and insurance fees.

- Part of managing stress is setting attainable goals and not taking on too many commitments at one time.

- Relaxation and humor are fundamental parts of any stress-management program.

## QUESTIONS FOR CRITICAL THINKING

1. Assume you worked in a shoe store, and a customer had a complaint about the quality of a pair of shoes she bought last week. What steps would you take in solving the customer's problem?

2. List two techniques that you use when managing your time. What are two techniques you are not currently doing that would improve time management for you?

3. Describe the behavior of a person you know who procrastinates when having a job to do or a class assignment to hand in on time.

4. Why are organizational skills important? Can you usually identify a person who exhibits these skills? What characteristics does the person possess?

5. What purpose does positive stress serve?

6. What are some methods a person can use to overcome negative stressors?

7. If you were asked to devise a plan that manages your stress level, what five actions would you include?

## On-line Research Activities

### Project 6.1: Time-Management Seminars

Research a number of web sites and locate several *time-management* consultants who provide onsite time-management seminars. Write a short paper that compares the content offerings of any three of these time-management seminars. Note in particular the seminars' similarities and any differences.

### Project 6.2: Stress- and Work-Related Illnesses 🖥

#### Situation

James Woo, vice president of human resources and customer relations, has been charting the incidence of absences at On-Time Technology Products. Each month, absences have been rising. As a result, he is curious to learn the extent to which stress-related illnesses affect workers today. He has asked Mary Graeff to assist him in this research.

*Go to various health-related web sites (e.g., Mayo Clinic, WebMD, medical training schools, or local hospitals) and locate seven factors or issues related to mounting stress-related health problems in the workplace. Using file PRJ6-2 on your student CD, key responses in the following table format that will inform Mr. Woo where you got your information and what factors or issues you were able to uncover.*

| Risks Web Sites | Factors/Issues Related to Health of Stress (One or Two Sentences) |
|---|---|
| 1. | |
| 2. | |
| 3. | |
| 4. | |
| 5. | |
| 6. | |
| 7. | |

## Communication Skills at Work

### Project 6.3: Time-Management Suggestions 🖥

Respond to the following six time-management suggestions with a personal example of how you either have implemented or would implement each suggestion.

*Retrieve file PRJ6-3 on the student CD and complete the following form by describing in column 2 a personal example of how you have implemented or would implement each time-management suggestion.*

| Time-Management Suggestion | A Personal Example |
|---|---|
| 1. Start with the most worrisome task. | |
| 2. Complete deadline work early. | |
| 3. Know your capacity for stress. | |
| 4. Stay organized. | |
| 5. Get physical. | |
| 6. Have fun. | |

## Decision Making at Work

### Project 6.4: How Would You Respond Positively to These Customer Scenarios?

Someone made a copy of an article from a customer service newsletter that Mary Graeff receives each month and has shared with all the CSRs at On-Time Technology Products. The article deals with solving customer problems. Specifically, the article presents several customer scenarios, gives a negative response to each scenario, and asks the readers to provide a more positive-sounding problem-solving response. How would you fill in these blanks?

*Provide a positive problem-solving response to each customer scenario:*

1. **Customer:** "I would like to be on the preferred customer mailing list." **Staff:** "You need to have spent $1,000 or more." (Sounds negative) **Your positive response:**

   _____

   _____

   _____

2. **Customer:** "Why haven't I received my refund?" **Staff:** "Because you filled out the form all wrong." (Sounds negative) **Your positive response:**

   _____

   _____

   _____

3. **Customer:** "Are there any more of these forms?" **Staff:** "I don't think so." (Sounds negative) **Your positive response:**

   _____

   _____

   _____

4. **Customer:** "How do I get to the exercise room?" **Staff:** "There's a map over there." (Sounds negative) **Your positive response:**

   _____

   _____

   _____

## Case Study

## Case Study

### 6.1 "If I Knew How to Solve My Own Problem, I Wouldn't Need You!"

As the floor manager, Mary Valentine, came around the corner at Baby's Little Store, she heard an angry customer say rather loudly, "If I knew how to solve my own problem, I wouldn't need you!" It was obvious that her new sales clerk of two weeks was in a tight spot with a customer.

As the situation revealed itself, this new mother had recently bought a baby mattress for her newborn and was very dissatisfied with the quality of the product after using it only a short time. She felt the mattress was made with unsafe materials and was concerned for her baby's health and safety. When the new mother said she wanted her money back, the new sales clerk said nicely, "I'll have to check with the store manager to see if we can take back this mattress for a full refund or not." At that point, the customer lost her temper and said, "If I knew how to fix my own problem, I wouldn't need you!"

#### Questions

*1. In your opinion, did the new sales clerk handle the situation the best she could under the circumstances?*

_____

_____

_____

*2. What suggestions could you make to this problem-solving approach, so that future dilemmas of this type have a more customer-oriented and positive solution?*

_____

_____

_____

_____

### 6.2 Making Time for What's Important

#### Situation

You had planned on getting to work early to finish the project that's due today, but now the car won't start. You know you wrote down the mechanic's name somewhere, but now you can't remember where you put it. You frantically search through your notes, but you can't find it anywhere. There's no way you are going to have time to finish your project (which you've had for two weeks or more). You start to panic, and the clock keeps ticking.

*First, indicate three time-management problems you can identify in this situation. Then, in column 2, respond with a suggestion that, in the future, could either eliminate the time-management problem or reduce the effects of it.*

| Time-Management Problem | Your Suggestion to Reduce or Eliminate the Problem |
|---|---|
| 1. | |
| 2. | |
| 3. | |

## Let's Discuss...

### Industry: Hospitality and Tourism

## Hospitality and Tourism Activities

1. Think about your total experience the last time you stayed at a hotel and respond with "yes" or "no" to the following questions:

| Yes | No | |
|-----|-----|---|
| | | Did the guest service agent (GSA) greet you with a smile and "Welcome to ____ Hotel"? |
| | | Did the GSA acknowledge guests who were waiting in line? |
| | | Did the GSA use each guest's name frequently? |
| | | Was the GSA knowledgeable regarding the property? |
| | | Did the GSA have frequent eye contact throughout the interaction with you? |
| | | When you checked out, did the GSA ask you, "Did you enjoy your stay?" |
| | | Did the GSA give an invitation for return by saying, "We look forward to seeing you again?" |

- How would you rank customer service at this hotel (1 = poor; 5 = superior)? _____
- From the material in Part 2, briefly explain why you evaluated the hotel as you did.

2. Briefly describe a situation at a restaurant where you or someone you know returned a meal because it was objectionable to eat.

- How did your server handle the complaint?
- What attempts were made to keep you as a satisfied customer?

3. Assume you are a director for a tour company that serves more than 500 tourists per week to Arizona's Grand Canyon. In that role, what are three time factors and three stress factors that you would need to manage and ultimately master as you serve customers well?

# PART 3

## GOVERNMENT PROFILE

by Theresa Alvarado, Human Resources
Director, City of Flagstaff

In past years, the city has always promoted customer service, and we had no reason to think of serving customers any differently. However, with the election of a new city mayor two years ago, who came from managing a large retail store, living customer service became Priority #1 for all 1,000 employees in the city government. As human resources director, I was asked by the new mayor to take on a new charge of establishing a customer service committee. The mayor's statement was "When walking through City Hall, I can't tell who is a customer and who is a city worker. Don't you think we need to fix that?"

It wasn't easy, but, after six months, and after giving each employee a choice about the type of and wording on their nametags, everyone wears a nametag every day. It is much more common now to see employees in city offices asking citizens, "Are you lost?" and "How can I help you?" It is prohibited to say, "It's not my job" or "I don't know" to any person in City Hall. Everyone in the city is now "in customer service"—with mind, spirit, and actions!

What makes this work is that critical elements for success on the job are tied to serving customers. By that, I mean the work of the customer service committee has been all encompassing in these ways:

- For every city employee, providing great customer service to both internal and external customers is now listed as a job duty and major component in each person's job description. This feeds naturally as an important piece of the employee evaluation process.

- On all job interviews, an applicant is asked a question dealing with customer service. For example, the question might be "In the position you are interviewing for, how will you demonstrate superior customer service?"

- Community customer service surveys are at many of our service-point counters in City Hall, where citizens give input on "How are we doing?" forms. We are looking to expand that effort and make it available at every service point. The survey results are tallied regularly,

# THERESA ALVARADO

and a report goes not only directly to the city manager but also to the mayor and each member of the City Council.

- The City Council has made customer service its #1 priority, and a recognition program is in place for the employees who give superior customer service.

In summary, we put a lot of emphasis on encouraging good customer service attitude and skills. We invest tax dollars in customer service skills training, even though our employees sometimes move to other jobs outside the city offices. When that happens, however, we still feel we have invested wisely and have made a contribution to the community by providing a better worker.

The skill set needed by any person working at federal, state, county, or city government goes beyond the rote smile and basic problem-solving abilities. It goes to the next level, which includes the following:

- Listening skills that show sincere empathy for a citizen's concern
- Problem solving that goes beyond a worker's own job parameters. That is to say, an employee needs to recognize when it is time to elevate the customer to another level to solve his or her problem. Employees must feel it's okay and safe to take that risk. Before, in our offices, it was rather "iffy," and city workers were reluctant to follow through to make sure a citizen's problem was solved.

Our mantra at the city of Flagstaff is "Community first, team second, and ourselves last." When facing any work dilemma and an employee applies this mantra, it helps clarify issues. I truly believe that, if you are going to be successful and have a career in government service, you have to put customers first, because they pay our salaries. We are really their servants; as such, it doesn't matter what it takes to serve the citizens, we are here to do *whatever it takes* to make sure citizens' needs are met through great service.

# Fundamentals of Communicating with Customers

*We are what we repeatedly do. Excellence is not an act but a habit.*

ARISTOTLE

## OBJECTIVES

**AFTER COMPLETING THIS CHAPTER,
YOU WILL BE ABLE TO:**

1. Explain the elements in the communication process.

2. Give an example of a mixed message.

3. Distinguish among the behaviors of people who communicate aggressively, passively, and assertively.

4. Associate the term *empowerment* with the task of serving customers well.

5. Compose examples of open, probing, closed, alternative choice, leading, and direct questions.

6. List tips to follow with customers before answering their questions.

7. Contrast the effects of using positive language with the effects of using negative language in oral and written communication.

8. Describe some communication techniques that bring about the resolution of conflict situations at work.

Communication is important to business. It is estimated that people spend about 80 percent of their work time deliberately communicating, when they write, read, speak, and listen. In every point of contact with customers, customer service representatives communicate something. As customers have more and more contacts with an organization, they combine their perceptions into an overall impression of the company's customer service. Typically, when serving customers, the three basic purposes of business communication are to inform, to persuade, and to build goodwill.

Part 3 covers all areas critical to communicating with customers, from the fundamentals of communicating to the importance of nonverbal communication, dress, and listening skills. Communicating in writing and on the telephone with customers is also discussed. Chapter 7 begins with the fundamentals of communicating when serving customers on a daily basis.

# Reviewing the Basics of Communication

The truth is, great service requires great communication skills. Think of the last time you experienced poor service from a service provider. What made the service poor?

- Didn't you get what you wanted?
- Were your expectations not met?
- Were you treated rudely?

As a working definition, we'll consider that **communication** has been successful if there is shared understanding between two or more persons, so what is the result of shared understanding? What are the implications of a lack of shared understanding? Let's examine what happens when we communicate, where the problems lie in the communication process, what we can do to improve our communication skills, and the types of communication. The reality is that communication is a process that takes place—for bad or for good—not only when we are trying to communicate well but also when we are not.

## The Communication Process

Understanding the communication process can help customer service representatives become better communicators. The process shows that each communication event is unique—that every mind is different from every other mind. This is what is called a frame of reference in communication when dealing with an audience. Unless the words or other signals used to send the message have the same meaning in the minds of both the sender and the receiver, communication suffers in some way.

The flow of communication in a business organization forms a complex and ever changing network. The human communication process follows this pattern:

1. A message arrives from a sender, and the senses pick up the message through signals and relay it to the receiver's brain. This is called the **encoding process.**

2. The receiver's brain filters the message and gives it a unique meaning. The meaning triggers a response, and the receiver returns (by voice, marks on paper, gestures, or the like) the shared understanding of this message to the sender. This is the **decoding process.**

3. The cycle may continue as long as the people involved care to communicate. When a message is transmitted back to the original sender, it is called **feedback.**

When we communicate, there are six elements in the communication process model: the sender, the receiver, a message, signals, the brain, shared understanding, and feedback:

- *The sender.* The sender has an idea to share with another person. Unfortunately, that information is in the sender's mind. The sender must get the information out of his or her mind and into the other person's mind.

- *The receiver.* The receiver is the person or persons with whom the sender is trying to communicate. The receiver has the responsibility of hearing, listening, and providing feedback to the sender.

- *A message.* The message is not just some words. The message is a combination of thoughts, feelings, words, and meanings. Many communication problems stem from the false notion that communication is simple.

- *Signals.* Signals are the means by which senders encode a message and broadcast it to receivers. Signals include more than the sounds of words; they include feelings, attitudes, facial and body gestures, and senders' unique personalities.

- *The brain.* All communication is filtered in the sender's and receiver's brain through personality, background, upbringing, culture, and current state of being. When we are tired, are stressed, or are in unpleasant circumstances, communication is that much harder.

- *Shared understanding.* The degree to which a receiver understands what a sender is trying to communicate depends on many factors. How much alike are they? Do they share any background experiences? Are their language skills, attitudes, and beliefs similar or dissimilar? What assumptions have they made about each other based on stereotypes and previous perceptions?

- *Feedback.* Feedback in our model is the receiver's reaction sent back to the sender. Each of us has experienced from time to time the feeling "He doesn't have a clue about what I'm trying to say." In most cases, we reach this conclusion by interpreting the verbal or nonverbal feedback the receiver is generating.

Communication theory attempts to explain what happens when we communicate successfully. The following is a real-world case in which communication with a customer goes sour. The company offers a high-quality product at a competitive price. Customer service policies and systems are flexible and user-friendly. Everyone in the organization

Are her thoughts that she doesn't believe a word he is saying?

one workstation to another in order to get "taken care of" may provide assembly-line efficiency for the company, but what it communicates to the customer is quite different. One person seeing to our needs feels warm and caring. When customers have to see different people, they don't feel nurtured and "taken care of;" instead, they feel processed.

## Service-Oriented Communication

What does service-oriented communication look and sound like? We've all experienced service-oriented communication. Think of a time when you felt you were the only customer the vendor had, or the time someone went the extra mile for you and you sent (or had every intention of sending) a note to his or her boss about the extraordinary treatment you received. In every story you can recall, think about the positive effect communication had when it was factored into the overall buying experience. Service-oriented communication looks like and takes on the following 10 dimensions:

1. Listening skills that make the other person feel heard
2. Questions framed in a respectful, nonaccusatory manner
3. A willingness to perform the work needed to reach the desired goal
4. An ability to remain calm and centered, despite chaos or challenge
5. Flawless follow-up by taking full responsibility for bringing communication full-circle
6. A demonstrated understanding of the other person's perspective
7. An ability to anticipate the client's needs
8. A calm and pleasant voice tone
9. Honest communication with good eye contact
10. Ease with admitting fault and a sincere desire to set right any misunderstanding

knows the value of the customer, and all accept the philosophy that the "customer is king"—yet the customer, based on his or her perception, may still not be satisfied. Often, the problem is mixed messages.

## Mixed Messages When Communicating

A **mixed message** is a single communication that contains two meanings. One part of the message—usually the verbal part—is positive. The other part of the message, usually the nonverbal component, contradicts the verbal portion and is negative. For example, a salesperson says, "Thank you," to a customer as she rings up the purchase, but she does so in a hurried tone and with no eye contact. When the verbal portion and the nonverbal portion of a message contradict one another, as in this case, the nonverbal portion almost always is believed. The reason is because nonverbal communication is perceived as less conscious, more honest, and harder for persons to fake.

Organizations unintentionally send hundreds of mixed messages to customers every day. One example is company policies that are intended for the convenience and protection of the customer but that many feel are actually designed to make life easier for managers and their employees. Procedures that require customers to move from

## Types of Communication

The best type of communication channel to use depends on the audience, the sender's purposes, and the situation. Written communication differs from oral communication in that it is more likely to involve creative effort, it has longer time frames between communications, and it has fewer feedback occurrences. Chapter 10 covers written communication more fully. This chapter, however, addresses more of the issues surrounding the oral communication process.

Much of the oral communication that goes on in business is person-to-person communication, which occurs whenever people get together. Most of us do a reasonably good job of informal talking. In fact, we do such a good job that we often take talking for granted. **Talking** is the oral expression of knowledge, viewpoints, and emotions through words. Imagine the best and worst speakers you have ever heard. This contrast should give you an understanding of the qualities of good talking—voice quality, speaking style, word choice, and adaptation to another person's communication style.

## Identifying Communication Styles

Good communication skills require a high level of self-awareness. By becoming more aware of how others perceive you, you can adapt more readily to their style of communicating. What this means is that you can make another person more comfortable with you by selecting and emphasizing certain behaviors that fit your personality. The selection you make should help you echo naturally with another person's communication style.

In business or personal life, there are three basic communication styles: aggressive, passive, and assertive. Although there are several personality tests, psychological assessments, and self-assessments to discover which style best fits you, the following descriptions of the three basic types can help in understanding each one.

### Aggressive Communication Style

A person who has an **aggressive communication style** is closed-minded, listens poorly, has difficulty seeing another person's point of view, interrupts other persons while they are talking, and tends to monopolize the conversation. Typically, an aggressive communicator feels he or she must win arguments and usually operates from a win/lose position.

In this room, there are participants who are using aggressive, passive, and assertive communication styles.

In other words, in order for that person to win, others must lose.

Unfortunately, this communication style fosters resistance, defiance, and retaliation. It costs a high price in personal and business relationships, especially when it comes to satisfying customers. Aggressive communicators express their thoughts and feelings in ways that violate or disregard the rights of others. For example, they tend to

- Humiliate and dominate other people
- Make choices for other people
- Show a lack of respect for someone else's rights
- Be sarcastic, insult others, and make unfair demands

### Passive Communication Style

Persons who communicate in the **passive communication style** tend to be indirect and at times hesitant to say what is really on their minds. By avoiding or ignoring problems, passive communicators tend to agree externally, while disagreeing internally. They often feel powerless in customer situations because they don't like to make waves or make people upset.

Passive communicators fail to express their feelings, thoughts, and beliefs. By being less than forthright about their true feelings, they typically give in to others. As a result, they allow others to make choices for them. In general, passive communicators

- Believe that other people are more important or more correct than they are

- Are concerned that they will anger someone if they express their true feelings
- Beat around the bush when trying to make a point
- Say nothing is wrong and then become resentful about the situation later

## Assertive Communication Style

A person who practices an **assertive communication style** tends to be an effective, active listener who states limits and expectations and does not label or judge people or events. By confronting problems at the time they happen, assertive communicators are open to negotiating, bargaining, and compromising in such a way that everyone involved wins.

The greatest advantage assertive communicators have is the ability to exercise their rights without denying the rights of others. Moreover, they express feelings honestly and directly while practicing mutual respect for others. Assertive communicators state their message without being blunt or rude and consciously practice good eye contact while using appropriate hand gestures and other suitable body language.

Clearly, the assertive style is the one to strive for when serving customers. However, the reality is that very few people use only one style. In fact, the aggressive style is essential at times, such as

- When a decision has to be made quickly or during an emergency
- When you know you are right and that fact is crucial to the outcome for both parties

The passive style also has its critical applications, such as

- When an issue is minor or when the problems caused by the conflict are greater than the conflict itself
- When emotions are running high, and it makes sense to take a break in order to calm down and regain perspective about the situation

Refer to Guideline 7.1 for more information about the behavior, nonverbal cues, and verbal cues of each communication style.

## Communicating with Customers in Person

Telecommunications, computerization, and self-service have reduced person-to-person communication to minutes and sometimes seconds. In order for CSRs to provide superior customer service in this fast-paced, competitive

---

**GUIDELINE 7.1    Communication Styles**

| Style | Behaviors | Nonverbal Cues | Verbal Cues |
|---|---|---|---|
| Aggressive | • Puts others down<br>• Has a know-it-all attitude<br>• Doesn't show appreciation<br>• Is bossy | • Frowns<br>• Squints eyes critically<br>• Glares and stares<br>• Is critical<br>• Uses a loud tone of voice<br>• Has rigid posture | • "You must [should, ought, or better]. . . ."<br>• "Don't ask why. Just do it." |
| Passive | • Sighs a lot<br>• Clams up when feeling badly treated<br>• Asks permission unnecessarily<br>• Complains instead of taking action | • Fidgets<br>• Smiles and nods in agreement<br>• Has slumped posture<br>• Speaks in a low volume<br>• Is meek | • "You have more experience than I do."<br>• "I don't think I can. . . ."<br>• "This is probably wrong, but. . . ."<br>• "I'll try." |
| Assertive | • Operates from choice<br>• Is action-oriented<br>• Is realistic in expectations<br>• Behaves in a fair, consistent manner<br>• Is firm | • Has open, natural gestures<br>• Uses direct eye contact<br>• Has a confident, relaxed posture<br>• Uses a varied rate of speech | • "I choose to. . . ."<br>• "What are my options?"<br>• "What alternatives do we have?" |

business world, they must be empowered. Relative to customer service, **empowerment** is the business process that authorizes an employee to do whatever he or she has to do on the spot to take care of a customer to that customer's satisfaction.

Many businesses mistakenly think of empowerment as giving employees the authority to make a decision to take care of the customer as long as the action they take follows the rules, policies, and procedures of the organization. This would mean that there actually is not empowerment. True empowerment in customer service means that customer service representatives can bend and break the rules to do whatever they have to do to take care of the customer. When communicating with customers in person, CSRs must be empowered to follow their best judgment in serving customers in the most excellent manner possible.

There must be limits in the use of empowerment. Empowerment doesn't mean that customer service representatives can indiscriminately slash prices to retain a customer. What it does mean is that they can take the initiative in solving customers' problems, so that customers will continue to do business with the company. CSRs need to feel confident that they will not be fired if they make a mistake and that it's okay to make mistakes in the process of working to win customer satisfaction.

An organization's mission should be to take care of the customer. In order to do so, employees must be trained in customer service and be trusted and empowered to provide exceptional service. One skill that goes along with empowerment is for CSRs to be able to appropriately gather information by asking and answering customer questions. When working with customers, how CSRs pose a question is often as important as what they ask.

## Asking Questions

Customers time and again call with questions. To answer customers' questions or to address their needs, you need to ask questions also. Typically, you question others in order to continue a discussion or to pinpoint and clarify issues to help in gathering pertinent information.

Asking a question skillfully increases the likelihood of quickly getting a good understanding of the issues. Remember that the person doing the questioning is usually the one who is in control of the discussion. Therefore, all questions should be asked in a positive way. A **positive question** is one that the customer is not afraid to answer. Avoid sarcastic or threatening language or tone in your questions by changing a "you" statement into an "I" statement. For example, avoid "What exactly are *you* getting at? or Could *you* get to the point a little quicker?" and say "*I* don't understand what you are trying to tell me. or Could you please try to explain it in a different way so *I* can understand better?" Relative to questioning techniques, there are certain approaches you should avoid when serving customers:

- *Bombardment-question approach.* Too many questions put customers on the defensive. You may control the conversation, but the approach may limit what you ultimately find out. "Why" questions, if improperly asked, often cause individuals to become defensive.
- *Multiple-questions approach.* If your question contains several questions, you may confuse the client. In addition, individuals from non-Western cultures do not receive rapid-fire questions favorably, as it creates distrust.

To get the response you want, you need to know how to choose the appropriate type of question to ask. Using effective questioning techniques allows you to get the information you need. It also helps you stay in control of the conversation. In normal conversation with customers, you will be using all types of questions to filter the vast amount of data you receive into information you can use. When working with customers, the following are the six types of questions you can ask, depending on the situation:

1. *Open questions.* An **open question** requests information in a way that requires a fuller answer than a simple "yes" or "no." Open questions encourage an individual to talk and elicit maximum information to identify causes and to help you work more quickly and effectively toward solutions. Open questions usually begin with "How," "What," "Why," or "Could." As a result of asking open questions, CSRs are able to gain enough information to give the customer a solution to a particular problem or at least to be in a better position to offer suggestions that help. Examples are "Could you describe the kind of engine noise you are hearing?" "How can I assist you?" and "What information were you given when you spoke with the CSR yesterday?"

2. *Probing questions.* A **probing question** uses information already established in order to clarify points and ask for more details. Often, these questions promptly follow up on a previous question and response. Two specific types of questions are those that request a piece of information and those that simply require a "yes" or "no" response. Examples are "Whom did you speak with yesterday?" "When did you purchase the product?" "Can you always be reached at this telephone number?" and "Tell me more about how you are feeling."

3. *Closed questions.* **Closed questions** usually elicit a "yes" or "no" answer. Closed questions can be useful in the closing minutes of a conversation with customers to confirm all the small details and to make sure that you have covered all the bases concerning the customer's query. They can be good for providing specifics and usually begin with "Where," "Are," or "Do." Examples are "Where do you live?" and "Are there other questions you have for me at this time?"

4. *Alternative choice questions.* **Alternative choice questions** provide alternatives for the customer to choose from. These questions can be particularly useful when dealing with difficult customers. Ask the customers what they would like you to do for them, but limit their responses by providing them with two or three alternatives that also suit you. Examples are "I could find this information for you and call you with an answer by the end of the morning, or would you prefer me to fax the information later in the day?" and "Would you like me to get our supervisor, or would you like to give me an opportunity to try to help first?"

5. *Leading questions.* **Leading questions** help speed up interactions with people who find it difficult to make a final decision. Leading questions help the customer confirm the information in an easy way. Examples are "You would like to receive the catalog updates on a monthly basis, then?" and "So, you would agree on a delivery this coming Thursday, if I can get you a discount?"

6. *Direct questions.* **Direct questions** can be open or closed; however, all direct questions have two characteristics in common: (a) When you pose a direct question, you always use the name of the other person, and (b) you pose the question as an instruction. Examples are "Tell me, Mr. Harkins, . . ." "Explain to me, Mr. Siskowski, . . ." and "Describe to me, Ms. Scott, . . ." By using the other person's name, you are in a great position to get his or her immediate attention. In phrasing the question as an instruction ("Tell me," etc.), you are subconsciously giving an order.

## CUSTOMER SERVICE TIP

**7.2** *Don't answer your twentieth question that day as if it were your twentieth question that day. Instead, answer the twentieth question that day as if it were your first question. It may be the twentieth time you hear the same question, but keep in mind that it's probably the first time that person has asked the question.*

## Answering Questions

Answering customer questions effectively is equally as important as asking the right questions. Following are eight tips to consider before answering customer questions:

- *Understand the question.* Pay attention to every word the customer uses when asking a question. Once you understand the question, then respond.

- *Decide whether you know the answer.* If you are not sure that your response is accurate, do not answer. Although quick responses are preferred, providing correct information is always the first priority.

- *Remember, you are an expert.* As a CSR, you know your job better than anyone else. If you are certain you are right, and you can back up your answer with facts, politely claim the truth of what you say. Again, do not promise something if you are not sure you can deliver.

- *Take enough time.* If a customer needs help, don't be too busy to help him or her. Don't refuse to help because you are too busy; and remember not to pass the questioner from person to person.

- *Smile.* If you've got a cranky customer, or one who thinks that what you say just cannot be right, bend over backwards to make him or her happy. Be pleasant at all times when answering the customer's questions.

- *Never answer a question with a question.* Questions should be asked only to clarify the original question; beyond that—answer, don't ask.

- *Be careful with your power.* Never belittle a customer or criticize a question you receive. In other words, don't say, "Don't you see the sign over the door that says...?" or "You mean you don't know?"
- *When you don't know, admit it.* When you've searched your mind, and you are sure that you don't know the answer, say so. Say you don't know, but try to send the questioner to another source, making sure ahead of time that the source is qualified to answer that question.

## ETHICS/CHOICES

**7.1** Assume you started a new customer service job and, after a week or so, determined that it was standard procedure at the company to promise customers products it couldn't guarantee reasonable delivery on. Would you express your concerns, or, instead, would you start thinking about finding another job?

## Using Positive Language

Language is an exceedingly powerful tool. Whether you communicate orally or in written form, the way you express yourself affects whether your message is received positively or negatively. Even when you must convey unpleasant news, the impact can be softened by the use of positive language. **Positive language** projects a helpful, positive feeling, rather than a destructive, negative one.

No doubt you are familiar with "the cynic." The cynic is the person who often offers criticism of ideas or always provides reasons that something won't work. If you've ever worked or associated with such a person, you know that this kind of negative communication is very fatiguing for those around this person. Additionally, the cynic's constant challenging creates a negative environment and increased confrontational situations.

Cynics don't always have negative attitudes. In many cases, they simply use language that gives the impression of negativity. They have not learned to phrase their comments in more constructive, positive ways. **Negative language** conveys a poor image to customers. Sometimes, it causes conflict and confrontation where none is necessary or desired. It is very easy to fall into the negative language

pattern. Many of us do so without being aware of it. Read the following dialogue that could take place at a business service counter:

> We regret to inform you that we cannot process your application to register your business name, since you have neglected to provide sufficient information. Please complete ALL sections of the attached form and return it to us promptly.

Note the high incidence of negative words—*cannot* and *neglected*—and the message has a tone that suggests that the recipient is to blame for the problem. Contrast this example with the following rewritten, more positive approach:

> Congratulations on your new business. To register your business name, we need some additional information. If you return the attached form, with highlighted areas filled in, we will be able to send you your business registration certificate within two weeks. We wish you success in your new endeavor.

Observe that the negative example tells the person what he or she has done wrong but doesn't stress the positive things that can be done to remedy the problem. The information is all there, but it sounds bureaucratic, cold, and negative. The positive example sounds completely different, although it contains almost the identical information. It has a more upbeat and helpful tone. Negative phrasing and language often have the following characteristics:

- They tell the recipient what cannot be done.
- They have a subtle tone of blame.
- They include words such as *can't, won't, and unable to,* which tell the recipient what the sender cannot do.
- They do not stress positive actions that would be appropriate.

Positive phrasing and language, on the other hand, have the following qualities:

- They tell the recipient what can be done.
- They suggest alternatives and choices available to the recipient.
- They sound helpful and encouraging, rather than bureaucratic.
- They stress positive actions and positive consequences that can be anticipated.

If you want to move to more positive communication, the first task is to identify and eliminate common negative phrasing. Guideline 7.2 describes some common expressions that should be avoided whenever possible when communicating with customers. However, if you are going to eliminate negative phrases, you will need to replace them with more positive ways of conveying the same information. See examples of positive phrasing in Guideline 7.3.

## GUIDELINE 7.2    Common Negative Language and Phrasing

| | |
|---|---|
| Expressions that suggest carelessness | • "You neglected to specify"<br>• "You failed to include"<br>• "You overlooked enclosing" |
| Phrases that suggest the person is lying | • "You claim that"<br>• "You say that"<br>• "You state that" |
| Expressions that imply that the recipient is not too bright | • "We cannot see how you"<br>• "We fail to understand"<br>• "We are at a loss to know" |
| Demanding phrases that imply coercion and pressure | • "You should"<br>• "We must ask you to"<br>• "We must insist that you" |
| Phrases that might be interpreted as sarcastic or patronizing | • "No doubt"<br>• "We will thank you to"<br>• "You understand, of course," |

## GUIDELINE 7.3    Examples of Positive Phrasing

- "If you can send us your bill of sale, we will be happy to complete the process for you."

- "The information we have suggests that you have a different viewpoint on this issue. Let me explain our perspective."

- "Might we suggest that you. . . [suggestion]."

- "One option open to you is . . . [option]."

## Handling Customer Requests

Sometimes, when handling customer requests, special service skills come into play. The best response to a request is "yes," but sometimes a "no" response is required, or occa-

sionally even an "I'm not sure" response cannot be avoided. Here's how to handle each circumstance:

- *Saying, "Yes."* Use friendly voice tones, combined with positive, cheerful words. Clearly tell the customer what you can do for him or her.

- *Saying, "No."* Empathize with the customer and help if you can. Explain why you cannot complete the request. Choose words that are calming and soothing. When customers are distracted or emotionally upset, they may not hear what you intended to say, so make every effort to use positive, clear, effective phrases. Avoid personalizing your sentences if your message is not positive.

- *Saying, "I'm not sure."* Use this phrase when you are not sure (1) if the request can be completed, (2) what options you can offer, or (3) if you have the authority to address the request. Say that there's an "off-chance" you can do this. The approach shows you are flexible and that you are trying to help the customer.

## CUSTOMER SERVICE TIP

*7.3   Use creative ways to say "no" to the customer. Make sure that, if you must use the word* policy, *that you do so only for matters of legal compliance, ethics, or absolute performance standards, such as "employee safety."*

## Communication Reminders

In the rush of doing our jobs, it is easy to forget that we are not just serving customers; we are in the business of serving people. When individuals approach us for assistance, we see just a snippet of their existence. We have no way of knowing what challenges or crises they are quietly coping with as they approach us. Providing rude or apathetic service is always bad business, but to provide it to a person who is suffering mental or physical pain is simply bad human behavior.

When serving others, it is safe to assume that some of the customers you encounter on most days are undergoing tremendous physical or mental trauma. Who these people are or what crises they face will likely never be revealed, but rest assured, your actions will make a positive or negative impact on their outlook for the day. The following are some sobering statistics about various crises people (customers) in America face every day. For each situation, reflect and then ask yourself, "How will you treat these people when they come to you for service?"

- *Death of a loved one.* Each day in America, more than 6,500 people die, and there are many customers walking around today, dealing with the shocking news about the death of a loved one.
- *Suicide.* Today, more than 90 people will take their own lives, whereas another 1,350 will attempt suicide. This means that, sometime today, hundreds of CSRs unknowingly have the opportunity to convince these people they are valuable human beings.
- *Divorce.* Today, 3,440 spouses will be served with papers for divorce. For many of them, this surprise will cause absolute devastation.
- *Missing children.* Today, more than 2,000 children will be listed as missing. How will you treat their parents when they come to you for service?
- *Rape.* Today, more than 250 women will report that they were raped, and hundreds more will suffer the same fate without reporting it.
- *Death of pet.* Today, more than 16,000 faithful house pets—dogs and cats with an average age of 10 years—will die.
- *Loss of job.* Today, more than 7,000 people will be laid off, fired, or otherwise removed from their jobs. How will you treat these people when they come to you for service?[1]

## Resolving Conflicts on the Job

People who never experience conflict on the job are rare. Although all workplaces suffer from conflict periodically,

[1] "You Never Know What Crisis Your Customer Is Facing," *A Supervisor's Guide to Improved Customer Service & Retention* (December 2000): 6.

some people think that workplace conflict has been escalating recently. Several factors may be tied to accelerated friction at work.

One factor is our increasingly diverse workforce. Sharing ideas that stem from a variety of backgrounds, experiences, and personalities probably leads to better problem solving, but it can also lead to conflict. Another factor is the trend toward participatory management. In the past, only bosses were expected to resolve problems, but now employees are making more and more decisions and having to deal with conflicts. Working together harmoniously involves a great deal of give and take, and conflict may result when some people feel that they are being treated unfairly.

To be good at resolving work-related conflicts requires a lot of practice. In Chapter 4, we discussed disagreement and conflict relative to serving customers. When you have interpersonal relationships with people at work, there may be conflicts that you are not aware of. For example, if someone who is normally upbeat and friendly toward you suddenly begins avoiding you and being rude, there is probably a reason. If the coworker has remained cheerful with everyone except you, chances are you are dealing with a conflict situation. In such instances, you will want to use your best communication skills and address the problem through the following process:

1. Try to determine if there is a problem between you and the other person.
2. If you think there is a problem, set up a private face-to-face meeting to discuss the problem with the other person.
3. In a nonconfrontational manner, ask the person if there is a problem. If the answer is "no," inform the person that you think there is a problem and explain what you think the problem is.
4. As you talk, ask for feedback. Do not attack the other person with accusations. Avoid finger-pointing.
5. Try to listen to each other with open minds.
6. Respect each other's opinions.
7. Take a few minutes to recycle the other person's opinions in your mind before responding.
8. Try to determine why the other person feels the way he or she does.
9. Try to work out a compromise that pleases both of you.

10. Find a way that both of you can walk away feeling like winners.

Remember that the goal is to reach a compromise that both of you can live with, as well as be happy with. Regardless of the type of conflict you are dealing with, there are several general rules of thumb you should follow when you are trying to bring harmony back into work situations. To review the rules for disagreeing diplomatically, refer to Guideline 7.4.

| GUIDELINE 7.4 | Rules for Disagreeing Diplomatically | |
|---|---|---|
| **Rule** | **When You Say. . .** | **It really says. . .** |
| 1. Reflect your understanding of the other's position or opinion. | "I feel [think, want]. . . ." | "I am listening to your opinion and I take your opinion into account before I state mine." |
| 2. Let the other person know that you value him or her as a person, even though his or her opinion is different from yours. | "I understand [appreciate, respect, see] how you feel that way." | "I hear you and respect your opinion." |
| 3. State your position or opinion. | "I feel [think, want]. . . ." | "I don't agree, but I value you—so let's exchange ideas comfortably, not as a contest for superiority." |

Handling a problem person takes a lot of skill but, most important, courage and time. Most of us avoid conflict so much that we ignore or walk away from these situations. Our thinking is that we don't have the time, emotions, or energy to put into confronting this person. Unfortunately, when problem people aren't confronted, they tend to repeat this bad behavior, because it works for them. If you are firm and assertive and use the techniques outlined in this section, you may not be able to avoid problem people, but you should be able to defuse them by coping rather than fighting or withdrawing.

## Concluding Message for CSRs

How important is practicing good communication skills with customers? More customers leave an organization because of poor customer service than because of dissatisfaction with a product. A lost customer is never just one sale, or even just one customer. When you lose a customer, that customer tells 10 to 12 others, possibly building on the story each time.

An unhappy customer tells people who might have been perfectly happy with you or who had planned on doing business with you in the future. Now, these other customers are not so sure, and your organization's future is not so bright. Keep in mind that it doesn't matter whether customers are right or wrong; it matters how they *feel* when they leave an interaction or a conversation with you. Before you leave an interaction with a customer, always ask, "Is there anything else I can do for you? If you need me, you can reach me by. . . ."

## Summary

- The six elements in the communication process are the sender, the receiver, a message, signals, the brain, shared understanding, and feedback.

- A mixed message is a single communication that contains two meanings—one verbal and the other nonverbal, which contradict each other.

- The best type of communication channel to use, written or oral, depends on the audience, the sender's purpose, and the situation.

- An aggressive communication style is one in which a person is closed-minded, is a poor listener, and tends to monopolize the conversation.

- A passive communication style is one in which a person tends to be indirect and is hesitant to express his or her true feelings, thoughts, and beliefs.

- A person who practices an assertive communication style tends to be an effective, active listener who confronts problems at the time they happen and is open to communicating in such a way that everyone wins.

- When a company practices empowerment, it grants an employee the ability to do whatever he or she has to at that moment to take care of a customer to the customer's satisfaction.

- Asking a question skillfully increases the likelihood of quickly getting a good understanding of the customer's concern.

- When clarifying issues with customers, consider the information you want to get and use a variety of the following six types of questions: open, probing, closed, alternative choice, leading, and direct.

- Answering customer questions well is equally as important as asking the right questions.

- Positive language projects a helpful, positive feeling, whereas negative language often tells the recipient what cannot be done and has a subtle tone of blame.

- The best response to customer requests is "yes," but sometimes a "no" response is required or occasionally even an "I'm not sure" response.

- When serving customers each day, it is safe to assume that some of those customers are undergoing tremendous physical or mental trauma. It is particularly important to be sensitive to the way each customer is treated.

- The purpose of resolving conflicts at work is to bring harmony back into work situations.

## QUESTIONS FOR CRITICAL THINKING

1. In your opinion, are there elements in the communication process that are more important than others? Explain.

2. Recount two situations you observed this past week in which mixed messages were sent.

3. Describe the behaviors of a person you know who predominately uses a passive communication style. an aggressive communication style. an assertive communication style.

4. From the perspective of a company president, would you be overly concerned with the extent to which CSRs were empowered to serve customers well? Explain.

5. Assume that a customer returns an article of clothing or a household item for a refund or credit. Develop six queries a CSR might use in this situation that make use of each type of question: open, probing, closed, alternative choice, leading, and direct.

6. Of the eight tips to follow before answering a customer's question, which three do you think are most important for CSRs to remember and why?

7. When someone speaks to you using negative language, how does it make you feel?

8. Why is it important to practice sound communication techniques with people at work? Do you think CSRs should have the right and ability to disagree diplomatically with coworkers?

## On-line Research Activities

### Project 7.1: Empowerment Policy

Research a number of web sites and locate several articles on *empowering employees as the key to customer service.* As a result of your research, develop an employee empowerment policy for a retail store, such as Sears or Home Depot.

### Project 7.2: Conflict Resolution Seminars 🖳

**Situation**

Lately, on entering the work area of the Customer Service Department at On-Time Technology Products, Mary Graeff has instantly felt a mood of stress and dissention among her CSRs. She imagines that it is because of a personal issue among Layla, Rosie, and Ruth. Wanting to get to the bottom of it and return harmony to her work area, Ms. Graeff is interested in researching the content of various conflict-resolution seminars offered around the country. She would like either to develop an in-service herself or to have an outside consultant come in and present a two-hour program for CSRs and others in the organization. She has asked you to assist her in this research.

*Enter "conflict-resolution seminars" in your favorite search engine. Using file PRJ7–2 on your student CD, key responses in the following table format that will inform Ms. Graeff where you got your information and what topics you would suggest be part of the in-service on conflict resolution.*

| Web Sites | Topics for Conflict-Resolution In-Service |
|---|---|
| 1. | |
| 2. | |
| 3. | |
| 4. | |
| 5. | |

## Communication Skills at Work

### Project 7.3: Language That Makes a Difference 🖳

Provide a more appropriate response to each of the following negative language statements. Hint: Use "I" statements, rather than "you" statements.

*Retrieve file PRJ7-3 from the student CD and complete the following form by describing in column 2 a more appropriate statement that uses positive language.*

| Avoid. . . | Try. . . |
|---|---|
| 1. "You didn't do this right." | |
| 2. "You are wrong." | |
| 3. "Wait here." | |
| 4. "It's not my job." | |
| 5. "What's your problem?" | |
| 6. "You aren't making any sense." | |
| 7. "Why are you so upset?" | |

## Decision Making at Work

### Project 7.4: Disagreeing Diplomatically

Assume you are a member of a strategic planning committee at On-Time Technology Products, and its goal is to review the wording and intent of the organization's mission statement. There is one individual on the committee who exhibits the following behaviors and attitudes during discussions: "I must have everything my way" and "Everything has to be perfect."

Using the rules for disagreeing diplomatically, as outlined in Guideline 7.4, describe three actions you and others on the committee should follow when working with this person.

1. _____

_____

_____

_____

_____

_____

2. _____

_____

_____

_____

_____

_____

_____

3. _____

_____

_____

_____

_____

_____

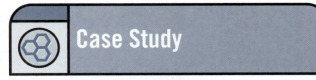

## Case Study

### 7.1  "I'll Take That Customer!"

Charlie Sampler has a reputation in the Customer Service Department at Haskin's Bookstore that he has always been proud of. He takes calls from customers with whom others in the department don't want to deal. In fact, at times when he is on the phone with a customer, he asks or motions coworkers to come near his desk to hear his side of the argument. It used to be cute when he sounded loud and belligerent with customers. He was happiest when he boasted of "winning." Things have changed, however, and Charlie is now in trouble with management because of a recent incident.

A loyal customer of 20 years, with whom Charlie spoke last week, just left the store and expressed in no uncertain terms to the owner, Mr. Haskin, why she was taking her business elsewhere.

#### Questions

1. In your opinion, should Charlie have been allowed to get away with this behavior with customers? Explain.

_____

_____

_____

_____

_____

2. As a coworker of his, did you have any responsibility to report to management his aggressive communication style with customers?

_____

_____

_____

_____

_____

## Case Study

### 7.2  "I Understand How You Might Feel That Way"

Doug went into work this morning at On-Time Technology Products and casually mentioned to his fellow CSRs that his wife had just been to a communications in-service for her company and that she learned the "feel, felt, found" technique in responding to customer questions and concerns. Doug wasn't sure how using this technique would work at this company, but he thought it was worthy of some discussion with his coworkers.

According to what Doug's wife told him, the technique works this way: When a customer expresses a concern, the CSR should respond by saying, "I understand how you might _feel_ that way. Others have _felt_ that way, too. Then they _found,_ after an explanation, that this policy protects them, so it made sense."

#### Questions

1. What is your first reaction to communicating with customers using the "feel, felt, found" approach?

_____

_____

_____

2. How extensively do you think it can be applied to most customer problems and concerns?

_____

_____

_____

3. Can you think of situations when it would not be advisable to use this approach with customers?

_____

_____

_____

# CHAPTER VIII

# Nonverbal Communication, Dress, Manners, and Listening Skills

*Your words tell me a story, but your body tells me the whole story.*

ANONYMOUS

## OBJECTIVES

**AFTER COMPLETING THIS CHAPTER,
YOU WILL BE ABLE TO:**

1. List the elements that constitute a person's body language.

2. Explain some interpretations of body language signals when serving customers.

3. Describe a common dress code for workers in today's workplace.

4. Give some examples of business etiquette and manners.

5. Distinguish among the three levels of listening.

6. Contrast active listening with passive listening.

7. Cite some guidelines to follow when practicing empathetic listening.

8. Discuss ways to become a better listener while non-native persons are speaking.

"Stop slouching and sit up straight. Stand with your back flat, your shoulders back, your head held high, and your feet firmly planted on the floor." How many times have we heard this from our mothers over the years? Well, as usual, they were right. When it comes to showcasing our intelligence and professional abilities, it is as much about presentation, including body language, dress, and listening skills, as it is about verbal communication.

Nonverbal communication is important, because you can get valuable information about your customer's state of mind by paying attention to what you see and hear. Customers are also able to read your response to them by observing your nonverbal messages. Understanding body language in the workplace isn't a game—it's a career necessity.

## Using Body Language That Is Customer-Friendly

When we communicate, we use nonverbal messages, called **body language,** that include tone of voice, eye movement, posture, hand gestures, facial expressions, and more. When really understanding the full meaning of a message, body language usually prevails over words. The reason is because nonverbal cues are more immediate, instinctive, and uncontrolled than are verbal expressions. They bring attitudes and feelings out into the open.

Clues we receive about a person's character come through the quality of that person's voice, the expression on the person's face, and the person's posture and hand gestures. However, although these behaviors are important to most Americans, they can be interpreted differently from culture to culture.

## The Importance of Body Language

Customer service often comes down to one person doing something for another person.[1] One study concluded that, when companies lose customers to their competition, 67 percent of the time, it happens because of one incident with one person. Every contact contributes to customers' impressions of a company. Each employee's communication skills contribute significantly to those impressions.

Without realizing it, we frequently send messages to customers with our posture, facial expression, tone of voice, gestures, and eye contact. Body language communicates our attitude to customers, and it can either reinforce or contradict our words. Understanding body language, therefore, can help reinforce verbal messages and can help us understand customers' messages better.

Nonverbal signals constitute a silent language that has about four and a half times the effect of verbal ones. Linguists who study the nonverbal elements of a conversation—including posture, eye contact, facial expression, and gestures—have concluded that these silent elements make up 55 percent of the message. Tone of voice contributes another 38 percent. This leaves 7 percent for the words you use.[2] In other words, 60 to 90 percent of every conversation is interpreted through body language. We react more to what we think someone meant than to the words he or she said. For example, you may tell a customer that you are happy to help her, but if you frown, slump, or refuse to make eye contact, the customer, in most cases, will not believe you. This is because people are more likely to believe nonverbal signals, such as a frown, than words.

---

[1]Carol Smith, "Face to Face with Customers," *Professional Builder* (June 2001): 20.
[2]*Ibid.*, 21.

Body language is a crucial communication tool, yet few people understand how to read it accurately. Guideline 8.1 describes several body language signs and their possible meaning.

| GUIDELINE 8.1 | Body Language Signs |
| --- | --- |

| Body Language Sign | Possible Meaning |
| --- | --- |
| Clenched hands | The higher the hands, the more frustration |
| Open palms | Sincerity, openness, interest, and involvement in the conversation |
| Leaning closer | Interest in or comfort about what is being said |
| Leaning away | Discomfort with the facts being presented or the person presenting them |
| Nodding of head | Interest, agreement, and understanding; women often nod to say, "I am listening to you"; men tend to nod only when they agree with the speaker |
| Tapping or drumming with fingers | Impatience or annoyance with the topic or person speaking |
| Fidgeting | Boredom, nervousness, or impatience with the situation |
| Clutching objects tightly | Anxiety or nervous anticipation about the interchange |
| Crossed arms and legs | Defensiveness, protection, the filtering of information |
| Placing of hand on cheek | Evaluation and interest in what is being discussed |
| Placing of hand on cheek with thumb under chin | Genuine interest, but with some negative thoughts or doubts |

Adapted from—Joy Davidson, "Office Ties: Understanding Body Language," *Men's Fitness*, July 1998, pg. 30.

## Interpreting Body Signs

Besides communicating an attitude of caring and cooperation, your body language conveys your professional stature and self-confidence. When you speak with conviction in a calm voice, listeners consider you to be competent, and they are more likely to trust what you say. The major elements of a person's body language include eye contact, tone of voice, smiling, posture, and gestures:

- *Eye contact.* The eyes communicate more than any other part of the human anatomy. For example, staring or gazing at others can create pressure and tension among people. Research suggests that an individual who can routinely outgaze another person develops a sense of control and power over that person. Shifty eyes and too much blinking can suggest deception, whereas people with eye movements that are relaxed and comfortable, yet attentive to the person they are conversing with, are seen as more sincere and honest. With increasing diversity in the marketplace, you might encounter customers from other cultures in which direct eye contact is considered offensive. Be sensitive and take your cue from the customer.

- *Tone of voice.* You might have noticed that you can "hear" a smile on the phone. The muscles that form your smile also cause your vocal cords to produce a warmer sound. Your tone of voice can sound either interested and caring or aggressive. Interested and caring works best for most customer situations. Notice the tone of voice of others with whom you speak and the feeling it creates in you. This is especially important on the phone, when other visual clues are missing from the conversation.

- *Smiling.* Show customers you enjoy helping them by smiling at appropriate times. If you smile even when you are not feeling your best, your brain does not know the difference; it thinks you are happy. The result can be that you cheer yourself up.

- *Posture.* Slouching and leaning postures send the wrong message—"I'm tired, bored, or uninterested in your concerns." A military stance is unnecessary, but an alert posture reinforces the customer's feeling that you are interested in helping.

- *Gestures.* The manner in which you gesture, especially in tense conversations, can mean the difference between sending a message of trust and cooperation and sending one of suspicion. Placing your hands on your hips typically conveys annoyance. Arms across your chest suggest distrust. Slamming something down abruptly can suggest you are angry.

By paying careful attention to body language, and noticing when someone makes a sudden transition from one attitude to another, you'll have a good idea of what the other person is thinking—whether or not that is what he or

## ETHICS/CHOICES

**8.1** A manager says he is very interested in receiving suggestions from you; however, while you try to outline to him an idea for reducing copier costs, he reads his mail and accepts incoming phone calls. How would you handle this situation? How would this exchange make you feel?

she is saying. The following are some typical interpretations of body language cues when serving customers:

- *Openness and warmth:* open-lipped smiling, open hands with palms visible

- *Confidence:* leaning forward in the chair, chin up, putting the tips of the fingers of one hand against the tips of the fingers of the other hand in a "praying," or "steepling," position

- *Nervousness:* smoking, whistling, pinching the skin, fidgeting, jiggling pocket contents, clearing the throat, running fingers through the hair, wringing hands, biting on pens or other objects, twiddling thumbs

- *Untrustworthiness/defensiveness:* frowning, squinting, tight-lipped grin, arms crossed in front of the chest, darting eyes, looking down when speaking, clenched hands, pointing with the fingers, rubbing the back of the neck

It isn't enough just to understand other people's body language—controlling your own nonverbal signals can improve your image and increase your success. If you want to appear confident, open, and in control, then practice the following moves in front of a mirror until they're second nature:

1. Walk with a brisk, easy stride and with eyes looking forward.

2. Stand evenly on both feet. Keep your arms relaxed and casual. For example, keep one hand in your pocket, and use the other one for gesturing as you speak.

3. Move slightly closer to others if you want to warm up the relationship. Avoid "commando" postures, such as hands on your hips or clasped behind your head. Also avoid "barrier" language, such as turning your body away from the listener or keeping your arms folded.

4. Look at others straight on. Meet their eyes, and then occasionally let your gaze drift elsewhere to keep from staring.

5. Keep your gestures loose, yet controlled. If those around you seem reserved or nervous, avoid excessively exuberant or frantic movements.

## CUSTOMER SERVICE TIP

**8.1** *Make the idea of being "the customer's champion" a primary factor in your success and career progression as a customer service representative.*

## Dressing to Make a Good Impression

In American business, there's never a second chance to make a first impression, and first impressions are lasting ones. How you dress and present yourself is a statement about you. Whether you will be interacting with fellow employees on the job or meeting with customers, your attire, behavior, and attitude say a lot about you. Those who aspire to leadership, or simply to move ahead in their careers, must think carefully about what they wear. Clothes can help or hinder goals.

Unlike decades past, workers today don't dress as formally as they once did, yet the concept of dressing for success is just as relevant today as it was 10 to 20 years ago, perhaps even more so because the workplace is more competitive. Knowledge and skills are instrumental, but one's image and appearance still continue to be key factors in moving into better jobs. If you want to achieve success, you must look successful. You must present an image of competency, self-confidence, and professionalism.

## Dress Code

By using common sense and exercising good judgment, you can easily dress to make a good impression. Following is a dress code for business today:

- *Hair.* Your hairstyle should be neat, and your hair color should be natural-looking and complementary to your complexion.
- *Nails.* Long, elaborately decorated nails may be frowned upon in many companies. Short, clean nails in a French manicure or one-tone polish (nude, baby

pink, earth tones) are always stylish. For men and women, clean and cared-for nails send a positive message to customers.

- *Makeup.* Your makeup should be subtle and complementary to your overall look. Choose shades that are flattering to your complexion.
- *Dress.* Remember that your clothes can say more about you than your words ever will. Your clothes should not be too short, too form-fitting, or too revealing in the office—it could send a message that you are not serious about your job.
- *Shoes.* Shoes should be polished and not run-down. Stockings and socks should be traditional and in shades that are compatible to your outfit or your skin tone.
- *Jewelry.* Jewelry should always be kept to a minimum in the office. Avoid facial jewelry. Nose jewelry, lip jewelry, or studs in the tongue or eyebrows are generally inappropriate in most businesses.
- *Accessories.* Invest in fun accessories that showcase your individuality. Colorful silk scarves or nice pins and bracelets can add a touch of individuality and interest to your wardrobe.
- *Perfume.* Use discretion and taste in choosing your office scents.

A dizzying array of opposing viewpoints swirl around the issue of business dress for women more so than for men. Rather than add to the confusion by presenting all the conflicting opinions, Guideline 8.2 presents recommendations in areas of agreement based on a broad consensus of opinion gathered from recent articles and other sources.

## Casual Apparel in the Workplace

Relative to casual apparel in the workplace, it is important for employees to get a clear idea from their company of what is expected. Your choice of work clothes sends a strong nonverbal message about you. It also affects the way you work. That's why many employers have mixed feelings about the current trend toward casual business attire.

If CSRs deal extensively with the public, it is fitting for organizations to require certain standards of appearance. If, on the other hand, CSRs have no contact with the public as in a telemarketing environment, then wearing more casual clothes is probably acceptable. When deciding whether a dress code is appropriate and what a dress code should be,

## GUIDELINE 8.2 Dos and Don'ts of Business Dress

| Dos | Don'ts |
|---|---|
| Always look professional. | Wear outfits that look haphazardly thrown together. |
| Dress to fit your audience, the company you represent, and yourself. | Wear too many accessories. |
| Dress for a look and for your comfort and confidence. Know what colors work for you in your environment. | Wear clothing that is overly revealing, too short, or too tight or clothing, accessories, or hairstyles that require continual adjustment. |
| Wear a mild fragrance, if desired. | Wear excessive perfume or perfumed hair products. |
| Wear heels (up to 2 inches) that you find comfortable and easy to walk on. Wear hose that are skin-color. | Wear heels so high or so thick and stacked that your walking is unsteady. |
| Wear one or two pieces of appropriate jewelry. | Wear jewelry that is large or gaudy. |
| Wear hair that looks styled and has a good cut for your face. | Wear the most trendy hairstyle if it doesn't complement your looks at work. |
| Make hands attractive by keeping nails clean and having a simple manicure. | Have nails too long or nail polish that is so bright that it is distracting. |
| Wear conservative makeup. | Wear heavy makeup. |

most organizations take into consideration the following three factors:

1. The business's public image
2. The nature of the work performed by the employees affected by the dress code
3. Safety standards

Some employers oppose casual dress because, in their opinion, too many workers push the boundaries of what is acceptable. They contend that absenteeism, tardiness, and flirtatious behavior have increased since dress-down policies began to be adopted. Moreover, and perhaps more important, they feel that casually attired employees turn off customers.

Regardless of what critics say, employees love casual-dress policies. As a result, 9 out of 10 employers have adopted casual dress days for at least part of the work-week.[3] Supporters argue that comfortable clothes and a more relaxed working environment lift employee morale, increase employee creativity, and improve internal communication. Employees also appreciate reduced clothing-related expenses.

The popularity of casual days is increasing in corporate America. Still, among those companies that allow casual dress, there is a need to have some type of appearance standards. In most companies, employees should go to work well groomed and dressed for a professional work environment. Clothes such as casual shorts, sandals, T-shirts, jeans, and sneakers are not appropriate. Your industry, age, geographical location, position in the corporate hierarchy, and personality will contribute to your determining what is appropriate dress. Regardless of how informal the outfit, clothes should always be clean and pressed, stain- and odor-free, and not ripped, torn, or frayed.

## Practicing Business Etiquette and Manners

Employers value well-mannered employees because they are a reflection of the company itself. Saying "please" and "thank you," warmly greeting customers and coworkers, speaking politely, and being patient are essential skills for anyone's success. Employees who are trained in the "soft skills" of business etiquette and manners will have the know-how and confidence to make a better impression.

People who have some polish make better impressions, and others want to be around them. People do business with people they like; it's that simple. Lack of proper etiquette when dealing with customers can have a major impact on business, according to a survey conducted by Eticon, a South Carolina-based consulting firm specializing in business etiquette. Fifty-eight percent of the respondents say they react to rudeness by taking their business elsewhere.[4]

Are punctuality, positive attitude, and cooperation really more important than knowing how to do your job? These skills are just as and maybe more important, because they help you become successful. A dependable worker

---

[3]Mary Ellen Griffey, "The Perils of Casual Apparel in the Workplace," *Business Communication Resources,* (December 1999): 38.

[4]Andrea C. Poe, "Mind Their Manners," *HR Magazine* (May 2001): 40.

If first impressions count, which CSR would you prefer to serve you?

most likely will be given more responsibility, advancements, and pay raises. Workplace etiquette in this area is simple—arrive on time every day with the intent of doing your best work.

People with good attitudes usually respect their coworkers, accept responsibility, and accomplish more each day. Your attitude is evident in your body language, the way you complete tasks, your attention to detail, your consideration of those around, the way you take care of yourself, and your general approach to life. Good manners, attitude, and self-discipline work together to make good things happen for customer service representatives.

## Developing the Habits of Good Listeners

Customers have needs beyond completing a simple business transaction; they have emotional needs as well. They need to feel welcome, important, valued, and understood. There is no better or easier way to show customers respect, concern, and understanding than by really listening to them. Successful customer service representatives understand the benefits of good listening, and they continually fine tune their listening service skills.

This section covers the most important service listening skills: engaging in active listening, listening effectively, practicing empathetic listening, overcoming barriers to effective listening, and communicating effectively with non-native speakers. Then it examines the benefits of listening. Before advancing to those topics, however, let's understand good listening by categorizing it into three levels.

### CUSTOMER SERVICE TIP

*8.2 Former President Lyndon Johnson had a plaque on the wall of his office that said, "You ain't learning nothing when you are talking."*

### Three Levels of Listening

People listen at different levels of efficiency throughout the day, depending on the circumstances, their attitudes about the speaker, and their past experiences. For example, most people have difficulty listening effectively when dealing with conflict or emotionally charged people, when having criticism directed at them, when being disciplined, and when feeling anxious, fearful, or angry.

A conscious awareness of your listening behavior will go a long way in helping you become an effective listener. Listening can be divided into three levels, which are characterized by certain behaviors that affect listening efficiency. These levels are not sharply distinct but, rather, are general categories into which people fall; they may and often do overlap, depending on what is happening.

As a person moves from the least effective level, level 3, to the most effective level, level 1, the potential for understanding and retention of what is said and for effective communication increases. The following descriptions of the three levels will help you understand the distinction between how each level is expressed in listeners.

- *Level 1.* A person at level 1 demonstrates the characteristics of a good listener. These listeners look for an area of interest in the speaker's message; they view it as an opportunity to gather new and useful information. Effective listeners are aware of their personal biases. They are better able to avoid making automatic judgments about the speaker and avoid being influenced by emotionally charged words. Good listeners suspend judgment, are empathetic to the other person's feelings, and can see things from the other person's point of view. Level 1 listeners use extra thought time to anticipate the speaker's next statement, to mentally summarize the stated message, to question or evaluate what was said, and to consciously notice nonverbal cues. Their overall focus is on listening with understanding and respect.

- *Level 2.* At level 2, a person is listening mainly to words and the content of what is being said, but the listener does not fully understand what the words mean. There are thousands of words in the English vocabulary, but the average adult in the United States uses only 500 of them. Each one of these words has between 20 and 25 meanings. This means that we are using 500 words with the possibility of 12,500 different meanings. Adding to the confusion is the variety of slang Americans use, double meanings of many words, and so on. The important factor in all of this is that words don't communicate; the meaning and the

understanding of words make communication work. For instance, level 2 listeners zero in on words, but many times they miss the intent—what is being expressed nonverbally through tone of voice, body posture, gestures, facial expression, and eye movement. As a result, level 2 listeners hear what the speaker says, but they make little effort to understand the speaker's intent. This can often lead to misunderstanding, incorrect actions, loss of time, and a variety of negative feelings. Since the listener appears to be listening by nodding his or her head in agreement and not asking clarifying questions, the speaker may be lulled into a false sense of being listened to and understood, when actually he or she is not.

- *Level 3.* At level 3, people are daydreaming, forming rebuttals or advice internally, faking attention while thinking about unrelated matters, and are more interested in talking than in listening. When level 3 is activated, it causes relationship breakdowns, conflicts, and poor decision making. Such listeners are busy finding fault in and being judgmental about what is being said. They do this by responding defensively or becoming overly emotional. All of this type of activity can result in either the speaker or the listener moving into the flight-or-fight mode.

About 20 percent of the working population spends most of their time at level 1, and the other 80 percent vacillate between levels 2 and 3, only occasionally making it to level 1.[5] There are many benefits for customer service representatives who listen effectively to the customers they serve. When customers know they are talking to an active level 1 listener, they openly state ideas and share feelings to work creatively as a team in solving problems instead of placing blame on others.

## Active Listening

Fully understanding the meaning of what someone says requires energy and discipline, both of which contribute to what is known as active listening. **Active listening** is listening with your whole mind and body—not just your ears. Two things happen when you practice active listening: The customer thinks you care, and you gain a more comprehensive picture of the service situation. Greater understanding

[5]Madelyn Burley - Allen, "Listen up: Listening is a Learned Skill," *HR Magazine*, (November 2001): 10.

allows you to respond more effectively and to meet the greatest need of customers—to be listened to.

Active listening requires putting one's own feelings aside while trying to understand what the other person is saying. Guidelines for active listening include maintaining eye contact, encouraging the other person to talk, and using one's own words to summarize what the person has said. Take the quiz in Guideline 8.3 to determine if your listening skills need a tune-up.

When you don't actively listen to your customers, you may assume that you know what they want, but you could be wrong. Don't conclude that you know what a customer wants after the first few sentences. You may need to ask for clarification before you fully understand the situation. The following are five strategies that will help you improve your active listening skills:

1. *Be ready to listen.* Do this with your eyes, head, and heart, as well as your ears. Have paper and a pencil handy, or clear your computer screen and be ready for the next customer contact. Eliminate all distractions, which are not conducive to an effective listening environment. Be aware of any internal, physical distractions that you personally feel can affect active listening, such as hunger, fatigue, headache, or emotional stress.

2. *Be ready to take notes, if appropriate.* If you are on the phone, let the customer know you are taking notes. Say, "I'm concerned about this, so I'm writing it down." When customers know you are taking notes, they are less likely to repeat themselves. This may also help them organize their thoughts, so that they state their message more clearly.

3. *Show that you are listening.* When talking on the phone, use attentive words, such as *okay* and *I understand,* to provide verbal reinforcement. This lets the customer know you are listening. If you are speaking to a customer in person, use your body language, stance, posture, and eye contact to show attentive silence. Concentrate on what's being said and avoid mental vacations.

4. *Ask questions.* Your goal is to get the customer to talk to you. Find out what he or she really wants by asking appropriate and thoughtful questions, such as those discussed in Chapter 7.

5. *Restate the customer's points.* Don't just repeat what the customer said—repeating is condescending and patronizing to some people. Instead, put the message in your own words and emphasize the main points, as you understand them to be. This way, you will know when you are on the right course, because restating what was said invites corrections from the customer.

## Effective Listening

Good listening skills enable a customer service representative to communicate more effectively and make better decisions. As human beings, we tend to filter the information we hear. All too often, what we hear is not what was said. **Filtering** is the tendency for a message to be watered down or halted completely at some point during transmission. Using our personal filters results in our deflecting or stopping the listening process.

Listening requires our participation and involvement. Effective listening is done with the whole body and necessitates our looking for the underlying feelings in messages.

Feelings are often more important than the words themselves. Proper eye contact and body posture can facilitate effective listening as well.

One of the best ways to clarify points made in the communication process is through feedback, or the receiver's response to the message. To understand better what speakers are really saying and to show understanding of the message, a listener can take advantage of three types of feedback: reflective, responsive, and reactive.

1. *Reflective feedback* mirrors content and intent: "If I understand you correctly, what you are saying is . . ." or "So, you feel that . . . because . . . ."

2. *Responsive feedback* characterizes the listener's feelings: "When you [action], I feel [reaction]."

3. *Reactive feedback* affirms the speaker's message: "I had a similar experience. It was. . . ." (Be careful, of course, not to use this technique to achieve "one upsmanship" over the speaker.)

We spend about half of our communication time in listening, yet our listening efficiency is gauged at about 25 percent. Some winning strategies for developing effective listening skills are

- *Realize that listening is hard work.* To listen well, you have to prepare yourself mentally, because it is an active, not passive, activity. Don't allow yourself to do other things as you listen, such as answering the phone, doing paperwork, playing computer solitaire, or checking your e-mail.

- *Make good use of the thought-speech ratio.* We can think about four times faster than a speaker can talk. As a result, we may have trouble concentrating on what another person is saying because we let our minds wander and start thinking about other things.

- *Seek to listen in more than one medium.* Listen with your eyes as well as your ears. Look for nonverbal clues to see if they reinforce or contradict what the person is saying.

- *Give the speaker space.* Strive to avoid invading another person's personal space. In a customer service situation, 4 to 6 feet is the optimum distance for helping another person feel at ease while talking with you.

- *Don't begin speaking the moment the person stops talking.* If you pause a moment before speaking, the person will realize that you are trying to understand what was said. As a result, the speaker will feel even more comfortable in sharing information with you.

- *Develop an open posture to encourage the other person to talk.* Lean toward the speaker. Gesture toward the person as you listen and respond. Use the speaker's name as you respond.

- *Be willing to empathize.* If the speaker is on a topic that has emotional overtones, empathize before you give an answer or advice. Basically, **empathy** is seeking to put you in the other person's position but without getting emotionally involved yourself.

Effective listening involves more than just hearing what the other person is saying. **Hearing** is the physical act of processing sounds. Effective listening means trying to find the real meaning of the words, as well as the unspoken message behind those words. Guideline 8.4 suggests additional techniques that you can use to become a better listener.

## Empathetic Listening

Empathy is critical in communication. Putting yourself in the customer's place can help you analyze the message from his or her perspective. The quality of the rapport between the sender and receiver determines, to a great extent, the ability to overcome roadblocks to effective communication and listening.

Empathy not only bolsters understanding but also is a powerful tool for customer loyalty. As an effective listener, you set in motion a positive, mutually rewarding process by demonstrating interest in the customer and what he or she is saying. This **empathetic listening** encourages honesty, mutual respect, understanding, and a feeling of security in the customer. The following are some guidelines for empathetic listening:

- *Be attentive.* When you are alert, attentive, and relaxed, the other person feels important and more secure.

- *Be interested in the speaker's needs.* Show you are listening with understanding and mutual respect.

- *Listen from a caring attitude.* Be a sounding board by allowing the speaker to bounce ideas and feelings off of you while you assume a nonjudgmental, noncritical manner. Be careful not to ask a lot of questions right away, or it may seem as if you are grilling the person.

- *Act as a mirror.* Reflect what you think the other person is feeling. Summarize by restating what the person has said to make sure you understand.

## GUIDELINE 8.4  Techniques for Becoming a Better Listener

| | |
|---|---|
| 1. Pay attention. | Concentrate on what is being said. This means putting aside whatever you are doing for a few minutes—including your thoughts, worries, and preoccupations—and listening to the other person. |
| 2. Be courteous. | Listen respectfully to everything that is being said, even if you do not agree. Don't interrupt or cut the person off in midsentence. |
| 3. Nod your head. | This nodding gesture indicates that you hear and understand—but not necessarily agree with—what is being said. A sincere "I see" or "Umhmm" will work also. |
| 4. Repeat the statement. | For clarification, repeat the ideas you hear. This lets the speaker know you are trying to understand. You could say, "So, what you are saying is . . ." or "If I heard you correctly, . . ." |
| 5. Don't be judgmental. | Allow the other person to state his or her case in full. Wait until you have heard the whole idea and have had time to think about its merits before you pass judgment. Try to set aside your own prejudices, frames of reference and desires, so that you can experience—as much as is possible—what is happening in the other person's world. |
| 6. Ask follow-up questions. | This action shows that you've been attentive. When you change subjects immediately after a person makes a statement, you send the message that you are not interested in what the person has just said. |
| 7. Listen with your entire body. | Sit up straight, lean forward slightly, and, as the other person is speaking, look at the person's face. Listen for the words between the words. Listen for feeling. Listen for meaning. Give the person your undivided attention as you weigh each word, each phrase, and each sentence being spoken. |
| 8. Respect each other. | Respect is shown, in part, by an inclusive, friendly, and sharing tone, rather than an exclusionary, hostile, and condescending tone. |

- *Don't let the other person get you personally involved.* Getting personally involved in a problem usually results in anger and hurt feelings, which can result in jumping to conclusions and becoming judgmental.
- *Use verbal cues.* Acknowledge the person's statement using brief expressions, such as "hmmm," "I see," "right," or "interesting." Encourage the speaker to reveal more by saying, "Tell me about it," or "I'd be interested in what you have to say."

## Barriers to Effective Listening

One of our greatest needs is to be understood and appreciated. The messages delivered by truly great communicators are clear, consistent, direct, human, and personal. It's important to be aware that people listen to, process, and react to messages in a variety of ways, depending on their behavior, cultural background, and relationship to the speaker.

Most people have the ability to be good listeners if their minds aren't cluttered, if they agree with what's being said, or if they like the person they are conversing with; however, if any one of these conditions does not exist, it is difficult for them to listen accurately. Communication barriers come in many forms, including passive listening and selective listening.

**Passive listening** is one-way communication, in which the listener does not give the speaker feedback. For listening to be effective, a two-way process must exist, so that the sender knows whether or not the message has been understood. Feedback not only regulates the learning process but also reinforces and stimulates it.

A speaker may be an excellent communicator, but the listener may be distracted by outside interference. **Selective listening** is hearing only what you want to hear—filtering out what's not important or not of interest to you. A selective listener finds concentration difficult, has a cluttered mind, may be tense with emotion, or is concerned about giving the wrong response. Effective listening under these circumstances is difficult, at best.

Unfortunately, people seldom listen carefully to each other. Although this is not intentional, it still happens for a number of reasons:

1. The reason may be as simple as the kind of day you are having and how you are reacting to it. It's important to recognize that, when you feel anger, joy, excitement, or boredom, each of these conditions affects how you listen to other people.

2. You may tune out someone who strikes you the wrong way because of dress, looks, ethnic background, or manner. When this happens, notice how little you hear of what this person says.

While listening, you transmit and you receive. As a CSR, you have a great deal of value to share with your customers. Listening errors can result in misunderstandings, wasted time and money, and missed business opportunities. Further, listening errors often result in the following five defensive communication events:

1. The listener perceives the speaker's expression, tone of voice, manner of speech, or content as criticism, judgment, or an attempt to control.

2. The listener perceives the speaker as being deceptive or manipulative and using strategies such as withholding information.

3. The speaker shows no concern for the welfare of the other person.

4. The speaker maintains poker-faced neutrality and appears to be playing a role, rather than behaving honestly and sincerely.

5. The speaker demonstrates an attitude of superiority.

## Effective Communication with Non-Native Speakers

Many workplaces require interaction between native and non-native English speakers. Interacting with customers who are foreign-born or who retain a strong ethnic identity has created difficulty in customer service departments across America. Once you start off on the wrong foot, it takes much longer to get to the final goal of great service. Serving a "world of customers" is here, and knowing how to provide sensitive service to these customers is vital for successful customer interaction.

### ETHICS/CHOICES

**8.2** Suppose you work with a person who, after serving certain customers, makes racial slurs or comments how slow to understand he feels certain ethnic groups are. Would this bother you enough to let your coworker know how you feel about his service attitude?

Workforce diversity is one of the most discussed management and communication topics. Demographic differences result in a workforce of customer service representatives and customers who hold different values and working assumptions. Combined, these often produce misunderstandings and disagreements. The culture we grow up in has norms for our behavior. The term **diversity**

is complex and in customer service describes differences two people experienced as a result of gender, race, age, disability, nationality, sexual orientation, and other topics.

As immigration increases and local businesses expand into global marketing, the chances are great that you will be listening to speakers for whom English is a second language. Although many non-native customers have studied English and generally comprehend it, they may have difficulty speaking it. Why? Vowels and consonants may be pronounced differently. Also, learning the inflection and sentence patterns of English is difficult when those patterns conflict with those of the speaker's native tongue. What can native speakers do to become better listeners while non-native persons are speaking?

- *Avoid making negative judgments about incorrectly accented speech.* Many non-native persons speak an insightful but complex variety of English. Although their speech may retain remnants of their native language, don't assume that their struggle with pronunciation means that they are unintelligent.

- *Be a patient listener.* Strive to overcome the urge to hurry the conversation along. Give non-native speakers time to express their thoughts fully.

- *Don't finish the speaker's sentences.* Allow non-native speakers to choose their words and complete their sentences without volunteering your help. You may find that customers end up saying something quite different from what you had expected.

- *Don't correct the speaker's grammar and pronunciation.* Although you might be trying to help a non-native speaker, it is better to focus on what's being expressed and to refrain from teaching English.

- *Don't pretend to understand.* It's perfectly all right to tell a non-native speaker that you are having a little difficulty understanding him or her and would he or she please express the thought again.

## The Benefits of Listening

Effective listening has many benefits. It saves time and money. People who listen well make fewer mistakes and create fewer interpersonal misunderstandings. Good listening skills result in happier customers and less employee turnover.

Of a group of people surveyed who were leaving their jobs, 80 percent cited management interaction as the primary

Remember, when helping non-native customers, that special care and understanding are sometimes required to serve their needs.

cause of their discontent.[6] When companies listen to their employees, three distinct benefits occur, which contribute to the bottom line: employees feel more valued and have higher morale, innovation flourishes, and company performance improves. Good listeners at work see tangible results: They get promotions, they are more frequently selected for prestige positions, and they are often better informed than are poor listeners.

Really listening to others will earn you respect, because good listeners are perceived by others to be patient, open-minded, sincere, and considerate. Good listeners stand out in a crowd. Employers, teachers, and friends cherish them, because they assist speakers in making their points and conveying meaning efficiently. Improving listening skills is never a waste of time; the benefits are tangible and vital to success and self-worth.

## Concluding Message for CSRs

Customer service representatives need to be aware of the impact of their body language on others. To become customer-friendly communicators, CSRs must comprehend body language signals in others and become cognizant of their

own nonverbal cues. When listening, it is important to lean forward slightly to show interest; be aware of your posture; not fidget; make eye contact; avoid crossing your arms, legs, ankles, or wrists when talking to a customer; and nod your head from time to time.

Your total communication—including your body language, tone of voice, and choice of words—helps you deal with important customer situations. As important as your verbal and nonverbal responses to your customers are, however, don't overlook the most important part of communication—listening. By listening attentively and making an effort to understand your customer's concerns, you show the respect and understanding that are important parts of providing the star service you know you can deliver.

## Summary

- When you communicate, you use nonverbal messages, called body language, including tone of voice, eye movement, posture, hand gestures, and facial expressions.
- Besides communicating an attitude of caring and cooperation, body language conveys your professional stature and self-confidence.
- When interpreting body language, you can get cues from customers of their openness and warmth, confidence, nervousness, or untrustworthiness.
- How you dress, show good business manners, and present yourself at work and with customers is a statement about you and the company.
- Regardless of how casual your work attire is, clothes should always be clean and pressed, stain- and odor-free, and not ripped, torn, or frayed.
- The levels of efficiency at which people listen throughout the day are influenced by circumstances, people's attitudes about the other person, and their past experiences.
- Active listening means listening with your whole mind and body—not just your ears.
- Filtering messages is the tendency to water down or halt understanding completely at some point during the transmission of a communication.
- To understand better what speakers are saying, listeners can take advantage of and use feedback that is reflective, responsive, or reactive.

---

[6]John Joyner, "Listening Increases Support from Co-Workers," *Computing Canada* (October 19, 2001): 29.

- When practicing empathetic listening, listeners put themselves in the customer's place in order to analyze the message from the customer's perspective.
- Listening errors can result in misunderstandings, missed business opportunities, and wasted time and money.
- Interacting with customers who are foreign-born or who retain a strong ethnic identity requires CSRs to be patient, nonjudgmental listeners.

## QUESTIONS FOR CRITICAL THINKING

1. Of all the elements that constitute body language, which three would you rank as the most important when serving customers? Explain.

2. If one customer expressed confidence and another customer expressed nervousness, what body language signals would you look for in each instance?

3. Why is it so difficult to establish a proper dress code in today's workplace?

4. List three advantages to a customer service representative who practices business etiquette and manners.

5. Relative to the three levels of listening, how would you characterize your listening skills the majority of the time?

6. Describe an incident with a friend in which active listening was taking place. Describe an incident you experienced in which passive listening was occurring.

7. In your daily life, when do you practice empathetic listening?

8. List two approaches you might use to become a better listener to non-native speakers.

## On-line Research Activities

### Project 8.1: Writing a Dress Code

Research a number of web sites and locate several articles featuring *appropriate dress for the workplace.* Suggested magazines to research include *Working Woman, Ebony,* and *HR Magazine.* As a result of your research, develop a simple dress code that would be appropriate in the banking and financial industry.

### Project 8.2: Listening Survey/Quiz 🖥️

**Situation**

For improvement purposes only, On-Time Technology Products would like for each customer service representative to take an online listening quiz to evaluate his or her current skill level. In fact, the results will become the basis of part of each CSR's yearly evaluation and improvement plan. Although most of the CSRs are not too bothered by having to do this, two coworkers are complaining that it is "just something else to do." In an effort to assist, locate at least three web sites you can recommend where workers can take a listening skills survey or quiz for free.

*Enter "listening skills survey" in your favorite search engine. Using file PRJ8-2 on your student CD, key responses in the following table format that first will inform management at On-Time Technology Products the web sites where these surveys are available. Second, take the quiz yourself and report in general terms your impressions of the survey/quiz, as well as how you did overall. To begin, key in the following URL and take the listening quizzes that are available:* http://virtualcampus.us-ace.army.mil/pmbp/pm10/html/pm10b3.htm#skill_3.

| Web Sites | Personal Quiz Results |
| --- | --- |
| 1. | |
| 2. | |
| 3. | |
| 4. | |
| 5. | |

## Communication Skills at Work

### Project 8.3: Words That Smile 🖥️

Note your reactions as you hear a classmate say the statements in the following table while frowning. Then have the classmate repeat the same messages with a smile. Assume that you were doing this role-play exercise for real with a customer. Are different messages communicated to the customer when you frown, as compared with when you smile?

*Retrieve file PRJ8-3 on the student CD and complete the following form by describing in column 2 your reaction to the three statements said with a frown and then with a smile.*

| Statement | "Frown/Smile" Reactions |
| --- | --- |
| 1. "Our commitment is to top-quality service." | |
| 2. "I'm glad you chose to do business with us today." | |
| 3. "What can I do to help you?" | |

## Decision Making at Work

### Project 8.4: The International Traveler

Assume that you are working in the hotel industry and an international traveler is asking directions. Although you have exactly repeated the instructions several times, the traveler just doesn't seem to understand. You are wondering what you should do next.

What are three creative steps you might suggest that your hotel take to prevent this situation from happening in the future?

1. _____

2. _____

3. _____

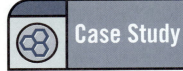

## Case Study

### 8.1 "I Know You Believe . . ."

Everyone in the administrative offices at the Peaks Medical Center was laughing so hard that many of the employees were near tears, as each person cited a real-case scenario that fit in with the meaning of a common quote. The anonymous quote that caused the laughter and subsequent discussion was "I know you believe you understand what you think I just said, but I'm not sure you realize that what you heard is not what I meant."

**Questions**

1. *How does this statement relate to the material covered in this chapter?*

_____

_____

_____

2. *To what extent do you think this statement is true in business?*

_____

_____

_____

3. *Relate a personal situation you experienced recently when the outcome was illustrative of this quote.*

_____

_____

_____

_____

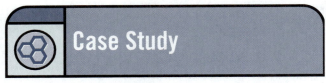

## Case Study

### 8.2 Casual Dress Debate

Mary Graeff at On-Time Technology Products is becoming increasingly concerned with the way CSRs are dressing. It seems as if the concept and application of casual dress are going from bad to worse, with workers in halter tops, ripped blue jeans, and extremely scuffed and dirty athletic shoes.

Today, Ms. Graeff has called 10 people from various departments to debate the following proposition: Business casual dress at On-Time Technology Products will be left up to each employee's interpretation and taste. You are one of those 10 persons.

**Questions**

1. *What are three support statements you could make in favor of this proposition?*

_____

_____

_____

_____

_____

2. *What are three opposition statements you could make against this proposition?*

_____

_____

_____

_____

_____

# Effective Telephone Communication

*Don't speak unless you have something to say. Don't be tempted to go on after you have said it.*

JOHN BRIGHT

## OBJECTIVES

**AFTER COMPLETING THIS CHAPTER,**
**YOU WILL BE ABLE TO:**

1. Detail the essential customer service skills needed when communicating over the phone.

2. Describe the processes to follow when transferring calls and putting customers on hold.

3. Discuss the purpose of voicemail and offer some suggestions for designing voicemail systems for customers.

4. Draft scripts to use when recording a voicemail message and when leaving a voicemail message.

5. List some general guidelines for using your voice effectively, especially on the phone.

6. Distinguish between outbound telemarketing and inbound telemarketing.

7. Cite examples of fraudulent telemarketing activities directed at consumers.

Despite the increased popularity of using the Internet to conduct commerce or simply to chat, the tried and true telephone continues to be our culture's most vital link between businesses and customers. This is evidenced by the fact that 95 percent of business communication occurs over the telephone.[1] It doesn't matter if a caller is asking a question about office hours or ordering merchandise, the politeness and helpfulness of the person on the other end of the phone are paramount to building relationships, instilling trust, creating a positive experience, and ultimately driving repeat business for the organization.

Companies spend good money on their *Yellow Pages* listings, their web sites, their stationery, and their marketing and advertising to get people to dial their phone numbers. All that money is wasted if the caller's first contact with those businesses is less than favorable. To the business enterprise, a first impression can mean the difference between a one-time interaction and a lasting relationship. Several studies have suggested that people decide whether or not

[1]Barry Spiegelman, "Impress Customers You've Never Even Met," *Direct Marketing* (June 2001): 33.

they "like you" within the first 10 seconds of meeting.[2] When companies choose employees to give that first greeting to customers, it is money well spent if they select individuals who sincerely care about the business and can convey that sentiment to customers who call.

When you think of the times you have had great experiences as a customer, you probably think of the people who made those experiences happen for you. We all know it instantly when we encounter a remarkable customer service representative, so why is it that some customer service professionals just stand out? The simple answer is that great customer service professionals make a choice. *Every day*, with *every* customer, on *every* call—they choose to do *all* they can to make their customer's experience as *positive* as it can be. Somewhere along the way, they learned that, to deliver exceptional customer service over the phone, it's essential to be

- *Connected.* Meet customers "where they are." Treat them as you would want to be treated.
- *Attentive.* Give every customer your full attention. Guide the call by listening and making your message clear.
- *Responsible.* Own the call, follow through, and never take remarks personally.
- *Enthusiastic.* Treat every customer as if he or she were your only customer.

## CUSTOMER SERVICE TIP

**9.1** *Because only sound is involved when speaking with customers on the phone, friendly voices are important.*

## Answering the Telephone

Telephone greetings are critical, because they help form first impressions. For example, new customers are deciding whether or not to do business with you, whereas irate customers are deciding how helpful and competent you are. When developing that all-important opening message, there is power in simplicity. For best results, incorporate

[2]*Ibid.*

into your first message three easy fundamentals by being pleasant, brief, and sincere.

The key elements of a telephone greeting are the department or company name, your name, and an offer of assistance. An example from someone in the customer service department might sound like this, "Customer service, this is Melissa. How may I help you?" It may sound simplistic, but practice saying your standard phone greeting until you can hear each word clearly.

A pleasant greeting is essential to a successful call, because it sets the stage emotionally. That is to say, listeners tend to mirror, or "catch," the emotional states of speakers. It is typical for people to respond in kind to what they are getting. For example, if you answer the phone gruffly, chances are the caller will become bad-tempered. If, on the other hand, you answer the phone in a pleasant manner, chances are the caller will be agreeable. We all know which caller is easier to work with.

## The Basic Process

Contact between customers and customer service representatives most often takes place on the telephone. Therefore, the manner in which CSRs handle themselves on the phone is all-important. Following are some tips to help CSRs become effective telephone communicators:

- *Stay close to the phone.* Try to answer the phone by the second or, at most, the third ring. When customers call, they do not want the phone to ring multiple times before somebody picks up. Nor do they desire to leave a message. They want to speak to a live person, conduct business, and move on to their next activity. Portable phones are not a good substitute, by the way. CSRs need to talk to customers from a quiet workplace, where all the necessary customer database information, notepaper, and writing materials are available.
- *Be friendly and pleasant.* State your name and ask how you may assist. This greeting tells clients that they have reached the right person and that you want to help.
- *Do not use technical language or abbreviations.* The caller may not understand the terms and that prevents sending an effective and clear message.

- *Always remain courteous, even if the caller is not.* CSRs often need to state firmly unpleasant truths—but, in doing so, they must know the difference between being firm and being impolite. Customers are people and always deserve to be treated with respect.
- *Have paper and pencil handy to take notes.* This will allow you to focus on solving the problem, rather than remembering a myriad of details.
- *Bring closure to the call.* Tell the caller what action you will take as a result of the call and when the customer can expect that the issue will be resolved.

In summary, everyone who answers the phone should be thinking that it is more than a call—it is a customer. Ten tips to sum up how to provide over-the-top phone customer service are shown in Guideline 9.1.

## Transferring Calls

In order to provide the best service for customers, you will sometimes have to transfer them to other persons or departments. Unfortunately, this is something customers usually don't like. If you are receiving a large number of transferred calls, perhaps information in response to

---

**GUIDELINE 9.1    On-the-Phone Customer Service Tips**

| | |
|---|---|
| • Use welcome words. | Answering callers requests with "I'll be glad to help you" makes customers feel more confident in your ability to help them. |
| • Treat each call as if it is the first call of the day. | From the caller's perspective, it is the most important call. |
| • Use the caller's name often. | Although prospects may not identify themselves without being asked, existing customers probably will. A caller's name is the most personal possession he or she has; by recognizing and using it frequently, you make the caller feel better about the service. |
| • Maintain an enthusiastic and personable tone. | Your voice is an all-important delivery system for your words. Speak distinctly and clearly while matching your talking speed and volume to that of the other party. |
| • Take great notes during each call. | Keeping a notepad next to the phone will help prevent you from forgetting important information. Such note taking not only will help keep names and facts straight during the call but also will serve as a good record afterward. Moreover, it will help you see if "patterns" develop that need to be addressed in a more systemic way in order to avoid similar problems in the future. |
| • Be flexible. | Callers want to know what you can do, not what you cannot do. Always look for any possible solution that stays within company guidelines and yet goes that extra mile for the caller. "First call resolution" is what the caller wants in the short run and the company needs to be successful. |
| • Keep language simple. | Present the best options to the caller rather than several different ones that could easily be confusing. Refrain from using technical jargon, industry buzzwords, and complicated explanations. |
| • Avoid negative and controlling words. | "Problem," "complaint," "You need to . . ." and "You should have . . ." are words and phrases that push hot buttons with callers and can illicit negative responses from them. People call customer service departments to resolve a problem, not to reaffirm that they have one. |
| • Give verbal clues to show you are actively listening. | Remember, over the phone people cannot see a nodding head or other visual signs of interest. Phrases such as "I see" and "Please tell me more" are welcome words to the calling party. |
| • Use probing skills wisely. | Use open-ended questions to "open up" a conversation and get full information. Use closed questions to focus on one area and pin down specific details, so that you can move more quickly to problem resolution. |
| • Promise to call back on unresolved issues and then follow through. | If a call involves some research of the facts, assure the person that you will call back before the end of the day. It may just be a telephone call to say, "I don't have the answer yet, but I'm still researching it." |

common customer inquiries should be provided to other team members in advance, so that they won't need to transfer to you so often and irritate customers needlessly. When you do have to transfer a call, however, keep it simple and positive, transfer with care, and follow these strategies:

1. *State what you can do, not what you cannot do.* Turn a negative into a positive by letting customers know you are acting for their benefit—for example, "I can help you by letting you talk to Jessica in Accounts Receivable. Should we get disconnected, her extension is 279. May I connect you now?"

2. *Avoid using the word transfer.* Customers don't like this word. Instead, say, "Let me connect you to . . ." or "I'll let you talk with. . . ." Communicate the benefits of your actions clearly to the customer.

3. *Pass along customer information.* When transferring a call to someone else, pass along the customer's name and any facts you have obtained so far. This will make customers feel that they are making progress, since they don't have to repeat their information. You can pass along customer information in two ways:

   • If you have conference call capability, you can hook up the caller to the desired party. Then, while all three of you are on the line, you can tell the receiving CSR why the person is calling.

   • Convey the message to the receiving person while the caller is on hold, so that the caller does not have to repeat the request in full.

4. *Stay on the line.* Attempt to become familiar with the general responsibilities of each department and person, so that you transfer the caller only once. Try never to transfer a call if you are not completely sure the next employee is able and available to work with that customer. Before transferring a customer's call, it's always good to ask for the customer's phone number. In that way, should you accidentally cut off the customer in the process, you are ready to call him or her back.

5. *Don't guess, if you're uncertain to whom to transfer a call.* Instead, collect as much information as you can from the caller and tell the caller that you will get back to him or her. Then call around your company, get the solution or information the customer needs, and call back. If another employee is going to call your customer back, make sure that employee follows through.

6. *Do not transfer the customer, if that is his or her preference.* Customers will tell you if they have already spoken to multiple persons to no avail. A good idea is to assume that, if you are the third person the customer has talked to, you should not transfer him or her again. You may not be the person with whom the customer needs to speak, but find out whatever you can about the situation and agree on a time when you will call the customer back. Then do the research yourself and call the customer back with the appropriate information that will move the resolution of the matter forward.

## ETHICS/CHOICES

**9.1** If an employee is not allowed to use a business phone to make personal calls, how can these calls be made? Many of these personal calls are important. In your opinion, what is a fair policy that companies should uphold about employees making personal calls while at work?

## Putting Calls on Hold

If customers don't like the idea of being transferred, they certainly don't like the idea of being put on hold. By pushing your hold button a little too quickly or a little too often, you can easily damage relationships with customers. The best alternative is not to put a customer on hold at all, but that alternative is not always reasonable. You should remember to ask if you can put the caller on hold and then wait for his or her response before doing so.

When you cannot avoid putting a caller on hold because you have a lineup of other callers or you need to transfer the person, follow these basic telephone courtesies:

• *Tell the caller why you would like to put him or her on hold and ask the caller's permission to do so.* Simply put, it's the polite thing to do. Also, maybe the caller doesn't have the time to wait and would prefer to call back or that you call him or her back.

• *Keep callers on hold no longer than 45 seconds.* Time moves more slowly when you're waiting on the phone; 45 seconds feels like 2 minutes to busy people, and they may simply become angry and hang up.

• *Thank the customer for holding.* Always say, "Thank you for holding," rather than "I'm sorry you had to hold."

The latter might invite the response "You should be sorry. Every time I call your company, I'm put on hold."

- *Offer to call the customer back instead of putting him or her on hold.* If you know the process is going to take a little extra time, offer to call the customer back within a certain time frame and then do it.

- *Get the caller's name and number prior to putting the call on hold.* This way, you know how to reach the person if an emergency forces the caller to hang up or if the caller gets tired of waiting.

- *Tell how long you honestly think the wait will take.* Customers need to feel they are in charge of how they spend their valuable time. Callers would rather know what they are truly up against than blindly assume that you'll be back to them at any minute.

- *Check in frequently.* If it is taking longer than you thought, return to the person at least every 45 seconds to let him or her know what's happening and to ask if he or she can continue to hold.

- *Question the use of canned music.* Supposedly, the practice of providing music while waiting is intended to soothe callers on hold. Often, however, it conveys the possibility of a lengthy hold, not to mention that it often displeases those who find a particular type of music annoying or would prefer to have some quiet time while waiting.

## Handling Irate Callers

With telephone technology expanding, customers are more sensitive than ever about the way they are treated on the phone. Customers are tired of being put on hold and getting transferred to voicemail or to the wrong person. They want their needs addressed by competent, caring service personnel. Even if you've heard the customer's question or complaint a dozen times that day, remember that this is the customer's first time. Show the irritated customer that the issue is important to you by

- Expressing empathy as the customer expresses his or her feelings about the situation.

- Resolving the problem with a smile in your voice.

- Using listening responses, such as "yes," "okay," and "I see."

- Using active listening techniques, such as paraphrasing, summarizing, repeating, and questioning for clarification.

- Telling the customer the issue is important to you—for example, "Thank you for bringing this matter to our attention."

- Expressing a sense of urgency and ownership regarding the customer's concern by saying, "I'll take care of this right away."

- Apologizing at least twice—once on hearing the problem and again after finding a solution.

- Thanking customers sincerely for doing business with your company.

Customer service surveys show that almost three-quarters of the people who complain will do business with the same company in the future if the problem is resolved quickly and to the customer's satisfaction.[3] Customers simply want a solution and to move on with other things that are important in their lives.

## Using Voice Response Units

All contacts with an organization contribute to a customer's perceptions about that organization, whether it is with an employee in a phone conversation or through **voicemail.** Voice response units, also known as voicemail, give customers an impression of a company. The sound of a caller hanging up before leaving a voicemail message should be viewed as dissatisfaction with your phone system and similar to a customer closing the door angrily as he or she leaves. Research shows that 34 percent of callers will not call back after hanging up, resulting in future lost revenue, which can be considerable.[4]

Although voicemail has grown increasingly popular, do not assume your customers will be satisfied with leaving a message. Instead, understand voicemail through customers' eyes. Customers want to feel that their telephone call is important to a company. What drives customers to frustration about some phone systems is not the fact that they are automated but, rather, that they think no one is paying attention to their needs. Make your system caller-friendly and you'll find that your customers feel they are getting even better service than before.

---

[3]Michael Bordner, "How to Get Unhappy Customers to Buy More," *Inbound Service and Selling,* (September 29, 2000): 4.

[4]John Tschohl, "Telephone Technology: Friend or Foe," *Service Quality Institute,* (November 2000): 11.

A well-designed phone system is fast, easy to use, cost-effective, and, most important, caller-friendly. Whether you are planning a simple voicemail system to take messages or a sophisticated "voice-processing" system that lets people choose from a menu of recorded information, the key is keeping your callers in mind and making it simple to use.

Voicemail, which functions much as an answering machine does, allows callers to leave a voice message for the called party. How does voicemail work? Unlike answering machines, a computer in the voicemail system converts the voice message into digital form. Once digitized, the message is stored in a voice mailbox, which is a storage location on a computer in the voicemail system.

A voicemail system usually provides individual voice mailboxes for many users (for example, employees in a company). By accessing a voice mailbox, the called party can listen to messages, add comments to a message, and reply or forward a message to another voice mailbox in the voicemail system. At many organizations, voicemail is the primary way employees communicate internally, even more so than with e-mail.

Some companies approach voicemail as a way to reduce headcount, and that's a good side benefit; however, if designed correctly, the real benefit of using voicemail is for customers. A well-designed system is a productivity and customer service tool that is responsive. Some tips on the fine points of designing voicemail systems are discussed in Guideline 9.2.

## CUSTOMER SERVICE TIP

**9.2** *To improve telephone communication, speak as if you were in a face-to-face dialogue—even smiling and gesturing if those actions make you sound more natural.*

## Recording an Outgoing Greeting

It is important that CSRs answer their phones whenever possible. If callers always get voicemail, they might become convinced that the company is trying to dodge them or is too busy to take care of their needs. Sometimes, however, voicemail is a necessary substitute. For example, CSRs cannot always remain at their desks. They do eat lunch and take care of other personal needs. They also talk to and help

| GUIDELINE 9.2 | Tips on Designing Customer-Friendly Voicemail Systems |
|---|---|
| Stay on top of it. | Update your voicemail greeting frequently and state the date, which lets callers know you actually use the system. Tell callers you check your messages frequently, so that they have confidence you will get their message and return their call. |
| Avoid "voicemail jail." | When callers bounce from message to message and can't reach a live person, they begin to feel uncomfortable, unsatisfied, and locked in to the event. Early on, give callers an easy way at any time to transfer directly to a receptionist by pressing one or two digits on their phone's keypad. If no one is available after business hours, be sure you switch to an alternative greeting that suggests callers leave a message, which will be returned early the next day. |
| Keep greetings and instructions short. | Strive for no more than 5 seconds for a voicemail greeting, and no longer than 15 seconds for instructions. Callers get impatient; they want action. |
| Attempt to give instructions the same way every time. | Always state the action first, then the correct key to press. For example, you could say, "To transfer to our receptionist, press zero." If you reverse the statement, callers may forget which key to press by the time you've finished telling them what will happen. |
| Limit menus and options. | A phone system is not a restaurant—callers can't remember more than three choices at a time. |
| Encourage two-way dialogue. | Ask callers to leave a detailed message or a complete request for information. |
| Sound as natural as possible. | When recording your greeting, vary your voice tone and speak more loudly or softly for emphasis. Be careful of background voices or music that are distracting to the listener. |
| Don't make technology a villain. | Voicemail should not be used to avoid phone calls. People expect that you will regularly answer your own phone. Most successful companies use voicemail as an exception, rather than the rule. |

other customers. Because voicemail has a strike against it—the caller wants to talk to a live person, not a machine—use the following suggestions to make it more efficient when recording an outgoing voicemail greeting:

- State your name and title and give reasons you cannot answer the phone at this time. Indicate how often you check your voicemail. Customer service representatives should return calls at least every hour and a half.

- Request key information from a caller, including full name, company's name and phone number, when the caller can be reached, and a brief explanation for the call.

- Above all, remember to return calls promptly. Even if you are not ready with all the answers, do not leave callers wondering whether you received their message. Calling a customer with updates can spread more goodwill than many companies realize.

## Leaving a Voicemail Message

When making a call, savvy communicators know that they'll probably have to leave a recorded message, so they adjust and plan before dialing the number. Be clear and brief in any voicemail message you leave. When a communiqué is delivered effectively, you move through it quickly, and you're clear about what's expected by the end. You appreciate the brevity and clarity of the speaker. Think of your reaction to long messages people leave for you. You may wonder, "When will Sam ever get to the point?"

Here's a plan that works well when leaving voicemail messages:

1. State your name, the date and time, your company name, and why you are calling.
2. Say what you would like the receiver to do. This is a statement or a request.
3. Give a reason for the statement or request.
4. Say, "Thank you."
5. Finish with "Feel free to call me back at the following number: 505-555-5111." Repeat slowly, 505-555-5111.

Finally, be aware that voicemail is company property. Voicemail messages can easily be forwarded, so, don't leave a message unless you're comfortable having it heard by other people.

## Evaluating Your Voice Qualities and Delivery

When you speak, customers listen to the tone of voice you use, your words, and your overall delivery techniques. Are you sincere? Do you sound kind in your approach with others? Do you show empathy and concern for their needs? A positive and caring tone in customer situations

says, "I understand how you feel and I'd be frustrated, too, if that happened to me."

## Voice Qualities

Following are some general guidelines for using your voice effectively, but especially while on the phone:

1. *Use a steady, moderate rate of speech.* Speaking too fast can suggest to the customer that you are nervous or in a hurry; speaking too slowly can signal that you are bored.

2. *Never allow your voice to become overly loud or shrill.* If a customer is yelling at you, you may be tempted to respond in kind, but don't. Maintaining a moderate volume and rate of speech can help calm an upset customer.

3. *Keep a smile in your voice.* The smile on your face is reflected in the sound of your voice. Keep smiling, even if you are speaking on the phone. Your customers will hear the difference.

4. *Increase the energy in your voice when speaking on the phone.* The telephone can rob your voice of some of its natural expressiveness and energy, so be sure to compensate adequately with more enthusiasm.

5. *With reference to the sound of your voice, reflect on the following questions and make the necessary adjustments:*
   - Does your voice become agitated or loud when you are angry?
   - Do you speak more quickly when you are nervous?
   - Do people describe your tone of voice as "upbeat"?
   - When you are in a serious conversation, does your voice sound warm and understanding?
   - Do you speak clearly, directly, and naturally?

## Delivery Techniques

Showing courtesy to others and incorporating good telephone etiquette can help businesses gain a competitive edge for one basic reason—people are more likely to return to a company and to buy more products and services when they are treated well. Moreover, customers are impressed when a customer service representative demonstrates friendliness, proficiency, and intelligence when delivering responses:

- *Friendliness.* This shows that you are genuinely interested in helping the caller.

Customers will have a good impression of you and your organization if you are pleasant, courteous, and helpful.

- *Proficiency.* You should be able to handle the caller's request without much delay through the use of a script or from lessons you learned in previous customer experiences.
- *Intelligence.* You need to be familiar enough with the various products and services to converse competently about them.

The following are eight essential tips for great customer service delivery while on the telephone:

1. *Check your attitude.* Be pleasant. Never be too busy to be nice. Being busy does not give you carte blanche to be rude. Neither does being in a bad mood. In truth, the caller doesn't care if you got stuck with a parking ticket while you were frantically running errands during your lunch hour.

2. *Answer the phone as soon as possible.* When you answer the phone by the first or second ring, you communicate enthusiasm, efficiency, and professionalism. An important call-answering organizational strategy is to ensure that a knowledgeable person always covers the telephone.

3. *Check your tone of voice.* Specifically, check your voice for warmth, clarity, enthusiasm, inflection, confidence, sincerity, volume, enunciation, and pace.

4. *Give the caller control.* Explain what the next steps will be that you are taking on behalf of the customer. Ask permission to put the caller on hold and wait for a response from the customer. For example, give the caller an estimated amount of time that he or she can expect

to be on hold. Offer to call back if you think it will take a while before he or she can be served.

5. *Identify the problem.* Keep the caller talking. The more you know about the caller and what he or she wants, the more opportunities will surface for helping to fulfill his or her needs.

6. *Listen for facts.* Reflect with words of understanding, probe for information, determine potential solutions, and provide options to the caller.

7. *Allow an angry person to express him- or herself.* This will calm down the person and provide you with valuable information to better serve the customer.

8. *Bring the call to a polite close.* Always thank the caller for giving you an opportunity to serve him or her.

Normally, the language, when using the phone for business or pleasure is rather informal; therefore, there are some noteworthy suggestions when speaking everyday English on the phone. Look at Guideline 9.3 for acceptable language and often-used phrases when using the telephone in business situations.

### GUIDELINE 9.3 Acceptable Informal Telephone Language

| Action | Acceptable Statement |
|---|---|
| Introducing yourself | This is Ken.<br>Good morning, Ken speaking. |
| Asking who is on the telephone | Excuse me, who is calling, please?<br>May I ask who is calling, please? |
| Asking for someone | May I have extension 321?<br>Could I speak to . . .? (Can I—more informal / May I—more formal)<br>Is Jack in? (informal expression meaning is Jack in the office?) |
| Connecting someone | I'll put you through (put through—phrasal verb meaning connect)<br>Can you hold on the line? Can you hold for a moment? |
| Taking a message | Could [Can, May] I take a message?<br>Could [Can, May] I tell him who is calling?<br>Would you like to leave a message? |
| Replying when someone is not available | I'm afraid . . . is not available at the moment.<br>I'm sorry but the line is busy. . . . [when the extension requested is being used]<br>Mr. Jackson isn't in. . . . Mr. Jackson is out at the moment. |

# Understanding Telemarketing Activities

Selling over the phone is never as easy as selling face to face. **Telemarketing** is the use of a telephone to sell directly to consumers. It consists of outbound sales calls, usually unsolicited, and inbound calls—that is, orders through toll-free 800 numbers or fee-based 900 numbers.

**Outbound telemarketing** is an attractive direct-marketing technique used by many organizations because of rising postage rates and decreasing long-distance phone charges. On the other hand, **inbound telemarketing** programs are used mainly by companies to take orders, generate leads, and provide customer service. Inbound 800 telemarketing is not new and has successfully supplemented direct-response TV, radio, and print advertising for several years. The more recently introduced 900 numbers, which customers pay to call, are gaining popularity as a cost-effective way for companies to target customers. One of the major benefits of 900 numbers is that they generate qualified responses. Although the charge may reduce the total volume of calls, the calls that do come through are from customers who have a true interest in the product, or they wouldn't be paying for the call.

## The CSR-Telemarketer Perspective

Most telemarketers are so busy following their own scripts that they often don't hear customers' needs or desires. In

Call centers do many types of telemarketing activities and contact hundreds of customers each day.

the future, should you work for an organization that telemarkets, don't forget these reminders when carrying out your work:

- *Display enthusiasm.* Second only to product knowledge, the most important asset telemarketers have is their enthusiasm. If there's any doubt your product is not what you claim it is, your prospects will sense it immediately. It will come across in your voice inflections and tone. Of course, the opposite is true as well. When you believe in your product, your prospects will believe in it, too. They trust that you know what you're talking about. Once you establish that belief, you are on your way to closing the sale.

- *It's all in the details.* People get calls from vendors all the time, so what makes one telemarketer different from all the rest? More often than not, it is the CSR's attention to detail. That attention might be really listening to what the prospect is saying, or it might even be sending a thank-you note after the call.

- *Anticipate objections to your sales presentations.* Telemarketers have probably heard every sales objection imaginable: "We're not interested." "We're happy with our present vendor." "It's too expensive." "I don't have time." As a CSR-telemarketer, you cannot argue with any of these points because, as soon as you do, you lose. That's when you should use the tried and true "feel, felt, found" approach to dealing with customers' objections.

When you hear an objection, pause and let it sink in. Don't rush to answer. Listen carefully, and then empathize with your prospect by saying, "I understand how you *feel*" or "I can appreciate that." Then build on the success you've had with other customers by saying, "Many of my present customers *felt* the same way, But, when they *found* out how much time they saved using our system, they were amazed. I'd like to find out whether we can do the same for you." This 3-F method has been used over and over in telemarketing sales and customer service activities—and it works. It doesn't work, however, when you do it by rote. You've got to know—inside and out—the benefits to your customer of the product or service you are selling.

## CUSTOMER SERVICE TIP

**9.3** *It takes 26 muscles to smile and 62 muscles to frown. Why not make it easy on yourself to provide top-notch, friendly service?*

## The Customer's Perspective

All of us from time to time have had telemarketers call us, and we've responded to them in various ways. Sometimes, it's been with interest; at other times, it's been with a slight edge to our voices, because we don't want to be bothered at that moment. This is not a very pleasant part of a customer service representative's job when telemarketing, but it is an aspect of the job that comes with the territory.

Unfortunately, other less than desirable things happen as well in telemarketing. Some customers have experienced very serious consequences from dealing with corrupt telemarketers. There are telemarketers who devise schemes to deceive customers intentionally into buying their products and services. The National Fraud Information Center (NFIC), a project of the National Consumers League, has published a set of general telemarketing tips that are intended to warn consumers of fraudulent activities and groups that may call them.

It is a wise step for telemarketing CSRs to be fore-warned about the fraudulent telemarketing practices and to become knowledgeable regarding the safeguards that organizations such as the National Fraud Information Center have published to alert and protect consumers. The following is a cautionary list to consumers in dealing with deceptive telemarketers taken directly from NFIC's web site:

- *Do business with those you know and trust.* If you aren't familiar with the company, ask for information to be sent to you about the products or services it is offering. A legitimate company will be glad to provide that information; a fraudulent marketer will not.

- *Understand the offer.* Be sure you know who and where the company is and how to reach it, what is being sold, the total price, the delivery date, the return and cancellation policy, and the terms of any guarantee. If that information isn't in a catalog or other materials that you have, get it in writing from the company before you buy.

- *Check out the company's track record.* Ask your state or local consumer protection agency if the company has to be licensed or registered and with whom, and then check to see if it is. You can also ask consumer agencies and the Better Business Bureau in your area about the company's complaint record. Keep in mind, however, that some companies open and shut quickly, so a lack of a complaint record is no guarantee that a telemarketer is legitimate.

- *Be careful to whom you give your financial or other personal information.* Don't provide your bank account numbers, credit card numbers, social security number, or other personal information unless you know the company is legitimate and the information is necessary for the transaction.

- *You may be better off paying by credit card than with a check, cash, or money order, as long as you know with whom you're doing business.* When you use your credit card for a purchase and there is a problem, you have the right to notify your card issuer that you are disputing the charge, and you don't have to pay it while your dispute is being investigated. Another way of looking at it is that it is easier to resolve a problem if you have not already paid for the product or service.

- *Take your time to decide.* Although there may be time limits for special offers, high-pressure sales tactics are often danger signs of fraud.

- *Resist pressure to send your payment by private courier, wire transmission, or overnight delivery.* These tactics are sometimes used to prevent you from changing your mind and to avoid law enforcement authorities, such as the U.S. Postal Inspection Service.

- *Don't enter contests or other games of chance unless you know the company or organization sponsoring them.* Fraudulent telemarketers often get lists of potential victims from entry forms for free trips or other prizes that consumers drop in boxes at fairgrounds or shopping centers, as well as from responses to mailings for sweepstakes, contests, and puzzles.

- *If you've lost money to a fraudulent telemarketer, beware of bogus "recovery services" that offer to get it back for you—for an up-front fee.* The same fraudulent telemarketers often target people who are victimized once again. Legitimate law enforcement agencies don't charge for attempting to help telemarketing scam victims.

- *You have some control over who calls you.* Under federal law, you can tell a telemarketer not to call again. If you are called again on behalf of those companies, report it to your state's attorney general and the Federal Trade Commission.

- *You can reduce unwanted calls.* Sign up for the Direct Marketing Association (DMA) Telephone Preference Service by writing to PO Box 9014, Farmingdale, NY 11735. DMA member companies that participate in this industry-sponsored program will put you on their "do not call" lists.

- *Don't be shy about hanging up.* Your phone is just like the door to your home or apartment. You don't have to open it or invite people in, and you can ask guests to leave at any time. Fraudulent telemarketers are very good at lying to, bullying, and sweet-talking their intended victims. The longer you stay on the line, the deeper they sink their hooks. Don't let a criminal in your home through your telephone line.

## Concluding Message for CSRs

Customers often feel powerless when they are on the phone. Customer service representatives must be ready to communicate the voice and spirit of the organization, as well as to develop that all-important initial relationship with customers on the phone. CSRs give an organization heart, soul, and feelings. They are often the first point of contact, a critical component in how customers judge an organization and, ultimately, whether they'll want to do business with that organization.

In response, organizations expect their telephone service to customers to provide the empathy, knowledge, and problem-solving abilities that keep customers happy.

Customers want to identify with someone as the voice of an organization, and they need to feel that sense of responsiveness by someone they can depend on to solve their problems. A major step in that process for companies is to identify a set of questions that customers regularly ask and then have those answers available in scripted form at each CSR's desk, so that the customer is served right away by one person without having to be transferred to someone else.

## Summary

- Exceptional customer service over the phone requires that CSRs be connected, attentive, responsible, and enthusiastic.

- The key elements of a telephone business greeting are the department or company name, your name, and an offer of assistance.

- When you have to transfer a call, keep it simple and positive and transfer with care.

- Remember to tell the caller why you would like to put him or her on hold and ask permission to do so first.

- A well-designed phone system is fast, easy to use, cost-effective, and, most important, caller-friendly.

- When you speak with customers over the phone, listen to the tone of voice you use, your words, and your overall delivery techniques.

- Telemarketing is the use of the telephone to sell directly to consumers; it consists of calls that are outbound, inbound, or a combination of both.

- When performing telemarketing activities, remember to display enthusiasm on each call, anticipate objections to your sales presentations, and pay attention to details before, during, and after the call.

- The National Fraud Information Center publishes a list of safeguards that consumers should be aware of when talking to telemarketers—particularly, telemarketers whose activities are deceptive.

1. If you were president of your company and were hiring a receptionist or customer service representative, what essential customer service phone skills would you look for in your top candidates?

2. What are some techniques you would keep in mind when transferring customer calls?

3. What are some techniques you would keep in mind when putting customers on hold?

4. Describe a voicemail system you have used that you consider to be customer-friendly. Describe one that you consider not to be user-friendly.

5. If you were recording a simple outgoing greeting on your company's business voicemail system, what would it say? Script an example.

6. If you worked in a telemarketing environment and had the choice of performing either outbound or inbound telemarketing activities, which would you choose and why?

7. If you were advising an elderly family member about protecting himself from fraudulent telemarketers, which 4 warnings out of the 12 listed in the chapter would you use?

# On-line Research Activities

## Project 9.1: Voicemail Update

Research a number of web sites and locate several articles about *recent developments in the installation and use of voicemail systems.* As a result of your research, develop a simple paper recommending additional features or upgrades to the voicemail system at your school or at work.

## Project 9.2: Evaluate Your Voice

### Situation

Mary Graeff, customer service supervisor at On-Time Technology Products, has received four complaints within the past six weeks about her CSRs' interactions with customers. Specifically, one comment said that, although the CSR used the proper words and phrases, she still conveyed the wrong impression over the phone. Needless to say, Ms. Graeff is very protective of her CSRs but certainly realizes how important it is to act on any customer concern as soon as possible. She has asked all of her CSRs to take and score the following quiz to evaluate their voices.

| Question | Yes | No | Question | Yes | No |
|---|---|---|---|---|---|
| 1. Does your voice sound high-pitched? | | | 4. Do you sound nasally—as if you are talking through your nose? | | |
| 2. Do you speak too loudly or too softly? | | | 5. Do you frequently clear your throat or make other irritating noises? | | |
| 3. Do you talk too quickly—or too slowly? | | | 6. Do you articulate words clearly, making them understood easily? | | |

# On-line Research Activities

## Project 9.2: continued 💻

| Question | Yes | No | Question | Yes | No |
|---|---|---|---|---|---|
| 7. Do you sound confident? | | | 9. Does your voice and manner convey a sense of authority? | | |
| 8. Do you say words in their entirety? (e.g., Do you say irritating noises? "goin'" for going?) | | | 10. Imagine that you are the caller. Would you enjoy listening to the person the caller is speaking with? | | |

Scoring: If you answered Yes to numbers 6–10 and No to numbers 1–5, you have an excellent speaking voice on the telephone. Work to improve the areas you answered incorrectly.

*Answer the previous 10 questions and evaluate your own voice, as though you were a CSR. Then enter "Improving Voice Quality" or "Effective Speaking Techniques" in your favorite search engine. Using file PRJ9–2 on your student CD, key responses in the following table format that first will inform Ms. Graeff which web sites contain information on improving voice techniques. Second, write three suggestions for improving voice quality and sound that you learned from your research.*

| Web Sites | Suggestions to Improve Voice Quality and Sound |
|---|---|
| 1. | |
| 2. | |
| 3. | |
| 4. | |

# Communication Skills at Work

## Project 9.3: Answering Telephone Calls 💻

Script the words you might use to respond to the following three telephone-answering situations.

*Retrieve file PRJ9-3 on the student CD and complete the following form by scripting in column 2 your responses to the three phone situations.*

| Situation | Script of Telephone Response |
|---|---|
| 1. Assume you are working for First City Bank. When calls come in, they go directly to your phone; there is no receptionist. How should you answer the calls? | |
| 2. Assume you are an employee in the registration office of a local career school. All calls are first answered by a receptionist and then transferred to your desk. How should you answer the calls? | |
| 3. Your boss is Mr. Clinger. He is not available, so you answer his telephone. What do you say when you answer, and what do you tell the caller if Mr. Clinger is taking a coffee break? | |

## Decision Making at Work

## Project 9.4: What Would You Say to a Friend?

Assume a good friend calls you on your direct line at work with the intent on chatting. While you two are doing some catch-up on personal news, she tells you that the other reps can handle your calls for a little longer. You are starting to feel uncomfortable with what is happening. Give a best case scenario how you should handle the situation. Then give a satisfactory case scenario response.

Best Case Scenario

_____

_____

_____

_____

_____

_____

_____

Satisfactory Case Scenario

_____

_____

_____

_____

_____

_____

_____

_____

## Case Study

### 9.1  The Phone Order Fiasco

Judy Martin is a CSR who receives a call from a new customer who wishes to place an order. Judy has a basketball game broadcasting very softly on the radio, and she thinks the customer cannot hear it. The customer begins to give the order, but Judy interrupts and puts her on hold because she cannot find anything to write with. Since the customer has a heavy accent, she needs to say, "Huh," quite frequently during the phone conversation. Judy concludes the transaction by saying, "Thanks for placing the order."

**Questions**

1. What would you have done differently during this customer dialogue, if you were Judy?

_____

_____

_____

_____

_____

_____

2. Is there anything that Judy did correctly when taking this phone order?

_____

_____

_____

_____

_____

_____

## Case Study

### 9.2  "Anyone Can Do Telemarketing"

In the southwestern college town where Angela lives, there is a company that specializes in telemarketing sales campaigns for major insurance companies across America. As a part-time college student and a new mother of a six-month-old infant, Angela desperately needs a job with some built-in flexibility. She has been told that the telemarketing company allows workers to set their own schedule within reason.

Angela wants to apply for the $12-an-hour job, but she is afraid that, with her rather strong Hispanic accent, she may not be hired. Someone told her that telemarketing companies would hire anyone and that she should apply.

**Questions**

1. In what ways does Angela sound like a good candidate for a telemarketing job in this college town?

_____

_____

_____

_____

_____

_____

2. In your opinion, do telemarketing companies hire just anyone?

_____

_____

_____

_____

_____

_____

# Communicating in Writing with Customers

*It is not enough to know what to say—one must also know how to say it.*

ARISTOTLE

## OBJECTIVES

**AFTER COMPLETING THIS CHAPTER,
YOU WILL BE ABLE TO:**

1. Discuss the importance of identifying the audience and purpose of writing when creating documents.

2. Describe how the tone in a written document affects the total message received by the reader.

3. Identify an effective method of writing rejection letters to customers.

4. List the three-step approach to the writing process.

5. Describe the actions that writers take in the revision, editing, and proofreading activities of the writing process.

6. List the advantages of using a computer software template or wizard when creating written business documents.

7. Format a typical business letter and memorandum.

8. Explain the major parts of an e-mail message.

From simple e-mails to more formal customer letters, CSRs will need to write documents that educate, persuade, inform, or enlighten the customer. Writing is an essential element of business communication. The ability to write effectively is a skill you learn; it comes naturally to only a few gifted individuals.

This chapter reviews the fundamentals of business writing and the steps in the writing process. In addition, the three most common business documents used to communicate with customers are presented—a letter, a memorandum, and an e-mail message.

## Reviewing the Fundamentals of Business Writing

Business writing experts say that the most important strategy behind good written communication is being clear. It is important to strive for clarity, even if the subject is difficult. In other words, it is much better to be as honest as you can be, within whatever limits you have to work with, rather than to write around the problem. Second to clarity is the skillful presentation of the written communication. Presentation reflects your company's professionalism, quality, and reputation. The costs of poorly written documents and spelling or grammatical errors can be staggering to organizations.

## Identifying the Audience

Clear writing is essential if you want your message to be understood by the recipient; what makes your writing clear will vary and is ultimately dependent on your target audience. Before you write, it is critical to understand to whom you are writing. One of the most common mistakes less experienced writers make is failing to consider the knowledge level of their audiences. Remember that the information, product, or service that you are writing about can be conveyed clearly at any grade level for any audience. Less able readers can understand complex information if it is written and edited in a way that is clear to them.

When conveying information, put yourself in your audience's shoes. What is important to them? How can you make sure that what you have to say becomes important to them? Answering these questions takes an awareness of your audience and an understanding of how people best receive messages. The vocabulary you use and the organizational structure you give the piece of writing depend on whom you want to say it to and what you want to say.

## Writing Clearly with a Purpose in Mind

Before you write one word, you need to know what you want your message to accomplish. Are you conveying information to an upset customer? Are you following up with a customer to clarify issues covered in a recent phone conversation? Do you want your reader to *do* something when he or she finishes reading? If you aren't sure what your purpose in writing is, neither will your reader. If you want your readers to do something, then illustrate in terms that are meaningful to them, by clearly stating the benefits *they* will receive by doing what you ask.

Like any assignment you tackle in your life, diving blindly into a writing project with no preparation or forethought is usually a recipe for disaster. When writing customers, for the most part the process involves putting together a well thought-out message. There are four things that clear business writing should be—brief and to the point, organized, accurate, and conclusive.

Because most people today spend less time reading, they want the whole picture in concise, easy-to-understand, and grammatically correct language. At the heart of effective writing is the ability to organize a series of thoughts. Once you've identified your true objective, take the time to list and prioritize the key points you want to make in support of that purpose. For some, an outline works best, since it allows writers to visualize their thought process on paper and in some detail. For others, the best ideas come from using a creative approach by simply jotting down ideas as they brainstorm the major elements of the message they want to convey.

Get to the point by presenting your primary message or call to action as quickly as possible. Few busy people today have the time to wade through long introductory paragraphs before coming to the point of a document. Provide just enough to capture readers' attention and let them know what is being asked of them. Guideline 10.1 offers additional suggestions for writing clearly with a purpose in mind.

## Using Proper Tone When Writing

Tone is present in all communication activities. The overall tone of a written message affects the reader just as one's tone of voice in everyday exchanges affects the listener. **Tone** in writing refers to the writer's attitude toward the reader and the subject of the message. A business writer should consider the tone of the message, whether writing a memo, a letter, an e-mail message, or a report. In writing documents, the customer service representative should strive for an overall tone that

- Is confident, courteous, and sincere
- Contains nondiscriminatory language
- Stresses the "you" attitude

Following are some general guidelines to keep in mind when considering what kind of tone to use in your written documents and how to present information in that tone:

- *Be confident.* You can feel confident if you have carefully prepared and are knowledgeable about the ideas you wish to express. The manner in which you write should assume a confident tone as well.

## GUIDELINE 10.1   Writing Clearly with a Purpose in Mind

| | |
|---|---|
| Start with the end in mind. | Decide what the result of your communication ought to be. List things you'd like to say and review them. Remove the ideas that do not effectively support the main idea. Good writing has a strong sense of purpose. |
| Get to the point early. | Don't delay. You should state the purpose of the message in the first paragraph. |
| Put yourself in your reader's place. | If the letter came to you, how would you respond to it? Be pleasant when you write and try to turn negative statements into positive ones. |
| Say it plainly. | Phrases such as "in compliance with your request" and "enclosed herewith" are too formal. Write as you talk—naturally and in a conversational tone. |
| Clear the deadwood. | Cut words and sentences that do not contribute to your message. Work hard to make your reader's job easy. |
| Use active verbs. | Passive voice is weak and confusing. Readers can sense your evasiveness if you write "Your order has been misplaced." Instead, write in an active voice, "I misplaced your order." |
| Be human. | Your message should read like a conversation. Address your reader by name: "Dear Ms. Hartman." If you can fit it in naturally, use Ms. Hartman's name in the body. You want her to know the message is personal. To achieve more informality and whenever you can, use pronouns such as *I, we,* and *you.* |
| Never write in anger. | Anger will evaporate over time; a letter won't. Devise a way to handle problems in an upbeat and calm manner. Your chances of success will multiply tenfold. |
| End with an action step. | The end of a business communiqué should suggest the reader's next move or your own next action. |
| Be professional. | The most well-written letters cannot survive bad presentation. Use a clean, logical format for your letter. A crowded or overdesigned page distracts from your message. |

- *Be courteous and sincere.* A writer builds goodwill by using a tone that is polite and sincere. If you are respectful and honest, readers will be more willing to accept your message, even if it is negative.
- *Use nondiscriminatory language.* Nondiscriminatory language is language that treats all people equally. It does not use any discriminatory words, remarks, or ideas. Moreover, it expresses equality among and respect for all individuals.
- *Stress the benefits for the reader.* A reader will often read a document, wondering "What's in it for me?" It is your job to write from the reader's perspective or with a "you" attitude. In other words, it's better to say, "Your order will be available in two weeks," rather than "I am processing your order tomorrow."

The only major exception to these guidelines is when you need to write a negative business message, such as when you deny a customer request. In writing a negative message, be sure to assume a tone that is gracious and sincere. Thank the customer for contacting you with the concern and carefully state that you cannot comply with his or her wishes. Then follow this response with an explanation as appropriate and necessary.

## Writing Rejection Letters

Nobody likes to receive a rejection letter, whether it pertains to a job, a query, or a contract for goods and services. In the same way, it is equally difficult to deliver bad news in writing. However, the old cliché remains true: "It's not what you say but how you say it."

The most effective approach is to give the refusal at the top of the letter, and then follow it with a brief explanation for the refusal. Be sure to suggest an alternative or a compromise, when possible. Your rejection letter should follow these guidelines:

1. *Refrain from the use of buffers.* **Buffers** are neutral or positive sentences that delay negative information. Unfortunately, they never fully prepare the reader for the bad news they are about to receive. Starting with the rejection doesn't make the reader happy, and most people can usually see right through a buffer.

2. *Remember that positive endings are not necessary.* Most businesses use this tactic as a way to maintain a customer relationship; however, if you don't really mean it, there's no need to end with statements such as "If we can be of assistance in another capacity...." Similar to buffers, insincere positive endings are easily spotted and not used. They may only upset the customer further. However, make a sincere attempt to exit your message gracefully.

# The Writing Process

Whether in writing or in person, being able to persuade others to accept your ideas or to act as you wish is one of life's most important abilities. A well-written letter or e-mail message generally demands that the writer attend to numerous activities, so where should one start? Many successful writers use a three-step approach to the writing process:

1. Plan and organize.
2. Draft and revise.
3. Edit and proofread.

## Plan and Organize

Planning is the first step in the writing process and embodies the brainstorming and organizing tasks that writers perform to generate ideas. When planning, consider the purpose of the document and know the intended audience. By organizing your ideas in a tidy package, you make your purpose sound more compelling to the reader. Suggestions for organizing ideas include

- *Begin with the end.* Business documents are very effective when the conclusion comes first, followed by the reasons, followed by an ending that counters possible resistance. For example, a defense attorney might start with the conclusion that the plaintiff had broken a contract. Then the attorney might give three reasons for taking this position. Last, the attorney might anticipate and rebut an opponent's arguments.
- *Group your thoughts into threes.* Thinking in threes forces you to boil down your comments into a concise, economical summary. Three ideas are far easier for the reader to remember and understand than five or more, and grouping in threes establishes a familiar cadence—for example, "We are Protestants, Jews, and Catholics" and "Of the people, by the people, and for the people."

## Draft and Revise

With a document plan, writers generally go to the next step in the writing process, which is to prepare the rough draft. This does not mean that writers start with the first sentence and continue their writing through to the last thought. The writing process best evolves on paper or at the computer and is creating a document that goes through several revision cycles before it sounds good enough to send to a reader.

When **revising,** most writers rethink their focus and develop points in greater detail. Determining the best possible order for conveying the message is part of this critical writing step, because it perfects what precisely the message should be to the reader.

## CUSTOMER SERVICE TIP

**10.1** *Some important books to have on hand are a good dictionary, a thesaurus, and one or two office handbooks. These reference books are also available in electronic form, either as a separate software package or as part of a complete word-processing software package, such as Microsoft Word.*

## Edit and Proofread

To produce quality documents, writers finish the process by editing and proofreading their documents. In short, they edit the language and proofread the documents' appearance and correctness. When **editing,** the concern is with the structure, conciseness, and clarity of the sentences. It is also the step in which the correctness and appropriateness of word usage and punctuation is checked. Here is where writers also look for redundancies, the overuse of particular words or phrases, and sentences that could be misinterpreted by someone not familiar with the topic. Questions to ask as you edit documents are

- What else does the reader need to know? Does the message sound complete as stated?
- Is the information in the most logical order, or should the ideas be rearranged?
- What extra details or unnecessary bits of information are in this document and should be removed?
- What words or details could be replaced by clearer or stronger expressions?

When **proofreading** documents, writers check for consistency in spacing, style, and other common errors, such as grammar problems and misspellings. No matter how targeted to the right audience and organized a written document is, if it contains spelling and grammatical errors, it can lose much of its impact. To many readers, documents with misspellings and grammar errors indicate sloppiness and inattention to detail—two traits no company wants to convey.

Proofing a document before you send it helps ensure that it is error-free, allowing readers to focus on its content. When you proofread, work from a printout instead of computer screen and read the message out loud. This is especially helpful for spotting run-on sentences, but you'll also hear other problems that you may not see when reading silently. Remember to end the proofreading process with using the spelling and grammar checkers that come with your word-processing program. Keep in mind, however, that a spell checker won't catch mistakes with homonyms (e.g., *they're, their,* and *there*) and certain typos (e.g., *he* for *the*). Use the following checklist to guide your proofreading as you check sentences for common writing errors:

- *Run-on sentences and sentence fragments.* Check each sentence to make sure it has a subject, a verb, and a complete thought. Have you run two sentences together incorrectly without a period, a conjunction, or a semicolon separating them?

- *Subject-verb agreement.* Check every subject and verb to make sure that, if you have used a singular subject, you have also used a singular verb. Similarly, a plural subject needs a plural verb.

- *Capitalization.* Have you capitalized the names of persons, cities, countries, streets, and titles?

- *Spelling.* Check any word you have doubts about. If you are unsure of the spelling of a word, look it up. Moreover, if you are using the recipient's name, be certain of the correct spelling.

Incorrect punctuation is one of the most common problems in business writing. It is best to refer to a comprehensive writer's handbook; however, the following are some handy tips:

- *Commas.* Use commas to separate items in a series ("I need a hard drive, a printer, and a monitor"); to separate clauses ("If I don't get my new computer soon, I'm going to be angry"); and to join independent clauses ("I want my new monitor, and I want it now").

- *Semicolons.* Use semicolons to join independent clauses. Generally, you should join clauses in this manner only when they are closely related ("My hard drive just crashed; it hasn't been working right for days").

- *Colons.* Use a colon to indicate an explanation of the main clause. A colon should always come after a complete clause ("I asked for three computer components: a keyboard, a monitor, and a printer").

Word-processing packages have several electronic tools to help you proof your documents. Such tools include spelling and grammar checker, thesaurus, and AutoCorrect proofing tools. By default, most word-processing packages automatically check the spelling and grammar in your document as you type.

The **thesaurus** tool allows you to substitute a word having the same or a similar meaning in place of the word that contains the insertion point. The AutoCorrect tool fixes common errors as you key in the text. For example, if you commonly key *adn* for *and,* AutoCorrect corrects the error as soon as you press the spacebar.

## Writing Business Documents

Word-processing software, such as Microsoft Word, has become so user-friendly that you can create many standard business documents based on a template. A **template** is a

Using word-processing software makes it easy to create documents from scratch or from preset templates.

master document or model that contains any text, formats, and styles that you want to include in a particular kind of document. Templates enable you to prepare documents more quickly, because they supply many of the settings that you would otherwise need to create—such as margins and tabs.

Document templates supply settings that automatically allow you to format letters, faxes, memos, reports, brochures, and newsletters. Often, organizations create their own custom templates by making changes to the current document and saving it as a template.

In the world of customer service, you can also use wizards to create letters, fax cover sheets, envelopes, labels, memos, and calendars. A **wizard** is a series of dialogue boxes that asks questions with structured responses; then it uses your answers to lay out and format a document. When CSRs write original business documents, most frequently those documents are letters, memorandums, or e-mail messages.

## ETHICS/CHOICES

**10.1** Evan works as a "floater" in a large hospital. Because of his excellent computer skills, he works in various departments when needed. One day, while working in admissions, he mistakenly deleted a patient's file from the hospital database. Because he works in this department only occasionally, no one will know he deleted the file. If you were Evan, would you tell your supervisor that you made an error and deleted the file? Why or why not?

## Letters

Companies want to make a good impression by the appearance of their external correspondence. Therefore, those who write to customers need to know the correct format to use when keying letters. Refer to Figure 10.1 as you read the following list, which describes how to format the basic parts of a business letter.

- *Date.* The date line is used to indicate the date the letter was written. Type the date 2 or 3 lines below the bottom of the letterhead. If you are not using letterhead, begin 12 to 14 lines from the top of the paper. Key the date using a word for the month, followed by numbers for the day and year. An example is December 11, 2004.

- *Inside address.* The **inside address** is the recipient's address; it includes the name, title, company, and address of the person receiving the letter. It is keyed four to eight lines below the date. The length of the letter determines the number of blank lines between the date and the letter address. Long letters require fewer blank lines; short letters require more.

- *Salutation.* Key the salutation two lines after the letter address. The greeting usually begins with the word *Dear* followed by the name of the person receiving the letter. A sample salutation is "Dear Mr. Chang." Use the same name as the inside address, including the personal title. Leave one line blank after the salutation.

- *Body.* The body of the letter begins two lines after the salutation. The body is the main part of a letter. It contains the reason for the letter, and it is usually at least two paragraphs long.

- *Closing and signature block.* Key the closing two lines after the ending of the body of the letter. The two most common closings used in business letters are "Very truly yours" and "Sincerely." Key the sender's name (the name of the person signing the letter) four lines after the closing. Four lines is enough room for the person to sign the letter. Usually, you will key the person's title on the line after the keyed name.

- *Typist initials.* Typist initials, keyed two lines after the signature block, are used to indicate the person who typed the letter.

- *Enclosures.* The enclosure notation is keyed two lines after the typist initials. If this notation appears on the letter, it means something is being enclosed with the letter. You key this notation only if something in addition to the letter is in the envelope. For example, a company may enclose a customer's refund check in the envelope with a letter.

- *Attachment.* The attachment notation is used in place of the enclosure notation when something is stapled or attached by a paperclip to a letter. This notation is keyed in place of the word *Enclosure*, two lines down from the typist initials.

- *Copy notation.* Sometimes, you need to send a copy of a letter to another person. If any copies are to be made for other people, a notation is made two lines after the enclosure notation; if nothing is enclosed, it is placed two lines after the typist initials.

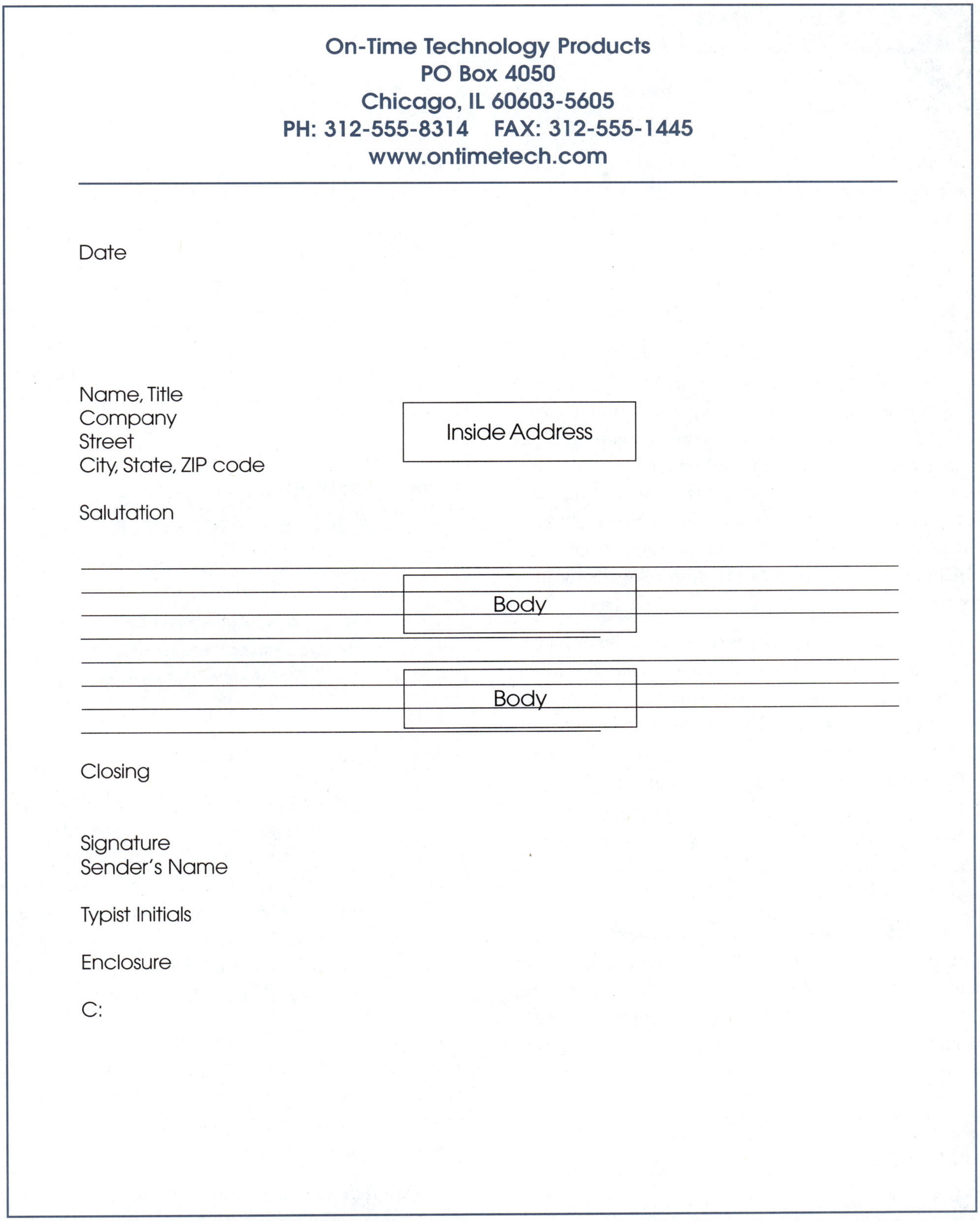

**On-Time Technology Products**
**PO Box 4050**
**Chicago, IL 60603-5605**
**PH: 312-555-8314    FAX: 312-555-1445**
**www.ontimetech.com**

Date

Name, Title
Company
Street
City, State, ZIP code

Inside Address

Salutation

Body

Body

Closing

Signature
Sender's Name

Typist Initials

Enclosure

C:

**FIGURE 10.1**
Parts of a business letter.

**ETHICS/CHOICES**

**10.2** Suppose that you work with a person, named Dolly, who has excellent writing skills and who willingly helps anyone in the Customer Service Department to draft letters, memos, e-mail messages, and so on. Even top managers ask Dolly to take a look at their work. You have noticed that Dolly is never given any credit and rarely even an honest thank you. Would you say anything to anyone about this lack of recognition of Dolly's skills?

## Memorandums

**Memorandums,** or memos, are internal documents that stay within an organization. They solve problems by informing a coworker about new information, such as policy changes or price increases. Memos are action documents when you write to persuade someone you work with to take an action, such as to attend a meeting, to use less paper, or to change a current procedure. When creating memos, you can use either the direct or the indirect approach:

- The *direct* approach, which is the most common, states the most important points first and then moves to the supporting details. This plan is useful for communicating routine information and for relaying news to coworkers.

- The *indirect* approach makes an appeal or presents evidence first and then arrives at a conclusion based on these facts. This plan is best used when you need to arouse your reader's interest *before* describing an action you want taken.

Figure 10.2 shows the parts of a memorandum. Although the heading section of a memo can be formatted in various ways, it usually contains the four headings To, From, Date, and Subject. The following example illustrates a popular heading format that CSRs can use when writing memos.

TO: (Readers' name and job titles)

FROM: (Your name and job title)

DATE: (Current date)

SUBJECT: (What the memo is about in five or fewer words)

When keying memorandums, keep the following points in mind:

- Do not use a salutation or closing.
- Use the block format, which is the entire document keyed even with the left margin.
- Triple-space between the subject line and the body of the memo. The body is the message part of the memo.
- Begin with the information that is most important. This may mean that you will start with key findings or recommendations in the first paragraph.
- Put important points or details into lists, rather than paragraphs, when possible.
- Key the typist initials, enclosure notation, and copy notation in the same locations as they are keyed on a business letter.

**CUSTOMER SERVICE TIP**

*10.2 Your boss may leave you a note, instructing you to make a telephone call or to write a customer an e-mail message. Always tell your boss when such a task is completed. One way to show that you have completed the task is to write "Done" on the note and return it to your boss.*

## E-Mail Messages

The twin challenges facing CSRs today are saving time and producing documents that enhance customer relationships. Imperfect as it may be, e-mail is critical to business communications, and CSRs must feel comfortable writing e-mail messages at a proficient level. Within customer service, e-mail messages are often written to convey much-needed information or to acknowledge receipt of an inquiry, so that customers know that their concerns are being handled promptly.

Within the e-mail functions, you can create, send, receive, forward, store, print, and delete messages. Well-written e-mails get to the point right away. They are clear, concise, and engaging; generate dialogue with the customer; and project a positive, professional image.

Too often, e-mail messages are unclearly written or have a stiff, overly formal tone. Many are full of grammatical mistakes, which erode credibility in the customer's eyes. These e-mails can cause misunderstandings and ill

**On-Time Technology Products**
**PO Box 4050**
**Chicago, IL 60603-5605**
**PH: 312-555-8314    FAX: 312-555-1445**
**www.ontimetech.com**

# MEMORANDUM

**TO:**
**FROM:**
**DATE:**
**SUBJECT:**

Body

Body

Typist Initials

Enclosure

C:

**FIGURE 10.2**
Parts of a memorandum.

feelings, and they can quickly undo established goodwill and loyalty.

Sometimes, e-mailing a message is not appropriate for the situation. For example, if you find yourself laboring over composing an e-mail, call or schedule a meeting instead. If you have something emotional to share, it is best to do it in person or on the phone. Understanding is gained through the voice, body language, and facial expressions. Too many people use e-mail as a shield to avoid unpleasant confrontations and end up alienating the recipient. The following are some tips on using e-mail well:

- State the purpose of the e-mail in the first sentence.
- Use short paragraphs and bullet points for easy reading.
- Keep e-mail messages to one screen, excluding attachments.
- Include your phone number and address in every e-mail message. Give the recipient the option to call you if it is warranted.
- Cover only a single item of business in every e-mail message.
- Make clear what actions are required. Ambiguity can cost precious time.
- Quote from a previous message to increase understanding of the response being given, as well as to lessen typing time.

Although the various e-mail systems differ somewhat, the components of a normal e-mail message are uniform. Figure 10.3 shows the typical composition screen for e-mail messages. The parts of an e-mail message include

- *To:* Here is placed the e-mail address of the recipient(s).
- *Copy.* If someone other than the prime recipient is to receive a courtesy copy, his or her e-mail address goes here.
- *BCC.* This abbreviation stands for blind courtesy copy. The recipient's message will not show this information; that is, he or she will not know who else is receiving a copy of the message.
- *Subject.* This line describes the message as precisely as the situation permits. The reader should get from the subject line a clear idea of what the message is about.
- *Attachments.* In this area, you can enter a file that you desire to send with the message. You should make certain that what you attach is really needed and that the attached file is free of viruses.

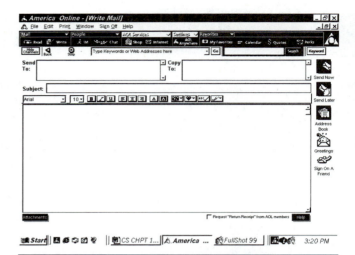

**FIGURE 10.3**
Parts of an e-mail message.

- *Salutation.* Whether to use a salutation or not depends on the writer's relationship with the receiver, corporate practices, and the formality of the message. At present, four patterns seem to be developing among e-mail writers:
  - Omission of salutations
  - Use of the receiver's name in the first line (for example, *Thanks, Pamela, . . .*)
  - Use of salutations such as *Dear Hank; Hi, Molly;* or *Greetings.* A comma, colon, or dash may follow these salutations.
  - If you are writing an e-mail message to a new client, use a formal salutation for a new client. For example, *Dear Mr. Newcomer* is generally appropriate.
- *Message.* The information you are sending goes here. In addition to following standard writing instructions, remember to
  - Organize short messages by presenting information in descending order of importance. In other words, the most important part of the message goes first, followed by the next most important part, and so forth.
  - Use language that resembles proper conversation that is well structured and organized. It is okay to use casual language (slang, colloquialisms) when writing to friends, but not when communicating with customers.
  - Cut nonessential thoughts and write concisely. E-mail messages should be as short as complete coverage of the subject matter will permit.

- Use the techniques of clear writing by using short, familiar words that are easily understandable. Your sentences should be short, and so should your paragraphs.
- Write correctly. Spelling errors, illogical punctuation, and awkward wording adversely reflect on the writer and his or her company.
- End your message with a simple closing statement and your name.
- Proofread. Before pressing the send button, proofread your message very carefully.

## Concluding Message for CSRs

In face-to-face communication, words, voice, facial expressions, gestures, and the like combine to determine the effect of the message. In writing, however, the printed word alone must do the job. The language used in a written message communicates more than the message. It also tells how friendly, how formal, and how careful the writer is.

To enhance writing skills, the CSR should be clear about why a document is needed and who is going to read it. Regardless, all writing should be clear, concise, and professional. Check grammar, spelling, and punctuation, including the correct use and spelling of names, titles, and numbers. Write documents that represent the tone of message that you would like to receive.

## Summary

- The costs of poorly written documents and spelling or grammatical errors can be staggering to organizations.
- Before you write, you must understand whom you are writing for and what you want your message to accomplish.
- Tone is the writer's attitude toward the reader and the subject of the message.
- The most effective approach when writing rejection letters is to give the refusal at the top of the letter and then follow it with a brief explanation for the refusal.
- The three-step approach to the writing process is to plan and organize, to draft and revise, and to edit and proofread.
- Two suggestions for organizing writing ideas are to begin with the end in mind and to group your thoughts into threes.

- Writing is a process that best evolves on paper or at the computer; documents usually go through several revision cycles.
- Word-processing packages have several electronic tools, such as spelling and grammar checkers, to help you proof documents.
- Document templates supply settings that automatically allow you to format letters, memos, and other business documents.
- The basic parts of a business letter are date, inside address, salutation, body, closing and signature block, typist initials, enclosures, attachment, and copy notation.
- When formatting memorandums, the header section contains the words *To, From, Date*, and *Subject*.
- You can create, send, receive, forward, store, print, and delete e-mail messages.
- Well-written e-mails get to the point right away and are increasingly used to communicate with customers to document situations, issues, and events.

### QUESTIONS FOR CRITICAL THINKING

1. Why is it important when creating documents to identify the audience and purpose for writing?

2. Describe your reaction to a letter you've received recently that you perceived as having an inappropriate tone. How did it make you feel?

3. What are two guidelines to keep in mind when writing rejection letters to customers?

4. In your opinion, is it always necessary, when writing customers, to use the three-step approach?

5. Indicate the particular activities involved in each of the following three writing practices: revising, editing, and proofreading.

6. Why do customer service representatives create business documents with a software template or wizard?

7. Describe the major parts or formats of a typical business letter and memorandum.

8. Why do businesses message with e-mail? What are some advantages to consumers of receiving messages over the Internet?

## On-line Research Activities

### Project 10.1: Improving Business-Writing Skills

Assume you are doing a report on *improving business-writing skills.* Launch your Internet service provider and browser software and enter http://www.findarticles.com. At that web site, locate information from at least four articles that you can use in this writing skills report. As a result of your search on the Internet, keyboard three paragraphs of cited material you might use in your report.

### Project 10.2: Popular Word-Processing Features

#### Situation

On-Time Technology Products is in the process of revising its correspondence manual in the Customer Service Department. Mary Graeff has decided to use many of the electronic writing tools in word-processing software packages when revising the current manual.

*Go to the web sites of companies selling the following three popular word-processing software packages: Microsoft Word, Corel WordPerfect, and Lotus Word Pro. Using file PRJ10-2 on your student CD, key responses in the following table format that compares the seven features listed for each of the three software packages. If possible, locate online a consumer report comparing the three packages feature by feature.*

| Feature | Microsoft Word | Corel WordPerfect | Lotus Word Pro |
|---|---|---|---|
| 1. Templates and wizards | | | |
| 2. AutoCorrect | | | |
| 3. AutoFormat | | | |
| 4. Spell checker | | | |
| 5. Grammar checker | | | |
| 6. Mail merge | | | |
| 7. Thesaurus | | | |

## Communication Skills at Work

### Project 10.3: A Blunt Refusal Message

Read the following e-mail message and suggest at least three ways you would improve the overall tone and wording to make it more customer-friendly.

*Retrieve file PRJ10–3 on the student CD and complete the following form by listing in column 2 at least three suggestions for improving the wording of the message.*

| E-Mail Message | Suggestions for Improvement |
|---|---|
| Subject: Your January 18 claim for damages.<br><br>Ms. Snider:<br><br>I regret to report that we must reject your request for money back on the faded upholstered office chair.<br><br>We must refuse because the fabric is not made for outside use. It is difficult for me to understand how you failed to notice this limitation. It was clearly stated in the catalog from which you ordered. Since we have been more than reasonable in trying to inform you, we cannot possibly be responsible and, therefore, will only credit your account with $50 of the original $122 amountyou paid. We trust you will understand our position.<br><br>Charlotte Bauer<br>Customer Relations | • <br><br>• <br><br>• |

# Decision Making at Work

## Project 10.4: The New CSR—Temporary Hire

A temporary, six-month CSR position has just been filled at On-Time Technology Products. The new hire is Abhey Patel, a very nice and bright person, who everyone agrees works very hard. Abhey has recently established citizenship in America from his homeland India. In realizing the need to write to customers using good English, grammar, and wording, the other CSRs have been covering for Abhey and doing his letter writing and e-mail messaging for him. He is trying very hard to learn English, but he hasn't mastered all the fine points yet.

*Respond to questions regarding Abhey's situation:*

1. Can you think of ways to help Abhey that would allow him to continue working at On-Time Technology Products?

_____

_____

_____

_____

_____

_____

_____

_____

2. Do you feel that the supervisor, Mary Graeff, should be informed that Abhey has not yet developed the skills in writing business documents and that others are doing his work for him?

_____

_____

_____

_____

_____

_____

_____

_____

## Case Study

### 10.1 Effects of the Increased Use of E-Mail Messages

Mr. MacGibson was recently told that experts predict the average number of commercial e-mail messages a typical consumer will receive in the year 2005 is 1,612 pieces. Most will be prompted by consumers' replies to online surveys. Half of the e-mails will contain advertisements. In anticipating the long-term needs of business communications with customers at On-Time Technology Products, several persons in top management are asking the question "Will letters and memos diminish in importance as e-mail messaging with customers and coworkers increase?"

#### Discussion Questions

1. Do you believe the prediction that there will be a staggering increase in e-mail messages to consumers? What effect do you think it will have on the way people spend their non-working time?

_____

_____

_____

_____

_____

2. If management asked you this question, how would you respond? In other words, do you think e-mail will overtake the need to send letters and memos in the not too distant future? Explain.

_____

_____

_____

_____

_____

## Case Study

### 10.2 Salutations in Letters

A coworker of Mary Beth's is taking a bereavement leave due to a death in her family and won't be back for three or four days. Since Mary Beth works in the same office area, the coworker has left a letter for Mary Beth to type. This letter, addressed to customer Lee Carolla, must go in today's mail.

As Mary Beth begins typing the letter, she gets to the salutation and stops. She does not know if Lee Carolla is a man or a woman. After checking, Mary Beth discovers that no one in her immediate area knows the customer's gender, either.

#### Discussion Question

1. What do you recommend Mary Beth do?

_____

_____

_____

_____

_____

_____

_____

_____

_____

_____

_____

_____

_____

_____

# Let's Discuss...

## Industry: Government

## Government Activities

1. Think about your total experience the last time you communicated with any government agency (examples: reporting a crime to police, paying a city water bill, getting tax information from the IRS, talking with a military recruiter) and respond "yes" or "no" to the following questions.

| Yes | No | Question |
|-----|-----|----------|
|  |  | Did you feel that the fundamentals of communication were followed well? |
|  |  | Was the nonverbal communication appropriate for and complementary to the total message? |
|  |  | Did you feel the person who served you was well dressed for that office and that he or she demonstrated good manners? |
|  |  | Did you feel your situation was understood by someone who displayed and used effective listening skills? |
|  |  | If you had occasion to telephone or receive a telephone call from the government agency, did it follow good techniques, as well as use voicemail effectively? |
|  |  | Were the written documents you received (letters, notices, or e-mail messages) during your transaction with the government agency appropriately written, formatted, and presented with a professional image in mind? |

- How would you rank the customer service provided by this government agency (1 = poor; 5 = superior)? _____

_____

_____

2. From the material in Part 3, briefly explain why you evaluated the government agency as you did.

_____

_____

3. Assume you are mayor of your city and are interested in creating a customer service policy relative to communicating effectively with the citizens of your community. What are three areas you would stress in your policy?

_____

_____

# PART 4

## HEALTH CARE PROFILE

by Denice E. Gibson, RN, MSN, CHPN, OCN; Good Samaritan Hospital; Phoenix, Arizona

As an oncology/hematology bone marrow transplant nurse, I have worked in a hospital as a staff nurse, providing bedside patient care; in a hospice organization as a clinical case manager; and in the public education system and the community, providing information and acute medical care.

From these experiences, I truly believe that great customer service in delivering health care is the essence of any health care institution. In basic terms, it directly affects the quality of patient outcomes. Simple things in providing great customer service mean a lot to those we serve—for example, making an effort to remember patients' names, not being afraid to ask "Is there anything else I can do for you today?" or giving a client your full attention. When delivering health care, I think of it this way:

The customer is always right—as long as it doesn't involve a safety or health issue.

Although health care professionals must, first and foremost, be proficient and competent in delivering care, the other critical skill sets that have an impact on the way customer service is delivered are

1. *Being culturally compassionate.* Given the culturally diverse society we live in, health care providers must be able to interact professionally within any culture and not allow their personal beliefs to develop barriers to serving their patients.

2. *Caring at a basic level.* Because delivering care in health institutions is increasingly dehumanized, it is essential to remember that the service rendered has a direct

# DENICE E. GIBSON

impact on the quality of life for the patient, the patient's family, and the community.

3. *Honoring integrity.* Moral principles are essential to maximizing the outcomes of quality and respected care. Not only can irresponsible behavior by health care providers result in direct harm to or mistrust from a patient, the patient's family, the community, or the health care institution, but the bottom line is that irresponsible behavior is simply not ethical and should not be done.

Finally, nurses, doctors, and other health care givers need an outstanding personal attitude that reflects exemplary customer service to the aggregate needs in health care. To be successful, I would advise those planning a career in the health care area to:

- Be committed to maximizing quality customer service
- Be willing to adapt to meet the challenges and changing needs of customer service in health care
- Work collaboratively with colleagues and other professionals
- Establish yourself as a person who is culturally compassionate, has integrity, and truly cares for patients at the most basic level

# Challenges When Serving Customers Online

*The most successful enterprises in the future will be those with the right blend of high-tech with high-touch.*

BILL GATES

## OBJECTIVES

**AFTER COMPLETING THIS CHAPTER, YOU WILL BE ABLE TO:**

1. List the opportunities for customer service that a technology-driven online store provides.

2. Describe the extent to which online services are growing.

3. Discuss some challenges facing companies involved in e-commerce.

4. Identify the major trends in e-commerce that affect the manner in which businesses operate.

5. Define customer relationship management and give reasons that its use in business is increasing.

6. List the multichannel communication methods used by online shoppers.

7. Make a distinction between the additional skills required of e-reps and the basic skill set needed by CSRs.

8. Describe the reasons that employee monitoring is becoming a more common practice in customer service organizations.

"Whether you sell stock or sell suits, the Internet has changed the world and how business is conducted," was a comment from Richard Grasso, chairman of the New York Stock Exchange. It is difficult to name a product or service that is not available on the Internet today. Consider books, health care, movie tickets, construction materials, baby clothes, music, electronics, toys, wine, cars, education, airline tickets, antiques, and more. Customer service is more of a challenge today, with the impersonal medium we've come to know and use called the Internet. However, when it's done right, online business offers consumers the best of both worlds—the old economy's one-to-one service and the new economy's immediacy, convenience, and cost-effectiveness.

From the consumers' point of view, the ability to buy merchandise *anywhere, anytime,* and *anyhow* they want is imperative in today's retail markets. One of the greatest

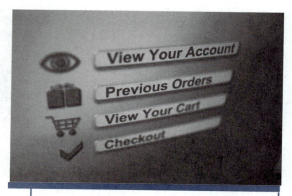

Today, more than 360 million users around the world connect to the Internet to access a variety of products and services in an assortment of ways.

challenges that electronic businesses, or **e-businesses,** face today is how to provide truly personalized service while taking advantage of the Internet's swiftness and interactivity.

Part 4 looks to the future of customer service by providing an understanding of the profound impact that new technology and improved telecommunications media are having on the delivery of customer service. This chapter begins by discussing the growth, opportunities, and challenges that businesses experience when serving customers online. Also discussed is the increased use of customer relationship management (CRM) software and the special qualifications organizations must consider and screen for when hiring online CSRs.

## Providing Customer Service on the Internet

Whether you are face to face with customers in a physical store or mouse to database with them in a virtual environment, customer service is still a universal principle of good business, because all customers are people. Customers can be located anywhere, but they still need or want something. Customer service and a customer-driven orientation are not new ideas. Taking steps to improve customer satisfaction in online transactions is, however. Online or not, the goals of companies are still to think and feel as their customers do and to try to develop knowledge about their total customer base.

The principle of first impressions is very strong in the virtual world. If traditional customers are not immediately impressed with a company or store, they must get back into their cars and drive across town to another one; however, virtual shoppers can click away in a matter of seconds. The odds are stacked against an online business unless it provides answers and solutions immediately. This can be done on a well-designed web site by providing a home page that loads quickly, provides security, and reassures customers that they are in the right place.

Used properly, technology offers opportunities for customer service that a traditional store cannot supply. For instance, the doors are always open, the search engines find products faster than rummaging through stacks of odd-sized and various colors of clothing, and rich layers of undiscovered information can be found on products the customer can browse at will. It's all a matter of how high a priority businesses give their customer service delivery and how well they apply technology to those service principles.

## CUSTOMER SERVICE TIP

**11.1** *Whether your business is online, at a physical location, or both, the same age-old principles of customer service apply, such as great service attitude before, during, and after the sale.*

## The Customer Service Experience

The Internet has become a new frontier for marketers and advertisers. Research shows that more than 25 percent of U.S. retailers have web sites. In 2001, an estimated $300 billion in commerce was conducted on the Internet. According to Nielsen/NetRatings, Americans spent $556 million in online auctions in June 2001, with E-Bay accounting for 67 percent of online auction revenues.[1]

The Amazon.com paradox proves that a selling relationship with *no* human contact can still be a great relationship. Customers love Amazon.com not because it offers the lowest prices, because it doesn't, but for the reason that the buying experience has been crafted so carefully that most

---

[1]"E-Commerce Guidelines for Merchants," Better Business Bureau Online (2002).

of us actually enjoy shopping at Amazon.com. It is not primarily a technological achievement; it results from Amazon.com headquarters staff obsessing over what customers want in a fundamentally new kind of relationship, called *the online experience.*

Few companies or industries are immune to the effects of the e-commerce tidal wave. In fact, some companies transact business only on the Internet. It has created new channels for customers, making land-based companies that were former leaders in particular industries sit up and take notice. E-commerce clearly has changed how many companies do business. Intensified competition and new e-commerce opportunities are pressing traditional companies to build e-business models that are flexible, fast-moving, and customer-focused. Guideline 11.1 lists the advantages to a business enterprise of conducting electronic commerce.

## GUIDELINE 11.1    Advantages of E-Commerce to Businesses

The global market is open 24 hours per day.

Businesses have access to more than 360 million people with Internet access.

Customers can conduct price comparisons easily.

Feedback to queries regarding the status of orders can be immediate.

Changing information can be updated quickly and can be made instantly available to customers.

FAQ (frequently asked questions) pages can provide easy access to customer support.

Companies can gather customer information, analyze it, and react on the basis of current data.

Companies have new and traditional approaches to generate revenue.

Manufacturers can buy and sell directly, avoiding the cost of the middleman.

Distribution costs for information are reduced or eliminated.

Society has a new option to create a near-paperless environment.

**Growth of and Opportunities in Online Services.** The uniqueness of the digital economy lies in its ability to provide choice and speed to buyers in order to access what they want. In this environment, transactions are over in a matter of minutes, if not seconds, before prospective customers

move on to the next web site. It is reasonable to understand that the remarkable power shift in a marketplace—from sellers to buyers—is driving online companies to value customer loyalty. When it comes to e-commerce, the cost of enticing customers to use an online service is heavy at the front end and light at the back end. In other words, the longer companies keep their e-customers and the more loyal customers are, the more lucrative sales become.

Online retailers, such as E-Bay, are changing the face of shopping—much as shopping malls did in the 1970s—and companies must master the new rules to keep customers coming back—in this case, to their web sites. Increasingly, companies must have at their fingertips the same customer data across *all* channels of customer interaction and must provide consistent service throughout each customer experience. Customer contact points are quickly multiplying and are using technology to reach more customers. Today, a customer may choose to contact an organization via the Internet, the telephone, e-mail, a fax, or a mobile device.

E-retailers have been good at attracting high levels of traffic to their sites but have been less adept at engaging these throngs of customers and converting them from browsers to buyers. Of necessity, e-retailers are turning away from pure customer acquisition to conscious efforts to build their customer bases through improved online customer service.

Customers rarely describe doing business over the Internet as a warm and fuzzy experience. However, never before has a business had an opportunity to be in such direct contact with its customers. The Internet allows a company to be in direct communication with every one of its customers—no matter where they reside on the planet (as long as they have an Internet connection).

Think of the Internet as a direct line to customers. For example, businesses can assess individual customers' needs, apologize, say "thank you," ask for input, and suggest new products or services suited to the individual, rather than to a whole market segment—all online. It's a new, exciting opportunity for any company that knows the value of listening and staying close to customers.

Customers are looking for easy ways to do business with companies. If a company can offer an online buying experience that is easy to navigate and superior in product and services to other online competitors, then customers will go back to shop again and again. In the online world, the consumer is king in a way that has never occurred before. That is to say, customers increasingly make buying decisions *without* vendors exercising any formal role. Why? Internet customers have access to sales information without the aid of a salesperson. Further, they tend to know exactly what they want. Being truly empowered, many customers now conduct their own research and trust their own judgment. To some extent, this circumstance provides new challenges to businesses.

**Challenges of and Trends in E-Commerce.** Although the way companies do business is changing rapidly to stay in step with evolving technologies, the fundamentals of excellent customer service have not changed. In fact, traditional service values are more relevant now than ever before in a world where a passion for technology seems rampant. Ultimately, the success of an enterprise has more to do with a company's core values and a commitment to delivering quality products and services than it does with the latest and greatest business trends.

What do e-consumers want? The answer to this question is perhaps the biggest challenge to online companies. It is reported that, currently, 50 to 75 percent of consumers do not complete online purchases of items they want because of poorly designed web sites. In fact, the most frequent button clicked on e-retail sites is the *back* button, which is an expression of people's frustration with poor site design and with the e-shopping experience in general.[2] Guideline 11.2 lists items on buyers' wish lists when shopping online.

> ### GUIDELINE 11.2   What Buyers Want While Shopping Online
>
> 1. Good site search tools, express ordering, and highlighted specials.
> 2. Assurance of on-time order fulfillment.
> 3. Order status information or, better yet, the ability to securely track their own orders.
> 4. The ability to exchange items purchased on a web site at any of the chain's physical stores.
> 5. The ability to buy merchandise anywhere, anytime, and anyhow the buyer wants.

---

[2]"What Do E-Consumers Want?" *USA Today Magazine* (May 2001): 8.

Negative experiences at an e-retail site make it less likely that the consumer will return there or to other sites. The top customer complaints about online shopping are slow web sites, unavailable products, late deliveries, and an inability to track order status. There are two types of online shoppers who require different buying experiences from each other:

1. Three-click shoppers are those who know what they want to buy and want the transaction to be as quick and simple as possible.
2. Online buyers who are uncertain about what they want to purchase need a more enriched shopping experience. For these customers, the e-retailer should have a range of items and offer easy methods of ordering and clarifying questions during the buying process and of making payments and receiving delivery.

The key to business longevity on the Internet is friendly help, not lowest price. Look at the dot-com graveyard, and among the commonalities are inaccessibility, unfriendliness, and the age-old business philosophy of "sell something first and service the sale second." When customers return to place a second or third order online, it is an indication that they feel it is easier for them to do business with that company than with its competition. Five rules to build strong online relationships with customers are listed to in Guideline 11.3.

## Trends to Watch in E-Commerce

Trends in e-commerce were planted in early days and are now starting to point the way toward its thriving future. In order to understand the growing magnitude of e-commerce, consider the following trends:

- *Multichannel retailing.* Shoppers are hopping back and forth freely among printed catalogs with 800 numbers, physical retail stores, and Internet sites. Customers want it all.
- *More satisfied online customers.* Customers now know what to expect from e-commerce. A few years ago, companies didn't know what they were doing online, and a lot of businesses failed for that reason. Most shoppers, who had bad experiences online with either poor customer service attitude or poor product delivery, have come back and have given the Web a second try, with positive results.

| | |
|---|---|
| 1. Excel at each stage of the customer buying cycle. | Once customers have found you in the virtual world, the next step is to give them a positive experience through the entire buying process. Whenever possible, make the web site simple and easy to navigate, make downloads fast, offer the kind of value that keeps customers coming back, and provide powerful searches. |
| 2. Empower customers to help themselves. | Most customers like to find out things on their own and on their own time. |
| 3. Help your customers succeed by empowering them to be in control of the buying situation. | Successful sites look professional, are easy to read and navigate, and work flawlessly. Broken links can destroy the trust of consumers. A webmaster must check the links to other web sites or web pages on a consistent basis. |
| 4. Protect the privacy of consumers. | Safeguard shoppers' payment information and any confidential details you gather about them. In addition, make sure that clear instructions on how to access customer service and how to return items are provided. |
| 5. Offer several types of free technical assistance. | Assistance can include using an online tutorial, watching a video, sending an e-mail message, or chatting with a customer service representative. Live chats with e-reps are gaining in popularity, because they answer customer questions quickly. |

- *More profits.* The number of profitable e-commerce companies continues to grow. A survey by Giga Research group indicated that about one-third of the top 40 e-commerce sites in terms of sales volume are profitable.[3]

Online customer service isn't just a good idea; today, it's mandatory for continued business survival. An even bigger challenge is striking the balance between high-tech and high-touch in serving customers. Basic Internet technologies for dot-com companies include a web site and server, a phone system, e-mail service, and customer relationship management (CRM) strategies.

---

[3]Keith Regan, "Five E-Commerce Trends to Watch," *E-Commerce Times* (April 3, 2002): 4–5.

## Customer Relationship Management

**Customer Relationship Management (CRM)** is a business strategy to integrate the functions of sales, marketing, and customer service that uses technology and wide-ranging databases of information. It is all about understanding the customer's needs and leveraging this knowledge to increase sales and improve service in a more personal way. Obviously, the overriding goal of companies is to increase customer share and customer retention through customer satisfaction. The new customer focus that CRM brings to a company is the direct result of the electronic world and the World Wide Web. No other approach can offer companies the unparalleled opportunity to personalize services, to provide multiple choices for customer support, and to track customer satisfaction.

How does the CRM system work? Rather than just collect, analyze, and report on customer information, CRM allows electronic measures to be taken automatically on the basis of the analysis of customer information. For example, if the CRM system detects a customer problem, it can immediately send the customer an e-mail message, alert CSRs to call the customer and apologize for the problem, and access the billing system to set up a credit on the customer's next invoice.

Customer satisfaction and customer loyalty are quickly gaining ground as reasons to get a CRM system up and running. In an economy that sees demand leveling off, making the most of the customers a company already has is the name of the game. In fact, to most businesses, maintaining or improving customer satisfaction can be more important than reducing budgets.

According to a report released in 2002 by Jupiter Media Metric research group, 26 percent of corporations say they plan to spend $500,000 or more on customer relationship management by 2004. This spending surge seems logical, in light of Jupiter's prediction that the total number of online customer service contacts will explode from 870 million in 2001 to 4.7 billion by 2006. Further, whereas just 2 percent of all customer inquiries were handled on the Internet in 2001, nearly 10 percent of all customer inquiries will take place online by 2006, according to Jupiter.[4]

**Purpose of CRM.** Customer relationship management is more than technology; it involves a change in philosophy and attitudes. To be effective, CRM needs to be viewed by organizations as an all-encompassing business strategy—a customer-centric philosophy of doing business that affects every consumer touchpoint. The new slogan is to do *whatever it takes* to delight the customer.

Consequently, a process for managing change must be instituted to help a company move from a product-centered focus to a customer-centered one. Companies cannot be customer-centered if they ignore the foundations of the CRM experience. For example, not answering e-mails is saying, "Don't bother us; we're not interested." For that reason, when companies desire to implement a successful CRM strategy, they need to consider thoroughly what each element of its implementation means:

- *Knowledge management.* At the heart of CRM implementation is the acquisition of information about each customer, as well as the analysis, sharing, and tracking of this knowledge.
- *Database consolidation.* This involves consolidating customer information from any form or type of contact into a single database. The goal is to have all interactions with a customer recorded in one place in order to drive production, marketing, sales, and customer support activities.
- *Integration of channels and systems.* The essence of online service is to respond to customers in a consistent and high-quality manner through the customer's channel of choice, whether that is an e-mail message, a phone conversation, or an online chat.

[4]Keith Regan, "Report: Online Customer Service Tops IT Shopping List," *E-Commerce Times* (February 25, 2002): 2.

**Benefits of CRM.** Customer service is traditionally viewed as an expense or a cost center. Because of this view, most operations typically put customers through an escalating series of hurdles when resolving a conflict in order to keep costs down. Companies justify their CRM investment cost by noting that strong, lasting relationships with customers encourage recurring revenue, which offsets these costs. CRM software is relatively simple to use, and the benefits are great, given our technology-using consumers; however, actually using it requires massive cultural changes in most organizations.

In review, customer relationship management software allows a company to collect information about customers, such as their account history and any questions or complaints they have had. Once that information has been collected, it can be analyzed using CRM software, and the company can more accurately gain insights into how to serve each customer better. In addition to a greater awareness of each customer's interests and problems, the biggest benefit CRM companies experience is less customer attrition and increased customer loyalty.

## CUSTOMER SERVICE TIP

**11.2** *Successful companies don't use technology to replace human relationships, only to enhance them.*

## Recognizing Cyberspace Customer Service Issues

The hardest part of traditional commerce is getting customers to come to your store location and make the decision to buy. Once the customer is in front of you, saying he or she wants to buy your product, the rest is easy, or at least more controllable. If there is a problem, the customer tells you about it by returning to the store, where you can solve it personally. With e-commerce, on the other hand, the easiest part is creating the web site, putting products on the site, and collecting the orders. The hardest part of e-commerce is dealing with the inevitable problems, such as sending out the right merchandise to the right address in a timely manner.

What level of customer service do online shoppers want? Consumers are telling researchers they want responsive, high-quality, and personalized customer service whenever and however they choose—day or night, online or offline. That is a tall order, but one that organizations can no longer ignore.

In response to growing customer complaints, many e-commerce companies are trying to make technological "fixes" to the customer service problem by investing in software and technology-based systems. Today's sophisticated buyers want and are getting answers through access to e-mail, chat rooms, instant messaging, voice over IP and collaborative browsing, traditional 800 phone service, Internet audio, and well-trained online CSRs behind e-services.

## Multichannel Communication

As pressure increases in call center environments to provide customers with around the clock availability and response, enterprises are forced to upgrade customer service and develop CRM strategies. Thus, the call center is evolving into a multichannel customer interaction center that integrates wired and soon to be largely wireless channels of customer contact.

Think about how a multichannel customer contact center differs from a traditional call center. In the traditional call center, customer contact is predominantly by telephone, either inbound or outbound. Customers know they can talk to someone who can resolve an issue if they just call. CSRs are usually well trained to talk to customers about products, services, systems, and processes. However, most CSRs are traditionally trained to handle only routine calls, referring more difficult or escalated situations to a specially trained team or lead customer service representative.

A very different situation exists when a CSR works in a technology-based multichannel customer contact center. Here, customers who may be working on their computers at the office, at home, or on the road expect to be able to start and finish an inquiry very quickly and with little hassle. Online customers want to talk to a person *only if* they cannot successfully address their situations electronically. When they do need to speak to someone, customers expect those CSRs to be very knowledgeable and skilled in managing their situations and in taking time with them to uncover and solve their problems on the spot.

Another major difference between traditional call centers and today's multichannel contact center is that the customer expects more control during the communication. Many customers today are tech-savvy and sophisticated. They move faster and with more confidence than in the past. Today, customers want to connect to a business's web site, navigate easily, complete an online order form or another appropriate mechanism for communicating what they want, and then have the solution documented for them in real-time on the spot. Further, customers expect the solution to be accurate, fast, and hassle-free, because they assume no human interaction will be necessary. In fact, many e-customers are seeking to *avoid* the human contact that was inherent in the traditional call center.

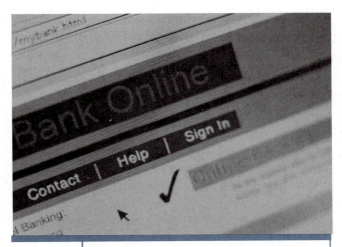

Many shoppers prefer to complete an online form, finalize a transaction, and receive delivery of the product or service without any human interaction.

Instead of regular classroom training programs that emphasize the company's products and service, the need now is for CSRs to have skills in solving problems and in "working" the multichannel contact system. Customers who need help from a CSR expect more, because they have already covered the simpler, more basic answers and solutions through the electronic avenues provided them on the company's web site. This makes it very important to keep call center agents on the job longer than their average 18-month stays, not to mention the challenge of keeping them trained in the latest service technologies. As a result, great attention when hiring and training online CSRs is considered critical and more necessary than ever before in today's business world.

## Hiring and Training an Online CSR

The idea of providing customers with numerous communication channels is enticing to many companies; unfortunately, less attention has been paid to the issue of how to handle the required human resources. With the popularity of wireless communication devices, e-businesses now need to be able to reach their customers through their pagers, PDAs, cellular phones, and other telecommunication devices. Although these technological advances help improve online experiences, many companies seem to have neglected one of the critical aspects of customer service quality—the customer service representative, or the human interface between the customer and the company.

How do you find, hire, and train new CSRs who can do more than just field phone calls? The ideal is to hire individuals who can handle everything a multichannel call center requires. However, the reality is that most companies are dividing the overall tasks, with one CSR group answering phones and another handling electronic communications. Few companies currently have CSRs who can handle it all.

The core skills needed in most customer service positions include work efficiency, problem-solving skills, social adeptness, effective communication skills, fact-finding abilities, and professionalism. Although many of the skill requirements for customer service personnel are the same, regardless of the method by which CSRs interact with customers, there are some differences.

For online CSRs (sometimes referred to as **e-reps**), who interact with customers by using e-mail and chat modes, good oral communication is important but is not as essential as good written communication skills. In addition, when CSRs use the chat mode to conduct real-time, text-based conversations, accurate and fast keyboarding skills are critical. Good customer service includes responding quickly to customers without typographical or spelling errors while using good grammar. Moreover, individuals who work in the online, real-time chat mode also frequently respond to several customers at one time; thus multitasking (a component of work efficiency) is critical.

No matter what industry best classifies a company, everyone who works there is in the business of customer service. If a company cannot give customers the appropriate information, response, or resolution within a reasonable

time frame, it doesn't matter what its services or pricing is—the company is on shaky ground.

Today's sophisticated buyers want e-mail, chat rooms, Internet audio, and well-trained people behind e-services. The key to serving online customers well is to treat them with the same respect as you would offline and in person. Five suggestions toward great online customer service are to provide:

- Customer self-service, such as a dynamic knowledge base or an FAQ section on the web site
- Prompt and efficient e-mail responses
- Text chat for immediate customer service needs
- A toll-free telephone number displayed on the web site
- Assistance available 24/7.

### ETHICS/CHOICES

**11.2** Many companies scan all employees' incoming e-mail for "R-rated" keywords and image file attachments. Colorful messages, pictures, and jokes can violate e-mail policies and land recipients in trouble—or, at the least, prompt an embarrassing discussion. In your opinion, what business ethics issues are prompting businesses to take this action? Further, in what ways does this monitoring advance the customer service a company wants to deliver?

## Understanding Employee Monitoring

All employers occasionally look over the shoulders of their employees. Increasingly, however, companies want more detailed knowledge of their employees' on-the-job computer and Internet use. Instead of supervision, some workers characterize this increased vigilance as "snoopervision." According to the consumer survey group Frost & Sullivan, about 90 percent of call centers use CSR monitoring through manual systems, a computer, or a type of recording product.[5]

As the Internet continues to dominate business communication, employee monitoring is on the rise. **Employee monitoring** is defined as the use of computers or other

---

[5]Teresa Burke Wright, "Workplace Privacy and Snoopervision," *Business Communication Resources,* (January 2001): 8.

electronic devices to observe, record, and review an individual's performance on the job. Employers know that 70 percent of Internet surfing is done at work. They also know that "cyberslacking" can put a significant dent in productivity.

A study by the American Management Association reports a startling increase in employee monitoring. Nearly 74 percent of major U.S. firms admit that they regularly record and review their employees' communications and activities on the job, including phone calls, e-mail, web usage, and computer file content. Twenty-five percent of these companies say that they have dismissed employees for misuse of telecommunications equipment. The main reasons for such terminations include viewing porn sites, trading stocks, and posting to chat rooms while on the job.[6]

Why such a dramatic increase in employee monitoring? Employers give the following reasons:

- E-mail and Internet access can be an entertaining pastime for workers, resulting in lower productivity.
- Companies can be sued for offensive e-mails sent by their employees.
- Employees can spread company secrets.
- Archived e-mail messages are increasingly appearing as evidence in lawsuits.

## Concluding Message for CSRs

The modern call center is a mix of low-tech telephony and the latest in online collaborative technology. Its capabilities range from simultaneous interactive voice and data access over the Internet to the use of a web page as the simple but timesaving first step in the service process. Web users who need extensive help click a callback button to have an agent call them. Customers with less complex questions use an instant text-chat feature to get answers from agents almost immediately.

At its core and despite all our technological advances, customer service involves human interaction between the customer and the company representative. The customer's perception of the service is directly affected by the nature of that interaction, which is directly affected by the skills of the company's customer service personnel—online or on-land.

[6]Margaret Heller, "Should Management Read Employee E-Mail?" *CIO* (May 2002): 248.

There are certain guiding principles that online customer service must still follow:

- *Respect customers.* Regard them as people who don't want to be deceived and who don't want to be interrupted by phone calls.
- *Build databases, but without violating a customer's privacy.* Always ask permission when requesting personal customer data and explain why you need certain information from customers.
- *Learn the importance of loyalty.* Loyalty prevents customer defection. Loyalty means staying with a company even after it makes a mistake. This act, however, is contingent on the company's doing a quick job of fixing problems.
- *Remember that the Internet makes word of mouth a mass medium.* There is much more at stake if an online customer becomes dissatisfied. Today, instead of telling only 15 persons face to face about a bad customer experience, customers can now easily share the information via monitor screens and the Internet with 1,500 to 15,000 individuals at once. Be honest and fair-minded while interacting in customer situations to minimize dissatisfaction and ill feelings, while resolving any problems that arise.

## Summary

- Customers today expect the ability to buy merchandise and services anywhere, anytime, and anyhow they want.
- Customer service is still a universal principle of good business, whether online or on-land.
- Used properly, technology offers opportunities for customer service that a traditional store cannot supply.
- The Internet allows a company the opportunity to be in direct communication with every one of its customers.
- Customers increasingly make buying decisions on their own, without vendors exercising any formal role.
- Top customer complaints about online shopping are slow web sites, unavailable products, late deliveries, and an inability to track order status.
- E-commerce trends include an increase in multichannel selling, a rise in satisfied online customers, and companies that are generating more profits than before going online.

- Customer relationship management is more than technology; it involves a change in philosophy and attitudes about doing business.
- Customer relationship management software allows a company to collect information about customers and to consolidate that database of information, so that it is integrated and available through numerous company channels and systems.
- The traditional call center is evolving into a multichannel customer interaction center, which integrates wired and soon to be largely wireless channels of customer contact.
- Today's sophisticated buyers want e-mail, chat rooms, Internet audio, and well-trained e-reps behind e-services.
- Employee monitoring is the use of computers or other electronic devices to observe, record, and review an individual's performance on the job.

## QUESTIONS FOR CRITICAL THINKING

1. What advantages do online stores provide that traditional stores do not?

2. What does current research identify as the extent to which online businesses are growing?

3. In your opinion, what are two major challenges facing companies that are involved in e-commerce?

4. To what extent do you think multichannel retailing is affecting the manner in which business operates?

5. Why are companies increasing their implementation of customer relationship management strategies?

6. Describe the multichannel communication methods you, your family, and your friends have used recently when buying online and receiving customer service.

7. Relative to the additional skills required of e-reps (as compared with the basic skill set needed by a CSR), do you think e-reps should be paid more, or is the acquisition of additional skills a normal part of most jobs?

8. What are the advantages to a company that regularly electronically monitors employee performance?

## On-line Research Activities

### Project 11.1: Growth of Online Product and Service Companies

Research a number of web sites and locate several articles on *the growth of online product and service companies.* As a result of your research, develop a simple chart (using computer software or by hand) showing trends of growth over the past five years.

### Project 11.2: Customer Relationship Management Software 💻

#### Situation

James Woo, vice president of human resources and customer relations at On-Time Technology Products, needs up-to-the-minute research on the advantages and disadvantages of incorporating customer relationship management strategies and software into the company and, more specifically, of adding those costs to next year's budget. He must get his recommendation to President Collin MacGibson within the week to be considered in next year's budget.

*Enter "Customer Relationship Management" in your favorite search engine. Using file PRJ11-2 on your student CD, key responses in the following table format that first will inform Mr. Woo which web sites contain information on the use of and/or advantages to businesses of using customer relationship management strategies and software. From your research, enter in the second and third columns, respectively, three advantages and three disadvantages that Mr. Woo should consider prior to making a CRM recommendation to Mr. MacGibson.*

| Web Sites | Advantages of CRM | Disadvantages of CRM |
|-----------|-------------------|----------------------|
| 1. | 1. | 1. |
| 2. | 2. | 2. |
| 3. | 3. | 3. |

## Communication Skills at Work

### Project 11.3: Multichannel Communication Methods 💻

Conduct a survey of your family and friends who shop online to determine the extent to which 20 people use multichannel communication methods when shopping online with retail establishments.

*Retrieve file PRJ11–3 on the student CD and complete the following form by breaking out the number of users in column 2 and writing a statement relative to the implications of such usage per method in column 3.*

| Communication Method | Number of Users | Implications |
|----------------------|-----------------|--------------|
| 1. E-mail | | |
| 2. Chat rooms | | |
| 3. Instant messaging | | |
| 4. 800-phone numbers | | |
| 5. Wireless communication devices | | |
| 6. Internet audio | | |

## Decision Making at Work

### Project 11.4: Employee Monitoring

RosaLee, a longtime e-rep, just found out today that, for the past three months, she has been monitored at work. Although she knew her company did such things, she never thought, because of her stellar reputation and demonstrated hard work, that she would be one her company wanted to monitor. She is very angry and offended and has called you (a good friend). On the phone, she sounds as if she is close to tears.

*Respond to the following questions:*

1. If you were in RosaLee's situation, would you feel the same way she does? Explain.

_____

_____

_____

_____

2. What are the advantages to an organization of monitoring employees' performance on the job?

_____

_____

_____

_____

_____

3. What are the advantages to employees of having their on-the-job performance monitored?

_____

_____

_____

_____

_____

## Case Study

### 11.1 "No Web Site Sales for My Company!"

Dudley and Sherol, retirees in their early sixties and co-owners of Sun City West Golf Carts, have been approached by a computer service company to develop a web site for their rather modest company. Dudley's first reaction is "We are fine the way we are. We don't need any more money from selling on that darn Internet. We can do business the same way we've been doing it for the past five years, in person and with hours we want to work in order to oversee our sales staff!"

On the other hand, his wife, Sherol, thinks there may be advantages they should consider when setting up a web site to have multiple channels for sales of their golf carts.

#### Questions

1. *Is Dudley's reaction to the suggestion for a web site typical of someone his age and station in life? Explain.*

_____

_____

_____

2. *What are two advantages Sherol might suggest to her husband for developing an e-commerce site?*

_____

_____

_____

_____

3. *If you were advising both of them about building a web site, what would you say?*

_____

_____

_____

_____

## Case Study

### 11.2 Hiring the Best E-Rep

On-Time Technology Products recently advertised for an e-rep; the company hopes the new e-rep will start on the job within the next few weeks. This is a new slant on the Customer Service Department, which formerly hired only CSRs. Of the 10 candidates who have applied, the following 3 applicants have been screened as the top candidates to be interviewed:

Candidate A is a former two-year employee of a competitor. She has excellent communication and keyboarding skills and a great customer attitude; however, she indicates on her application that she is technology illiterate.

Candidate B is a recent high school graduate with a GPA of 3.8 and plans to be a part-time student majoring in computer information systems at the local community college. She has taken several business courses and was in Honors English class throughout high school. She needs this job to work her way through college and to help with expenses in caring for her invalid mother.

Candidate C is a current CSR at On-Time Technology Products who has been with the company for three years. She has excellent communication skills and loves working with computers. It is rumored that she has told others that, if she doesn't get this job, she will quit and go to work for On-Time Technology Products' major competitor. Over the past three months, she has received two customer complaints for not following up as promised and for shouting at a customer.

#### Questions

1. *What criteria would you use to select the top candidate for the e-rep position at On-Time Technology Products?*

_____

2. *In your opinion, who are the top two candidates?*

_____

3. *Which candidate would you recommend hiring and why?*

_____

_____

# CHAPTER XII

# Using Technology to Communicate with Customers

*A new idea is first condemned as ridiculous, and then dismissed as trivial, until finally it becomes what everybody knows.*

WILLIAM JAMES

## OBJECTIVES

**AFTER COMPLETING THIS CHAPTER, YOU WILL BE ABLE TO:**

1. Describe the use of web-based technologies in customer service departments.

2. Identify the advantages to organizations of using the business-to-consumer e-commerce model.

3. Discuss some design principles when developing a web site.

4. List some advantages and disadvantages of exchanging messages with customers through e-mail.

5. Explain the importance of netiquette while using the Internet with customers.

6. Describe the application of instant messaging and chats when serving customers online.

The Ford Customer Service Division has a representative that fields questions from dealership technicians (internal customers) 24 hours a day, 7 days a week—without stopping to eat or to sleep. We are talking about Ernie, a *virtual* representative that fields e-mail questions on the Ford dealer web site, giving answers in plain sentences, just as a human representative would do. The goal is for Ernie to be able to answer 70 to 80 percent of the questions and to refer questions he cannot answer to his human counterparts at the Ford call center.[1]

The software Ford uses saves the call center time because the "live" CSR receives a transcript of the online dialogue; the technician does not have to repeat the inquiry a second time. Although this is an example of technology to the extreme, it is good to recognize that organizations are spending money and customizing their software in order to provide round-the-clock assistance and service to both external and internal customers.

Many consumers now rely on the Internet for product research, daily purchases, bill payments, and communication with customer service representatives via e-mail. That's leading some companies to deploy sophisticated customer service tools that can filter and sort e-mail messages,

---

[1] Donna Harris, "Ernie Is Chatty, a Know-It-All, and Ford Likes Him Like That," *Automotive News* (June 4, 2001): 22.

provide a sophisticated knowledge base, and introduce advanced call center tools that are seamlessly integrated with the Web. As a result, customers can chat with a specialist online or click a button in the browser and receive a call back within seconds. Some systems also allow a CSR to synchronize browsers and then walk a person through a web site by pushing web pages to the customer's computer that are needed in order to make a sound buying decision.

This chapter discusses the technology used to communicate with customers and the importance and effective use of web sites. Special communication considerations when serving customers using fax, e-mail, and other Internet activities are also discussed.

## Identifying Customer Service Web-Based Technologies

The Internet has opened plenty of options for providing exceptional customer service. Companies use the following methods to serve customers through web-based technologies:

- *E-mail* allows a customer to send a message quickly and effortlessly. Companies that have a system to filter, route, manage, and respond to incoming messages are able to serve customers more quickly.

- *Instant messaging and chats* allow a customer to engage in one-on-one, real-time text chat with a customer service representative by simply clicking a button.

- *FAQs* permit customers to quickly view online the most common product and service issues through a list of frequently asked questions. Since 80 percent of the questions handled by live customer service representatives in an online environment are routine, automated responses to these repetitive queries makes a lot of sense.

- *Knowledge base* offers current and detailed information about products and services that customers can access instantly through a natural language query.

- *Online forums* allow users to share information and post responses to one another in an online discussion group. These discussions are not in real-time the way chats and instant messages are. Instead, they are referred to as threaded discussions, ongoing over a few days as the need exists.

- *Voice call-back* permits customers to click a button at the customer service site and receive a call back from an e-rep in a call center. A variation is IP telephony, which works directly through the computer's Internet connection as a phone call.

## Considering Web Site Issues and Design

E-commerce has changed the way organizations serve customers and, in general, how people carry out an assortment of business-oriented activities each day. Electronic commerce, also known as **e-commerce,** is a financial business transaction that occurs over an electronic network, such as the Internet. It requires a business to have a web site. Conducting business online virtually eliminates the barriers of time and distance that slow down traditional in-person transactions. Now, with business-to-consumer e-commerce, purchase transactions occur instantaneously at any time and from anyplace in the world.

### Business-to-Consumer E-Commerce

A popular use of e-commerce by consumers is known as **business-to-consumer** (**B-to-C** or **B2C**) **e-commerce.** B-to-C consists of the sale of goods and services from a business entity to a consumer or the general public. For example, a customer (consumer) visits an online business through its web site, also known as an **electronic storefront.** An electronic storefront contains text and graphic descriptions of products and services and a **shopping cart,** which allows the customer to collect purchases electronically. When ready to complete the sale, the customer simply enters personal and financial data through a secure web connection and completes the sale. Fulfillment of the order and delivery are the final steps.

Businesses that use a B-to-C e-commerce model eliminate the middleman. They sell products directly to consumers without using traditional retail channels. This enables some B-to-C companies to sell products at a lower cost and with faster service than a comparable bricks-and-mortar business that has a physical location where consumers must go to shop.

Not only do businesses derive benefits from this online B-to-C business model, but consumers do as well. Consumers have access to a variety of products and services

An online purchase allows consumers to complete a purchase in a matter of minutes from anywhere and at any time.

The best electronic storefronts plan for convenience. They are efficient and easy to use. Consumers want to navigate easily and quickly through a site with instructions that are clear and easy to follow. Studies indicate that Web customers will click to another site if they must wait more than eight seconds for an item, an image, or a page to download to the screen.[2] Furthermore, the fewer clicks it takes for a customer to find a product and place an order, the more sales an online store will make.

In designing a web site, several questions must be asked and thoughtfully considered by an e-organization:

1. *What is the purpose of the web site?* Is it simply to provide information or to support a complete line of e-commerce functions, such as marketing, selling, information, and customer service?

2. *What graphics are needed to capture and maintain customer interest?* A web site should be easy to navigate and require no more than three clicks to access key data, such as company address and phone number, as well as a customer support link. It is critical to design a web site so that the download speeds of the design elements are acceptable.

3. *How easy is it to navigate and perform search functions?* The site should allow visitors to move back and forth from the current page to other pages. It should have a link to the site map and easy pull-down menus. These features allow the customer to go directly to the content desired or to be easily linked to other related content sites and web pages.

without the constraints of time or distance, and they can easily comparison shop to find the best buy in a matter of a few minutes. Many B-to-C web sites also provide consumer services, such as access to product reviews, chat rooms, and other product-related information that helps when making informed buying decisions.

## Creating an E-Commerce Web Site

With the Internet offering such tremendous business potential, many consumers and companies are venturing into the worldwide horizon. Depending on the nature of the existing business, the approach used to establish an online presence varies. The goal of a successful web site is to attract customers and keep them returning to the site for additional products. Guideline 12.1 lists factors that lead to e-loyalty and can affect whether an e-commerce customer will return to place future orders.

[2]Gary Shelly, Thomas Cashman & Misty Vermeat, *Discovering Computers 2003*, Thomson/Course Technology, Boston, MA, 2002.

4. *Will customers feel secure with the buying experience?* To enhance this feeling of safety, tell customers when they are in secure transactions and that transmitted data will be protected through encryption during transmission. Provide all options from credit cards to online shopping carts, because poor checkout experiences cause people to abandon shopping in the middle of their e-purchases.

5. *Is the web site fun, current, interactive, and interesting?* Stay current by updating the web site with new information at least once a week or more often. At the same time, check for any broken links and fix them immediately. Customers are busy people and resent having their time wasted.

## Service after an Online Sale

Surveys indicate that a large percentage of customers are dissatisfied with customer service at online businesses. Online businesses, therefore, need to consider carefully how to provide service after the sale. Following up with a customer after a sale can generate return business and thoughtful recommendations for improvement. E-retailers can improve after-the-sale communication by

- Using technology to activate an automatic e-mail message that confirms orders within minutes of placing them
- Displaying a list of frequently asked questions (FAQs)
- Sending online surveys to receive customer feedback quickly
- Answering customer queries speedily and accurately
- Offering live chat rooms for sales assistance
- Providing a means for customers to track shipments
- Establishing return policies that allow customers to make returns and exchanges quickly and conveniently

Many e-commerce sites use e-mail publishing to keep in touch with customers, in addition to the methods just mentioned. **E-mail publishing** is the process of sending newsletters via e-mail to a large group of people with similar interests. For example, an e-retailer can use e-mail publishing to offer loyal customers discounts and promotions, to announce new products, or to deliver industry news.

How does this work? Increasingly, B-to-C businesses create **electronic customer profiles.** These profiles collect buyer information by tracking preferences as consumers browse through the web pages. This individu-

alized profile then enables the B-to-C business to target advertisements, determine customer needs, and personalize offerings to a particular customer.

### CUSTOMER SERVICE TIP

**12.1** *It is much easier to offend or hurt someone in an e-mail message. That is why it is important to be as clear and concise as possible to avoid misunderstandings.*

## Messaging Customers with E-Mail

The recent growth of the use of e-mail in customer service areas has been phenomenal. The following are most significant reasons for the rapid growth of e-mail messaging:

- E-mail eliminates **telephone tag,** or the problem of trying to contact busy people who are not always available for telephone calls.
- Conversely, e-mail saves time. Consumers are protected from the interruptions of traditional telephone calls while they are attending to other matters.
- E-mail speeds up the process of making business decisions, because it permits rapid exchanges from all parties involved in the decisions.
- E-mail is inexpensive. It permits unlimited use at no more than the cost of an Internet connection.

It is prudent to mention that e-mail is not without its disadvantages. The following drawbacks stand out:

- E-mail is not confidential. Some describe e-mail as just about as private as a postcard you drop in the mailbox.
- E-mail does not communicate the sender's emotions well. Voice intonations, facial expressions, body movements, and such are not a part of the message, when compared with communicating on the telephone or face to face.
- E-mail may be ignored or delayed. The volume of e-mail often makes it difficult for some respondents to read and act on all of their messages.

Guideline 12.2 describes some common e-mail terms that have evolved over time and their appropriate use in customer messages. These terms are *emoticons, abbreviations, flame, shouting,* and *bounced message.*

GUIDELINE **12.2** **Common E-Mail Terms**

| | |
|---|---|
| Emoticons | Emoticons, also called smileys, are characters that express emotions and gestures in messages. They represent human faces if you turn them sideways. These are not advised for use in business e-mail messages. |
| Abbreviations | Abbreviations are commonly used in electronic messages to save time as you type. For example, BTW means by the way. FYI means for your information. Again, these casual abbreviations are not advised for use in business e-mail messages to customers. |
| Flame | A flame is an angry or insulting message directed at one person. A flame war is an argument that continues for a while. Avoid starting or participating in flame wars. Certainly, it is never appropriate to flame customers. |
| Shouting | A message written in capital letters is annoying and hard to read. This format is called shouting. Always use upper and lowercase letters when typing messages to customers, just as you would do in normal correspondence. |
| Bounced Message | A bounced message is a message that is returned to you because it cannot reach its destination. A message usually bounces because of typing mistakes in the e-mail address. Before sending a message, remember to check for correctness and any typos you may have made. |

## The Use and Misuse of E-Mail

The use of e-mail has revolutionized the way the working world communicates. We continue to learn more about how to use it efficiently. For example, scrolling through e-mail as it arrives is a big time waster. Instead, set aside certain times each day to read e-mail and act on each message.

E-mail is used to save time, not diminish professionalism and the proper use of writing. Although writing e-mail messages was covered in Chapter 10, the following are some tips you may wish to review:

- *Place deadlines in the subject line.* You grab attention and increase comprehension by putting deadlines in the subject line as well as in the body of the message.
- *Refrain from using a salutation.* Many writers save time with quick salutations, such as "Greetings" or simply by addressing the message to the recipient's name.

- *Frontload the main idea.* Give recipients the main idea of the message in the first paragraph. Support the main idea with details in the middle paragraphs and end with any action items or requests.
- *Use common e-mail features effectively:*
  - Reply to a message: You can reply to a customer's message when answering questions or supplying additional information.
  - Forward a message: When you receive a message and read its contents, you may think of someone else who would be interested in reading the message. E-mail programs allow you to send a copy of the message, along with your comments, to another person.
  - Delete a message: You can delete a message you no longer need. This prevents mail from accumulating in your electronic mailbox.
  - Store a message: You can store important messages so that you can review them later. Storing messages also provides a paper trail of a transaction, which can be very useful documentation. E-mail programs permit you to create folders to organize all your stored messages.
  - Print a message: You can print a message to produce a paper copy.

An audit of 79 online retailers found that, although consumers' average wait for e-mail replies is 12 hours, only 40 percent of questions are answered accurately, compared with 63 percent for questions answered correctly by staff over the telephone.[3] The point is that customers who make inquiries by e-mail often tire of waiting for a reply and pick up the phone instead. This action forces companies to pursue customer service on two fronts instead of one.

## ETHICS/CHOICES

**12.1** What if you worked in a Customer Service Department with a young person who had just graduated from high school, and she found it amusing to chat with friends and to speckle her e-mails to customers with "smileys." Would you say anything to her or your supervisor?

---

[3]"E-Mail Response Says It All," *Inc.* (April 1, 2001): 36.

Employers are learning the hard way that the estimated 1.3 trillion e-mail messages sent every year make up a visible and potentially perilous communication medium. Following are some examples of e-mail communication pitfalls—both practical and legal:

- Based on incorrect assumptions of privacy, e-mail users write things they would never even say aloud, much less say in a business record that may be saved, forwarded, and printed.

- Employees (and even highly placed executives) use startlingly candid or flippant language, without realizing that "delete" doesn't mean gone. In fact, the document can be produced years later in a courtroom, because the e-mail messages still reside on the computer server until Information Technology Department personnel choose to delete them permanently.

- E-mail is more conversational than face-to-face communication and is often sent in haste. Loose language, slang, and inappropriate jargon compound communication problems. Further, the send button is often pressed too quickly without an adequate or careful rereading of the message. This results in messages that readers often interpret as inappropriate in tone or wording.

## CUSTOMER SERVICE TIP

**12.2** *Return e-mails in the same amount of time that you would return a phone call.*

## E-Mail Etiquette and Safeguard Considerations

A U.S. Department of Commerce report says that more than half of the nation is now online.[4] **Netiquette,** which is short for Internet etiquette, is a code of acceptable behaviors that users should follow while on the Internet. Netiquette includes rules for all aspects of the Internet, including the World Wide Web, e-mail, chat rooms, instant messaging, and discussion forums.

**E-mail etiquette** is a set of dos and don'ts that are recommended by business and communication experts

in response to the growing concern that people are not using their Internet's e-mail feature appropriately. E-mail etiquette offers some guidelines that CSRs can use to facilitate better communication between themselves and their customers. Since e-mail is part of the virtual world of communication, many people communicate in their e-mail messages the same way they do in virtual chat rooms—with much less formality and, at times, too aggressively.

One overall point to remember is that an e-mail message does not have nonverbal expression to supplement what we are saying. Most of the time, we make judgments about a person's motives and intentions based on his or her tone of voice, gestures, and body language. When those clues are absent, it is more difficult to figure out what the message sender really means.

Before clicking the send button on your e-mail, it is always important to know who will receive your e-mail. This helps in two ways. First, it helps you think about the tone of your writing. For example, you will want to follow the traditional rules of writing, but e-mails you send to external customers will probably be more formal and brief, whereas e-mails to an internal customer or colleague might be less formal. Second, it helps to decide whether you need to use a person's title or if writing the first name or using a generic greeting is more appropriate.

Despite the fact that you may send an e-mail to someone privately, remember that e-mails are public documents. Therefore, include only statements that you can openly defend, should your e-mail message be circulated or shown to nonintended parties.

Three ways companies can minimize the rise of e-mail abuse and can safeguard its best and highest use is for companies to enact policies, to enforce them consistently, and to educate employees and managers on what is and is not appropriate when using company e-mail. When using a business e-mail system, all employees should bear in mind these pieces of advice:

- The employer owns the e-mail. All messages created, sent, or received using a company system remain the property of the employer.
- The e-mail system is for business communications only. Personal business is unauthorized and should be conducted at home, rather than at work.

---

[4]Brian Sullivan, "Netiquette," *Computerworld* (March 4, 2002): 48.

- Offensive and inflammatory messages are strictly prohibited. These actions can be grounds for termination in some organizations.

- The use of passwords does not indicate that a message is confidential or that the company will not be able to intercept it.

- Send an immediate reply to each person who sends an e-mail message. In essence, your message should convey "We received your message, and we promise to respond within one business day."

## ETHICS/CHOICES

**12.2** In your opinion, is it right for companies to create electronic profiles on customers' preferences as a result of web sites visited and forms completed when buying merchandise?

## Other Customer Messaging Systems

Although e-mail appears to be the online communication medium of choice, other means of communicating with customers also exist. Internet Protocol Private Branch Exchange Systems, instant messages and chat rooms, and fax documents are increasingly used by customer service representatives to communicate with customers.

### Internet Protocol Private Branch Exchange Systems

Today, low-cost call centers funnel e-mails, web inquiries, and phone calls through a single computer that blends the power of the Internet with the muscle of a corporate telephone system. At first glimpse, these call centers seem rather mundane, because they consist only of standard desktop computers, digital phones with small screens, and software; however, the ability of call center equipment—known as Internet Protocol Private Branch Exchange Systems, or IP-PBXs—to route inquiries automatically means that fewer customers get lost in the shuffle.

IP-PBXs can also do clever things such as redirect calls to home-office workers without getting the phone company or an information technology staff person involved. Their most dazzling feature is a popup computer screen window, which, once programmed, reveals the name and sales his-

tory of each incoming caller or e-mail message sender. This element allows CSRs to begin personalized service at the start of each customer contact.

## CUSTOMER SERVICE TIP

**12.3** *According to Frost and Sullivan Research, online customer service sales will grow to $800 million by 2007, up from $94 million in 2000.*[5]

## Instant Messages and Chat Rooms

For many people, shopping alone is not as much fun as interacting with someone during the experience. Customers are starting to use instant messages and chat room technologies to share the buying experience. **Instant messaging (IM)** is a real-time Internet communications service that notifies you when one or more people are online and then allows you to exchange messages or files or to join a private chat room with them. Instant messaging, a kind of super e-mail, allows two or more people to hold a real-time, typed conversation online. First introduced by America Online in 1997, the technology is now enjoyed by 40 percent of the U.S. online population, up from 27 percent in 1999, according to researchers at Cyber Dialog.[6]

Devotees of instant messaging spend 15 hours a week online, compared with 11.5 hours for average users. The advantage of IM for customers is that, when they have a question prior to finalizing a buying decision, they send a message to an e-rep in the Customer Service Department and get a quick reply.

Too many companies defeat the point of good customer service by not having enough reps on hand to keep impatient surfers from clicking away while waiting for a response. Successful online retailers have learned that live messaging and chats boost sales in an instant. The essence of this technology is simple. It consists of just two components:

1. *Synchronicity* involves the ability for two people to exchange information in real time.

---

[5]Customer Care Institute Factoids. http://www.customercare.com/library/research/studies.htm

[6]"Chat Me Up...Please," *Business Week* (March 19, 2001): 10.

2. *Presence awareness* lets you know whether your correspondent is online or disconnected. It can even let you know if that person is away from the desk or is typing you a message.

How does instant messaging help CSRs? IM allows you to collaborate with colleagues in the following ways that improve customer service:

- You can send a message to a colleague for help with a query as you are answering a customer's request.
- You can inform colleagues of an incoming call, allowing them to end a less important call.
- You can send a message to more than one colleague at a time for information while serving a customer.

## Fax Documents

A **facsimile machine (fax)** is a device that transmits and receives documents over telephone lines. Fax documents can contain text, drawings, or photographs. At a time when e-mail is dominating written communication and Internet documents are replacing hard-copy forms in business, faxes can seem like a throwback to a time when everything was hardwired and nobody had heard yet of e-commerce.

What's keeping fax not merely alive but active in the face of competing technologies is the sheer number and pervasive use of fax machines. E-mail and the Internet probably will erode fax volume in the United States, but that's not the case elsewhere. In a global customer service economy, the use of fax machines is exploding in Latin America and Europe and shows no sign of slowing down. The main reasons, of course, are that Internet access is not nearly as available in those regions, along with telecommunications and technology that are still quite costly. Today, companies in America must keep fax equipment if for no other reason than to communicate with their foreign trading partners.[7]

Faster is better, and one of the key tools for life in the fast lane is a new trend in faxing called the Internet fax. In Internet faxing, the service provider supplies the user with a personal fax number, which is tied to the user's e-mail account. Faxes sent to that number are received as e-mail

In a global customer service economy, fax machines continue to transmit documents around the world.

attachments in the user's e-mail. Sending a fax, therefore, is as simple as addressing an e-mail or printing a document to the fax machine's phone number. The result is an amazingly fast and flexible personal fax system.

## Concluding Message for CSRs

For years, customer communications have been funneled into well-staffed and highly automated call centers with phones. Online customers, however, have changed that, and today Customer Service Departments are swamped with e-customers. The greatest advantage of companies keeping up-to-date on their e-mail is they have a chance of staying ahead of the competition.

E-business and e-commerce are evolving rapidly, if not explosively. The Internet and the Web level the playing field, making it possible even for small companies to quickly establish a business presence in worldwide markets and to serve customers in a way not previously imagined. No doubt about it, web-based technologies are the way of the future. Employees who have the skills to effectively communicate with customers online will be the ones who reap the most rewards now and in the future.

---

[7]Bob Mueller, "Competing Technologies: No Match for Fax," *Purchasing* (February 22, 2001): 25.

# Summary

- Many consumers rely on the Internet for product research, daily purchases, bill payments, and communication with customer service representatives via e-mail and other methods.

- Companies make available the following communication web-based technologies when serving e-customer needs: e-mail, instant messaging and chats, FAQs, knowledgebases, online forums, and voice call-back systems.

- E-commerce is a financial business transaction that occurs over an electronic network.

- Business-to-consumer e-commerce consists of the sale of goods and services from a business entity to a consumer or the general public.

- The goal of a successful dot-com web site is to attract customers and keep them returning to the site for additional products.

- Following up with a customer after a sale can generate return business and thoughtful recommendations for improvement.

- E-mail is the exchange of text messages and computer files transmitted via a communications network, such as a local area network or the Internet.

- Netiquette is a code of acceptable behaviors that users should follow while on the Internet.

- Although e-mail appears to be the online communication medium of choice, Internet Protocol Private Branch Exchange Systems, instant messages and chat rooms, and fax documents are also used to communicate with customers.

- Instant messaging is a real-time Internet communications service that notifies you when one or more people are online and then allows you to exchange typed messages or files with them.

## QUESTIONS FOR CRITICAL THINKING

1. Of all the web-based technologies used in Customer Service Departments, which two do you think are the most efficient from the standpoint of a consumer?

2. Why do organizations use the business-to-consumer e-commerce model? In your opinion, will more businesses sell to customers using this approach?

3. Using the design principles in developing a web site that were covered in this chapter, locate and provide the web addresses of two companies that you think best follow these principles.

4. From a customer's point of view, what are the top advantages of using e-mail to send messages to companies?

5. Of what value are the rules of netiquette to consumers who use the Internet?

6. In your opinion, are there differences between consumers' use of instant messaging and chats to buy products and their use of these technologies to share information with friends and family?

## Project 12.1: Debate the Issue: Electronic Customer Service

Research a number of web sites and locate several articles about *customers' acceptance of electronic-oriented customer service.* As a result of your research, role-play with a fellow student the pros and cons of companies using technology to communicate with customers.

## Project 12.2: Web Site Design Considerations 🖥

### Situation

President Collin MacGibson at On-Time Technology Products wants to develop an effective web site for his company to sell to and communicate with customers. You are among several employees he would like to serve on a team to develop ideas and guidelines for the home page.

*Enter "Web Site Design Considerations" in your favorite search engine. Using file PRJ12-2 on your student CD, key responses in the following table format that first will offer Mr. MacGibson three web sites to visit that are good examples of strong online pages. From your research, enter in column 2 some suggestions to consider when developing the web site relative to the design features listed. Place your suggestions to the right of each design feature.*

| Good Web sites | Design Suggestions for Web Site Features |
|---|---|
| 1. | 1. Use of graphics: |
| 2. | 2. Ease of navigation: |
| 3. | 3. Interesting and fun web site: |

## Project 12.3: E-Mail In-Service Seminar Materials 🖥

Assume you have been asked to put together a list of seven training topics you think would be appropriate to cover in a seminar entitled "Use of Company E-Mail Systems."

*Retrieve file PRJ12-3 on the student CD and complete the following form by recommending seven topics you feel should be covered in an in-service seminar at On-Time Technology Products. In column 2, state the reasons or justification for including the topic as part of the training.*

| Training Topic | Justification for Training Topic |
|---|---|
| 1. | |
| 2. | |
| 3. | |
| 4. | |
| 5. | |
| 6. | |
| 7. | |

## Decision Making at Work

### Project 12.4: Replacing Traditional Forms of Business Communications

In a recent survey, respondents compared e-mail with the more traditional forms of business communication. Each of the following three statements indicates part of the survey results.

*Respond to the following survey results. Do you believe the results are accurate, relative to the way that business correspondence is changing?*

1. Eighty percent said that e-mail has replaced *airmail* (snail mail) for the majority of their business correspondence.

_____

_____

_____

_____

_____

2. Seventy-three percent say that e-mail has replaced *faxing* for the majority of their business correspondence.

_____

_____

_____

_____

_____

3. Forty-five percent say that e-mail has replaced *phone calls* for the majority of their business correspondence.

_____

_____

_____

_____

_____

_____

_____

## Case Study

### 12.1 Online Sales Lost

Sammy Jimenez, a rather spirited colleague at On-Time Technology Products, took to work a recent Datamonitor report estimating that more than $6 billion in online product sales was lost last year in the United States due to inadequate customer service, costing businesses dearly in terms of sales and customer goodwill.

#### Questions

*1. Do your own research to either support or refute this statistic. Cite your reasons.*

_____

_____

_____

_____

_____

*2. If this report is to be believed, should American businesses be concerned?*

_____

_____

_____

_____

*3. What can you recommend that businesses do to improve online sales and customer goodwill?*

_____

_____

_____

_____

_____

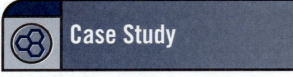

## Case Study

### 12.2 After-Sales Support

On-Time Technology Products recognizes it does not do enough to connect with customers after a sale. Beyond extending a warranty and maintaining a technical support call center, it has done little else in this important customer support area.

#### Questions

*1. What are some techniques you would recommend On-Time Technology Products incorporate in their quest to go beyond their current offerings of after-sales support?*

_____

_____

_____

_____

_____

_____

_____

_____

*2. In your opinion, in what ways can the Internet more effectively provide some innovative methods to support an after-sales transaction?*

_____

_____

_____

_____

_____

_____

_____

# CHAPTER XIII

**13**

# The Future of Delivering Superior Customer Service

*Do less than customers expect and service is perceived as bad. Do exactly what customers expect and service is perceived as good. . . . But do more than customers expect and service is perceived as superior.*

JOHN TSCHOHL

## OBJECTIVES

**AFTER COMPLETING THIS CHAPTER,
YOU WILL BE ABLE TO:**

1. Explain the role of management in customer-oriented cultures.

2. Give examples of measurable standards in customer service.

3. Describe the working environment for most customer service representatives.

4. Identify reasons companies should train, empower, and reward service professionals.

5. Cite customer situations in which role-playing serves as an effective training method.

6. Suggest ways that companies can recognize and reward a CSR.

7. List four factors that have an impact on employee retention and encourage loyalty on the job.

8. Describe the talents that a good customer service manager demonstrates.

Looking to the future is always exciting and fun. Companies that attribute their success to exemplary customer service do so as a result of setting realistic and forward-looking goals and standards, which serve and value customers. These companies give more than just words to the importance of training, empowering, and rewarding customer service representatives. Chapter 13 discusses those areas, as well as the role of managing the effectiveness of customer service areas in organizations.

## Setting Standards in Customer Service

Successful companies are made, not born. Setting standards, or benchmarks, in customer service doesn't just evolve. Standards are painstakingly conceived and delivered with care. In successful companies, the employees appear to be a cut above others because they are courteous and always seem to be smiling. In addition, service professionals in these companies never fail to ask if they can be of assistance.

They always seem to be having a great deal of fun doing the job. These employees achieve a higher level of productivity for their employer. Was their employer just fortunate to have that many happy and enthusiastic employees apply for jobs? Assuming that's not the case, how did it happen?

## CUSTOMER SERVICE TIP

**13.1** *Here's a simple secret of serving customers: Find out what they want, and how they want it, and give it to them just that way!*

## The Role of Management

A customer-oriented culture starts at the top and is consistently reinforced throughout all levels of management. Good managers are responsible for hiring employees with great attitudes. These managers must work very hard to create a workplace environment where these employees are satisfied. By the same token, it might also be surmised that, to arrive at this core group of cheerful and enthusiastic employees, these companies have hired and fired numerous employees who did not meet their expectations.

There are two keys to an organization's success: solid customer relationships combined with trusted performance, which is delivered accurately and on time. These cornerstones to success are not new; they have been true for many years. What has changed is this: Technology has increased the speed of information and production. It has also brought efficiencies and has heightened customer demand and requirements. When organizations today draft their company mission statements, specifically with regard to the customer service activity, the mission statements

- Articulate what the Customer Service Department is expected to contribute to overall company's goals
- Provide guidelines for the behavior of various departments involved in customer service situations
- Provide a sense of identity, continuity, and pride in customer service representatives

Customer Service Departments need direction also and usually write their own mission statement. Of course, departmental goals are always aligned with those of the organization. An example of a strong mission statement particular to a Customer Service Department follows:

The mission of the Customer Service Department at XYZ Company is to establish, maintain, and improve the company's position in the marketplace through developing strategies for customer retention and new account growth by providing high levels of service offered to customers, prospective customers, and the general public.

As we can see, the overriding purpose of Customer Service Departments is to satisfy customers. Conventional wisdom says an organization must have satisfied customers if it is to survive. According to study results published in the *Journal of Retailing*, satisfied customers are pleased with an organization's delivery in five ways: tangibles, reliability, responsiveness, assurance, and empathy:

1. *Tangibles* are the physical aspects of a service experience, such as the appearance of the facility and staff, as well as any written communication items, such as letters, e-mails, flyers, and advertisements. In short, this is the image that an organization projects.

2. *Reliability* means performing the promised service dependably and accurately, keeping promises, and doing it right the first time.

3. *Responsiveness* refers to the timeliness of service and the willingness of service personnel to help. The loyalty factor is set in motion when an organization responds to a customer's need before he or she even realizes that a need exists. In addition, when an organization goes above and beyond the call of duty in responding to a customer request, customers feel well served.

4. *Assurance* is the knowledge, courtesy, and professionalism of the service specialist that builds a customer's trust. Ensuring that customer service representatives are knowledgeable requires that an organization invest in effective training initiatives on a continuous basis.

5. *Empathy* is the caring and individualized service that makes a customer feel valued. Acts such as remembering customers' names and their likes and dislikes build loyal customers.[1]

## Standards for Customer Service

Exceptional customer service must be a primary business goal and core value of an organization. This commitment is reflected in company policies, procedures, and standards.

---

[1]"Customer Service Doesn't Cut It Anymore," *Journal of Retailing* (Spring 2001): 12.

**Standards** tell workers what is expected of them, both in the quality and in the quantity of their work. When organizations have a baseline of service performance standards, they deliver, regardless of who the customer is or the amount of the purchase. In customer service, there are three commonly used work standards based on production, accuracy, and performance. Examples of each one appear in Guideline 13.1.

| GUIDELINE 13.1 Examples of Customer Service Work Standards | |
| --- | --- |
| **Work Standards** | **Examples** |
| Production work standards | • Complete X number of work units in a specified time frame. |
| Standards of accuracy | • Error rate should be no greater than a specified number per 1,000 transactions. |
| Standards of performance | • Attitude toward customers should be enthusiastic, empathetic, confident, tactful, and professional. |
| | • Information provided to customers must be accurate. |
| | • Paperwork and call backs to customers must be completed in a timely manner. |
| | • Demonstrate a willingness to cooperate and lend assistance to other areas when asked in order to achieve departmental and company goals. |

In organizations, customer service begins with hiring the right people.

Every customer service operation is unique. Despite their individuality, however, all customer service centers need to measure the same key areas to gauge how well they are doing and the specific areas they can improve upon. Companies measure specific performance standards in the following ways:

- Operations management measurements calculate the following customer service statistics:
  - Cost per call or cost per minute
  - Earnings per representative
- Service level measurements determine
  - How well $x$ percent of calls are answered in $y$ seconds
  - The percent of calls abandoned

- Customer service representatives are usually measured by the following identifiers:
  - Quality—which is measured when monitoring calls and checking data accuracy
  - Productivity—which is measured by calls per hour and amount of dollars achieved per sale
- Employee satisfaction measurements commonly used are
  - Employee retention rate
  - Employee surveys
- Customer satisfaction measurements include
  - Customer surveys
  - First-contact resolution rates
  - Customer retention rates

Effective customer service standards reflect an understanding of what customers need, want, and are willing to pay for—and what the competition is offering. To have any meaning, standards must be stated in numbers and be measurable. Words such as *excellent* and *superior* are good motivators, but they need to be translated into specifics of performance. For instance, three types of measurable standards in customer service can be written these ways

- Ninety-eight percent of online customer inquiries will be answered live and within five minutes of their receipt.
- Credits will be posted to customer accounts within two working days.

- Complaints involving $500 or less will be resolved within five working days or less.

The best way to evaluate and write standards is by looking at service situations from the customer's point of view. Some say it is difficult to teach customer service standards to employees if they don't have the right personality in the first place. That's why customer service begins in organizations with hiring the right people in the first place.

## Understanding the Evolving CSR Position

HELP WANTED. Individual of high intelligence and personal charm, capable of working under extreme pressure with frequent interruptions, resourceful and flexible, cheerful and even-tempered. The individual selected for this position must be completely trustworthy, as he/she will be entrusted with millions of dollars of company's business, and must be able to represent customers' best interests with the company while remaining completely loyal to the company. Must be a self-starter with high initiative and an excellent team player. Must be willing to work long hours in a confined spaced under less than ideal conditions. Must be willing to work for low pay with little opportunity for advancement. This is a nonexempt clerical position. Equal opportunity employer M/F. Apply Box 4050; Anytown, USA.

As this fictitious, but only slightly exaggerated, classified ad suggests, most companies expect a great deal from their front-line customer service representatives. However, beyond the usual benefits packages, many companies don't always give a great deal in return. Formal training is often sketchy, and the general companywide perception of CSRs as low-grade clerical workers is compounded by a perception that they are also troublemakers.

The reason for this perception is that CSRs show up in other departments only when there is a customer service problem that they cannot handle. Mix these elements with the typical pressures of the customer service environment, and it is not hard to understand that problems of morale, stress, burnout, and turnover are common to the customer service function in businesses. The following

sections examine CSRs' duties, working environment, salaries, and promotion opportunities.

## Duties and the Working Environment

CSRs perform a variety of duties that require them to communicate effectively and to work under little direct supervision, but in cooperation with others. Typically, they work inside comfortable offices or cubicles between 35 and 40 hours per week with occasional overtime, night, and weekend hours. Often, they work under stress from angry or upset customers.

The physical job requirements require CSRs to sit for long periods while using their arms, hands, and fingers. They need to speak, hear, and see well. To carry out their duties, CSRs use the telephone, calculator, and computer to produce correspondence, invoices, e-mail messages, and other product information for customers.

The employment outlook for this career is good. As the population and the service economy grow, there will be a strong demand for customer service workers. However, the increased use of voicemail and electronic telephone interchanges will have an impact on the number of jobs. According to the Association of Support Professionals' Customer Care Institute, the average rate of increase from 1997 through 2005 is projected to grow at 16 percent. On an average, employment of customer service representatives is expected to grow faster than the average for all occupations through the year 2005.

## Salaries and Promotion Opportunities

The approximate pay for CSRs ranges from $896 to $2,560 per month nationally. Starting salaries in 2002 for senior customer service representatives remained relatively flat at the range of $28,000 to $41,000, only a .7 percent increase from 2001.[2]

Promotion opportunities for CSRs tend to be limited. However, this entry-level job is a good occasion to learn solid business skills, which often lead to the prospect of filling administrative and sales positions within organizations.

---

[2]"Admin Salaries to Remain Flat," *Administrative Assistant's Update* (April 2002): 2.

Certification is becoming the mark of professionals in many career fields. In the world of customer service, CSRs can pursue professional certification, sponsored by the International Customer Service Association (ICSA). The ICSA Professional Certification Program is a self-paced, 30-hour training program consisting of six coordinating modules. CSRs who take specified training and participate in extracurricular customer service activities receive points toward the designation of CCSP (Certified Customer Service Professional). Log on to *http://www.icsa.com* to obtain further information regarding certification and professional activities available for CSRs.

## Retaining CSRs and Other Loyalty Issues

Employees working in customer service areas should be recognized and rewarded for their efforts every day. Although too often they are on the lowest rung of a company's pay scale, CSRs' contributions to an organization's bottom line are invaluable. Companies show customer service employees that they are valued and appreciated when they take three simple measures: train them, empower them, and reward them.

> **CUSTOMER SERVICE TIP**
>
> **13.2** *Effective job performance is best acknowledged on the basis of* outcomes *or* results produced *for the customer, rather than on internal performance criteria.*

### Train CSRs

Customer service training begins with the way in which an employer screens candidates for hire. With today's new generation of workers and accompanying new attitudes about the role of customer service, training is taking on greater importance. For example, when pre-employment assessment questions on customer service were examined, it was determined that, of those applicants surveyed,

- Forty-five percent said they believe that customers should be told when they are wrong.
- Forty-six percent said customers have to follow the rules if CSRs are going to help them.

- Thirty-four percent said they would prefer to work behind the scenes, rather than with customers.
- Thirteen percent said they believe that, if customers don't ask for help, they don't need it.
- Ten percent said they do not feel it is necessary to help a customer if the request falls outside their area of responsibility.[3]

These survey results pose great concerns in business today. For better or for worse, companies are most often judged by the performance and perceived attitude of their front-line personnel. There is a tendency to blame poor service on poor training. Many corporate executives spend a fortune on advertising, inventory, and capital improvements while essentially ignoring the importance of employee training.

Ongoing education is necessary for quality customer service representatives. Training is an essential component of any effective quality control program. Companies that say they can't afford the time or money to give their customer service representatives and managers regular training sessions end up paying far more for the lack of training than they would have paid for the training itself.

When companies make the investment to train their customer service employees, they show that they value them and the work they do. One estimate is that a good training program has a value of at least five times its cost, because employees who feel valued are more motivated and more productive.

The return on investment for training is great in another area as well. Most people don't go in search of new jobs in order to make more money. The real reason they leave is that they haven't been trained to handle the job. According to the Department of Labor, only 11 percent of American workers get any formal training, and only 14 percent receive even informal training.[4]

Employees who are not trained to provide good customer service find themselves frustrated in their attempts to deal with rude, difficult, and irate customers. If they are

---

[3]Brenda Paik Sunoo, "Results-Oriented Customer Service Training," *Workforce* (May 2001): 84.

[4]John Tschohl, "Wanted: Loyal Employees," *Service Quality Institute* (November 19, 2000): 2.

trained in how to diffuse those situations, there is a much greater chance good workers will stay, because they can handle the job better.

**CSR Training Curriculum.** According to Customer Service Consultant John Tschohl, companies should provide at least 40 hours of training each year and establish clear objectives, so that employees know what they should be able to do once they've completed that training. To be effective, training must be consistent and continuous and must involve everyone in the organization. Training is especially important for front-line employees, however, whose knowledge and behavior influence clients and customers to return with additional business.[5]

What should a curriculum that teaches good customer service skills look like? It should emphasize developing phone skills and interpersonal communication that fosters a teambuilding environment. Further, the customer service curriculum should include training on the latest customer care technologies, such as live interactive chat, intelligent e-mail response systems, telephone services, and robust self-service search engines. One of the main customer service training goals is to enable employees to be knowledgeable about the company's products. When employees are unable to answer a customer's question about a product or service, credibility suffers and the consequences of lost sales are evident.

**Training Methods.** Role-playing is one of the most effective methods for training CSRs. It helps teach them how to talk with customers and how to make sales by using cus-

One of the best training methods to use with CSRs is to role-play customer situations, because it is like a "dress rehearsal before the performance."

tomer scenarios encountered in the real world. By acting out situations, employees learn how to eliminate on-the-job shyness, prevent intimidation, extract personal information from shoppers, handle irate customers, overcome objections, and share product knowledge. Working on awkward customer scenarios and handling obnoxious customers are good topics to role-play.

Rehearsing in this way helps employees eliminate verbal fillers, those cumbersome "ums" and "you knows" that can creep into our speech when we are uncertain what to say. Role-play, however, is not the easiest type of training to do. Some employees are reluctant to participate, because the thought of acting in front of an audience—even a tiny group—makes them nervous. To be effective, the training technique requires dedicated time. The benefits gained, however, are worth the time and effort, because they boost employee confidence.

In summary, Guideline 13.2 offers some additional tips when establishing an effective employee customer service training program.

---

[5]John Tschohl, "Employee Training Offers Bottom Line Benefits," *Service Quality Institute* (November 19, 2000): 4.

GUIDELINE 13.2  Tips for Organizations to Establish Ongoing Service Training

- Use 10 percent of the company's advertising budget to train customer service employees.
- Spend a minimum of 40 hours per year training each employee in the art of customer service.
- Introduce a new training program every six months in order to create a culture change and keep enthusiasm high.
- Provide at least six hours of customer service education, with a follow-up session a month or two later for front-line employees.
- Establish clear objectives, so that employees know what they should be able to do once they've completed the training program.
- Recognize communication, cooperation, and commitment—from top-level management to front-line employees—as critical to the success of any training program and to the changing of a company's culture.

**Source:** John Tschohl, "Employee Training Offers Bottom Line Benefits," *Service Quality Institute* (November 19, 2000): 3.

## ETHICS/CHOICES

**13.2** Suppose you overheard someone you work with say, "If you've got to have seven layers of management signing off on every minor decision, what's the sense of having a customer service center?" What is your reaction to this statement? Explain the position you take.

## Empower CSRs

Empowerment is an enormous employee motivational tool, which can give a business the competitive edge it needs to survive. When you empower employees, you give them the authority to provide exceptional customer service. That means bending, even breaking, the rules to do whatever they have to do to take care of customers to their satisfaction.

Without empowered employees, no service, or very little service, reaches customers. When there is little or no service, customers will not return to your business. A recent Technical Assistance Research Program study found that each problem a customer encounters causes a 20 percent decline in his or her long-term loyalty to that company.[6]

Employees who are given the authority to satisfy customers are crucial to the success of any business. Start with giving CSRs the authority to handle customer complaints and concerns on the spot. Then allow them to use that authority by assuring them that they won't be fired if they make a mistake in the process of working to win customer satisfaction.

When managers, for whatever reason, do not empower or delegate responsibility for getting the job done, employees tend to react in some fairly predictable ways:

1. Often, they become apathetic; they develop a "So what?" attitude. Energy drains off and productivity slows down.
2. If people are unable to exercise their talents, those talents waste away. Without challenge, no new talents are acquired.
3. If an employee is given no responsibility, the unvoiced assumption is "I'm not good enough to take control of this job." This leads to the employee being less motivated or less likely to take responsibility at a later date.
4. Employees with limited responsibility tend to break rules, be absent more often, or increasingly show up late for work.
5. The organization has no backup, because no one is trained to think independently. This creates problems of succession and poses threats to the long life of the company.

## Reward CSRs

Customer service employees know they are valued when companies use positive reinforcement and public praise. Workers need to know that their contributions are noticed and appreciated. Well-trained customer service employees, who feel they are valuable members of the corporate team, create the magic inside the business that keep customers coming back.

It's unfortunate, but too often top *sales* performers earn sizable bonuses or expensive prizes, whereas top *service* performers go unrecognized or are recognized on a much smaller scale. It is unwise for companies to send the message that service is less important than sales. Even small successes should be celebrated, because it gives companies the opportunity to recognize employees on a regular basis.

[6]John Tschohl, "Customer Service: A Year-Long Commitment," *Service Quality Institute*, October 2000, 4.

A recognition event doesn't have to be extravagant. A pizza party, a small gift, a money certificate, a balloon bouquet, or a special parking spot often does the job. Some companies use a system called "Stories of Success" coupons. It works like this. A coupon is awarded each time a manager sees or hears a CSR performing one of the following behaviors:

- Demonstrating teamwork
- Offering to help someone
- Taking ownership of a problem
- Making a suggestion for cost savings
- Having perfect attendance for the month
- Teaching someone something
- Going beyond the call of duty
- Providing excellent customer service
- Making a suggestion that increases productivity
- Finding a potential problem and fixing it

Most coupons are worth one point (one point = $1). The CSRs collect the coupons and can trade them in for a merchandise gift certificate, a restaurant certificate, or a cash payout at the end of each month.

## Other Loyalty Issues

Customer service centers are notorious for high turnover, but that doesn't mean organizations have to accept turnover as a given. When employees leave, it's not just about money. Certainly, money matters, and, if you don't compensate employees fairly, good employees will leave. However, research shows that four main factors have an impact on employee retention and encourage loyalty on the job when:

1. *Organizations provide meaningful work.* Having work that is meaningful keeps people excited about their jobs. If a CSR feels that her work isn't meaningful, managers should spend time with her, brainstorming how to make the situation better. Sometimes, that simply means helping a CSR find a different way of thinking about the job.

2. *Organizations provide chances to learn and grow.* Employees need opportunities to learn, change, and grow. Offering growth opportunities used to be a nice thing to do, but now, when corporate loyalty is diminishing, it is a necessity. Managers need to ask frequently, "How else can we offer a rewarding work environment?"

3. *Organizations provide good bosses.* To most employees, a good boss is one who shows respect, demonstrates genuine caring, gives good direction, and shares information in a timely fashion.

4. *Employees feel that they are part of a team.* Employees need to feel as if they are part of something bigger than themselves, that their individual contributions make a difference to a greater whole.[7]

Staff loyalty is critical to a company's success. Three of the most common crisis situations experienced by employees that cause them to leave a job are

- *New-hire hysteria.* This condition can be brought on by a number of new job circumstances, including overwhelming assignments, friction with a new boss, or an unusually heavy workload. To alleviate this situation the new recruit can be paired with an experienced associate who can help guide the employee through this difficult transition time.

- *Promotion peril.* An employee is vulnerable to defection when he or she is ready for a promotion but a slot is unavailable. Ambitious, upwardly mobile employees waiting for promotions are ripe for the picking by competitors who are only too happy to give them those next steps up on the ladder. Managers can buy themselves some extra time by putting the employee in a special project role, for two or three months, that recognizes his or her achievements.

- *Boredom blues.* The most productive employees typically don't tolerate boredom well. New jobs and golden opportunities outside their company will start to look more and more attractive. Management should find out what specific areas most interest the employee and find ways to tailor at least some of his or her assignments around those areas.[8]

Research suggests that replacing key employees costs between 70 and 200 percent of their annual salary, and that doesn't even take into account the costs of losing key customers who leave because their favorite CSRs are no longer at the company.[9] That's why it's necessary to view retaining CSRs through a reward system as a critical business strategy.

---

[7]Sharon Jordan-Evans, "The Four Reasons Employees Stay in Their Jobs," *Customer Service Manager's Letter* (April 15, 2000): 2–3.

[8]Sharon Jordan - Evans - pg. 3.

[9]Michael Lowenstein, "Securing the Service with a Smile," *Customer Loyalty Today* (October 2000): 6–7.

In summary, some best practices for retaining employees and building loyalty include

- Build a climate of trust that works both ways.
- Train, train, train, and cross-train.
- Make sure each employee has a career path.
- Provide frequent evaluations and reviews.
- Recognize and reward initiative.
- Ask employees what they want.
- Have fun.
- Hire the right employees in the first place.

## Advancing into Managing a Customer Service Department

Some of the best managers in organizations come from the ranks. Put another way, a company that promotes CSRs from within have great managers. Good managers are comfortable assigning tasks to CSRs because they know the job inside and out. They are good at facilitating cooperation between departments as well as with customers because they have "walked the talk," as the saying goes.

A strong leader understands and motivates workers. Customer service managers must be well organized and capable of helping the department organize itself in order to accomplish goals. One of the strengths of a good leader is the ability to see a future for the department that is better than what currently exists. Managers who create an environment that works for the customers and staff set the stage for customer service excellence. Good managers of customer service do five things well:

1. *They generate a spirit of service by*
   - Encouraging laughter, humor, warm greetings, smiles, and compliments
   - Demonstrating belief in people through positive words of encouragement
   - Casually visiting with staff, seeking their input and then incorporating that information into observable actions
2. *They build trust by*
   - Keeping people informed of change and letting affected people be a part of any change
   - Demonstrating flexibility and interest in the personal situations of employees

- Sharing information about the organization, so that people feel a part of things and in the know
- Defining boundaries and providing reasonable expectations for all workers

3. *They develop people by*
   - Providing timely feedback through effective coaching
   - Adapting communication techniques based on the needs of employees
   - Rewarding successes and addressing problems promptly
4. *They lead by example by*
   - Practicing the behaviors and ethics expected of front-line workers
   - Giving direction in a respectful manner
   - Listening attentively and responding to feedback from staff
5. *They stay focused on customer needs by*
   - Recognizing individuals for giving great customer service
   - Implementing employee suggestions that improve service

## Customer Service—a Final Word

What's happening in today's business world is a shift in power to consumers because of the Internet and other available telecommunications devices. Customers are in a much stronger position these days because of the increased access to information and an abundant choice of suppliers. In a recent book review, Caitlin Mollison offers some practical ways for companies to become fanatical on behalf of customers. In your current or future job, you cannot go wrong by applying these suggestions:

1. *Offer customers choices.* You have to provide customers with choices and multiple decision points: e-mail, fax, the telephone, and the Web.
2. *Practice accountability.* Your customers will lose faith in you if your service isn't up to par. Admitting your mistakes and trying your best to rectify them will go a long way toward winning customer loyalty.
3. *Empower employees.* Give them the ability to make others jump in defense of customers. Customer service is mostly a process and a commitment. It cannot be an afterthought.

4. *Know your customers.* Serving your customers is a lot easier when you have a sense of who they are and what they are interested in. Set up a feedback mechanism, so that you actually communicate with your customers and they can evaluate you.

5. *Maximize loyalty among your current customers.* Not only does going the extra mile for customers mean that they will want to do business with you again, but they will probably recommend you to their friends as well.

6. *Recognize how much the human touch matters.* The best technology in the world and the shortest call times possible won't mean a thing if customer service representatives don't treat customers like human beings.

7. *Measure customer satisfaction it.* What gets measured usually gets improved. If you don't use quantitative methods to determine how well you are succeeding, you probably aren't putting your customers first.[10]

## Concluding Message for CSRs

There was a time when customer service meant hiring an individual to sit behind a complaint desk. Today, customer service is more comprehensive. It requires that employers hire the right employees, create a customer service culture, view customers as high-maintenance "guests," and train employees on certain technologies without sacrificing the human touch.

Knowledgeable, courteous, helpful employees bring in—and retain—customers. Advertising brings customers in the door, but poor service turns them away and points them in the direction of a competitor. Employers must hire good people and then train them, coach them, empower them, and reward them.

Consumers are more knowledgeable and have higher expectations than most other people. When a company improves its service delivery, the satisfaction bar is raised. The challenge for the twenty-first century is not just serving customers,

1. It's understanding customers as people.
2. It's being prepared to serve customers right the first time.
3. It's helping angry customers immediately.

4. It's asking customers for information the right way.
5. It's listening to customers with empathy.
6. It's being responsible for your actions when a customer calls.
7. It's living up to your commitments and always following through.
8. It's being memorable by going a little beyond what customers expect.
9. It's surprising customers with unexpected acts of kindness.
10. It's striving to keep customers for life.
11. It's regularly getting unsolicited referrals from customers.

## Summary

- Setting standards for performance is a conscious effort and involves able direction from customer service managers.
- An organization's mission statement integrates the expectations of good customer service.
- Standards tell workers what is expected of them, both in quality and in quantity of work.
- Three commonly used work standards in customer service are based on production, accuracy, and performance.
- Effective customer service standards reflect an understanding of what customers need, want, and are willing to pay for.
- The first step in providing great customer service is to hire the right people.
- Typically, a CSR works inside comfortable offices or cubicles between 35 and 40 hours per week, with some occasional overtime, night, and weekend work.
- CSRs can pursue professional certification, sponsored by the International Customer Service Association.
- Companies are often judged by the performance and perceived attitude of their front-line personnel.
- Role-playing helps customer service representatives, because it allows them to act out situations in a training setting prior to interacting with an actual customer.
- Empowering employees motivates them to provide exceptional customer service.
- It is unwise for companies to send the message that service is less important than sales.

---

[10]Caitlin Mollison, "Driving Customer Service," *Internet World* (September 15, 2001): 8–9.

- Four main factors that encourage loyalty on the job are meaningful work, chances to learn and grow, good bosses, and inclusion in a team.
- Some of the best customer service managers come from within an organization, are loyal, and appreciate the value of exceptional customer service.
- Good customer service managers generate a spirit of service, build trust, develop people, lead by example, and stay focused on customer needs.
- Relative to expecting great customer service, customers today are in a much stronger position because of increased access to information and an abundant choice of suppliers of products and services.

## QUESTIONS FOR CRITICAL THINKING

1. What is the role of management in customer-oriented cultures?

2. Why is it important to use measurable standards in customer service?

3. Describe the pros and cons of a typical working environment for customer service representatives.

4. What is the incentive to companies that train, empower, and reward service professionals?

5. Give one advantage and one disadvantage of organizations that use role-playing when training customer services representatives.

6. Out of the several ways that companies can recognize and reward a CSR, which two would you prefer receiving and why?

7. Prioritize four factors that have an impact on employee retention and that encourage loyalty on the job. Explain your reasons for listing them in that order.

8. What talents do you possess that might make you a good customer service manager?

# On-line Research Activities

## Project 13.1: Job Qualifications for CSRs

Research a number of web sites, such as *Monster.com,* to locate several *job descriptions currently available for CSRs.* As a result of your research, develop a list of the top eight qualifications and job skills that employers are seeking in customer service representatives. Present your findings to the class, using a visual aid, such as a PowerPoint presentation, charts, or overhead transparencies.

## Project 13.2: Managing a Customer Service Department 🖥

### Situation

Mary Graeff has decided to move out of state next month to take care of her father, who is in poor health. As a result, On-Time Technology Products must advertise for a new supervisor for its Customer Service Department.

*Enter "Customer Service Manager" in your favorite search engine. Locate several job positions that are open and specifically look for the qualifications that those jobs require. Using file PRJ13-2 on your student CD, key responses in the following table format, listing seven of the most critical job requirements for a customer service manager. From your research, enter in column 2 at least three reasons that On-Time Technology Products should consider filling Ms. Graeff's position from within the organization.*

| Job Qualifications | Three Reasons to Promote from Within |
|---|---|
| 1. | • |
| 2. | |
| 3. | • |
| 4. | |
| 5. | • |
| 6. | |
| 7. | |

# Communication Skills at Work

## Project 13.3: Communicating Standards to Customers 🖥

Assume you have been asked to put together a script for the following six service benchmark characteristics. This script would be used to train new CSRs in standards of performance, accuracy, and production at On-Time Technology Products.

*Retrieve file PRJ13-3 on the student CD and complete the following form by recommending, in column 2, a standard method or action by which a CSR can demonstrate each of the six benchmark characteristics.*

| Benchmark Characteristic | Method or Action to Meet the Benchmark Characteristic |
|---|---|
| 1. Value | |
| 2. Communication | |
| 3. Attitude | |
| 4. Reliability | |
| 5. Empathy | |
| 6. Exceptional service | |

## Decision Making at Work

### Project 13.4: Career Advancement or Job Security?

Of late, there is a question among managers of Customer Service Departments as to whether it is best to hire a CSR who is more concerned with job security or one who is more interested in career advancement. Respond to the following two statements by offering reasons that a CSR might prefer job security over career advancement and vice versa.

1. **Defend:** When hiring, it is better to offer a CSR stability and longevity on the job over any other factor. You get a better employee.

_____

_____

_____

_____

_____

_____

_____

_____

2. **Defend:** When hiring, it is better to offer a CSR advancement through a career path and promotion opportunities over any other factor. You get a better employee.

_____

_____

_____

_____

_____

_____

_____

_____

_____

## Case Study

### 13.1 Cost of Nonservice

A woman was mistreated by a salesperson in a store where she had been shopping once a week for 3 years. The poor service caused her to switch stores. After 12 years, she returned and decided to tell the owner what had happened. He listened intently, apologized, and thanked her for coming back. Then he went right over to his calculator. He estimated that, if the woman had spent only $25 a week and never increased her buying, over the 12 years his store would have made $15,600. He had lost her business to the cost of nonservice.

**Questions**

1. *In your opinion, can or does nonservice affect businesses today?*

_____

_____

_____

_____

_____

2. *What methods can companies use to prevent this seemingly insignificant incident of poor service from causing such economic disaster?*

_____

_____

_____

_____

_____

_____

## Case Study

### 13.2 Customer Service Fallacies

During an interview for Mary Graeff's position, an applicant made the following two statements. Most of those on the interview team recognized that these statements represent two customer service fallacies that exist in business today. For the following two fallacies, argue them false.

1. *Customer service means adding more people to the payroll.*

_____

_____

_____

_____

_____

_____

_____

2. *You must pay people more money in order to improve customer service.*

_____

_____

_____

_____

_____

_____

_____

_____

# Let's Discuss...

## Industry: Health Care

## Health Care Activities

1. Think about your total experience the last time you, a family member, or a friend received health care services and respond "yes" or "no" to the following questions:

| Yes | No | |
|---|---|---|
| | | Did the health professional customer service (HPCS) person greet you in a pleasant way on your arrival at the office, clinic, or hospital? |
| | | Did the HPCS person treat you with dignity and respect your rights to privacy? |
| | | Did the HPCS person use technology to access confidential data about you or previous visits you may have made? |
| | | Did it take an excessive amount of time to provide written information or to update your medical files? |
| | | Was your time valued by the HPCS person by not having to wait too long to be served by a doctor or nurse practitioner? |
| | | Was the HPCS person knowledgeable in providing answers to the questions you asked? |
| | | Did it seem to you as though the customer service provided was well managed, organized, and customer-driven? |
| | | If given a choice, would you return to that health care provider again? |

- How would you rank customer service at this health care facility? (1 = poor; 5 = superior)? _____
- From the material in Part 4, briefly explain why you evaluated the health care experience as you did.

2. In your opinion and relative to the customer services offered, are the health care services that are provided by HMOs preferable to those provided by nonparticipating medical practices? Explain.

_____

3. Assume you are the customer service director for a local hospital. In that role, how would you design the Customer Service Department to use technology, while serving patients in a caring and considerate way?

_____

# Index

t = *indicates table on page*
f = *indicates figure on page*